FACES
OF PERSIAN YOUTH

FACES
OF PERSIAN YOUTH

A SOCIOLOGICAL STUDY

BY

A. REZA ARASTEH

Professor of Analytic Psychology
University of Tehran

LEIDEN
E. J. BRILL
1970

TABLE OF CONTENTS

62514

CYRUS

IN SEARCH OF SELF

SEMA

ENCOUNTER WITH THE WEST

INTRODUCTION

THE REBIRTH OF YOUTH IN THE AGE OF CULTURAL CHANGE[1]

My interest in the study of awakened youth grew out of my study of the state of maturity.[2] This study convinced me that the process of maturity requires an awareness of the interplay of being a productive participant as a social man and as a unique person expressing intimacy with both the human and non-human world. At the same time I discovered that in the past the road to harmonizing these two contradictory poles was open to courageous and inquisitive men, whereas in our age the disintegration of traditional forms and increased cultural interaction has better prepared youth to reintegrate into a positive form and to live by creativity and a peaceful attitude, provided the opportunity is available. As I have stated in my book,[3] the

---

[1] This article is the last two chapters of my recent book, *The Renaissance of Youth in the Age of Cultural Change* (in Persian), Tehran: Elmi Publishing Co., 1966. This study was done when the author served as an advisor to the Prime Minister of Iran in the area of potential manpower.

[2] Professor Arasteh is currently Visiting Professor of Analytic Psychology, University of Tehran and previously was on the faculty of the Department of Psychiatry, George Washington University, Washington D.C. He is also the author of *Final Integration in the Adult Personality* (1965), *Man and Society in Iran* (1964), *Rumi the Persian* (1965), and *Education and Social Awakening in Iran* (1962).

[3] Published as *Final Integration in the Adult Personality: A Measure for Health, Social Change and Leadership* (E. J. Brill, 1965).

1

period of youth offers a great opportunity for harmonizing one's search for meaning and one's search for an adult role in society. It is a period when youth is full of energy—a representation of wholistic expression. The complete submission of youth to exploration in sex, politics and communial living indicates that the whole organism is being formed into a new being. Ordinarily, if one is born within a closed cultural pattern where people have a strong social superego, the urge to transform into a new being is weak, and character formation takes place without much revolt. However, in an age when the sense of relatedness to a specific pattern is weakened (as in our own era) then youth fall into a suspended state—representing a true state of man. More and more youth throughout the world are falling into such a state, although the cause may be existential in the West, historical deprivation in the developing nations, and historical awareness in communist societies. When an individual, especially a youth, falls into the mentally suspended state, he usually faces one of two situations. If the older generation and the society provide security and opportunity and accept the change, the youth, instead of rising against the previous generation, will use his energy to discover his own interests and utilize the favorable cultural conditions to give form to his own images, thereby growing into a productive adult. If such a condition appears collectively it can become the dawn of a new historical epoch—a renaissance. However, if the society and the older generation resist change and anxiously yearn for the "good old days," then such a situation will provoke youth to trade their positive and constructive outlook for destructive urges culminating in crime, social revolt and all kinds of deviant behavior.

In my Persian book, *The Renaissance of Youth in the Age of Cultural Change*, I have tried to expand this theory in order to

2

explain the significance of the "state of awareness" in history, society and man; identify the national problems of youth pertaining to growth; indicate the specific problems of youth emerging from cultural factors relating to America, the Soviet Union, Japan, France and Italy; and finally analyze the youth problems of developing nations, with an emphasis on Israel and Iran.

Therefore, this article discusses the general trend of youth in developing countries with an objective study of the problems of youth in the changing society of Iran.

Some general assumptions

Generally speaking, the evolution and revolution of developing nations in the twentieth century has arisen from a series of social and political revolts in the second half of the nineteenth century. The first contact with the West was based on traditional ways and took place when Afro-Asian societies knew little of the mechanisms of Western societies. In fact, the communication was between government agencies, not the people. In the second state, some cultural and social exchanges took place and this was intensified by two world wars culminating in an awareness of the people of non-Western societies. The impact of the West on the Afro-Asian nations was such that it awakened the latter and released their energy, especially the energy of the youth.

In the first period the released energy was concentrated and utilized for the achievement of national independence. In countries where such an ideal was actualized the awakened individual youth was subdued by the national demands and his restlessness calmed by national unity. This new relatedness filled the vacuum which had arisen out of the separation from

3

the traditional value systems. In the early 1950's this urge for national unity was so strong that it even satisfied the religious sense of belonging, and it would have disolved any social divergencies that existed.

In the second state, this is, after the attainment of political independence, the awakened energy under the direction of identifiable leaders was used for economic reconstruction—a process which is still continuing. In countries where this transference of energy has realistically been adopted (regardless of social systems) the energy of youth has manifested itself in terms of constructive projects and their actualization for the purpose of attaining immediate common goals directed toward material comfort. This is true, in a sense, of Yugoslavia, Egypt, Indonesia, India, and even China. In their reconstruction such countries, unlike those of the West, have not yet permitted the divergent energies of youth to coalesce and seek out a meaning to life; nor is the negative trend visible either. However, if the trend is directed toward the attainment of material culture, it will eventually lead the next generation to either pursue physical pleasure, hobbies and entertainment or, if guided by visionary leaders, to attain the unification of creativity and happiness thereby arriving at a more transcendental state of life.

The case of Israel

The best example of this theory, that is, the use of released energy for the solution of political, then economical, and finally existential problems (but which is now frozen because of the limited scope of a national philosophy) is the nation of Israel.

Historically, we know that years before the establishment of the present state of Israel, the Jews were scattered throughout the world, and those in Europe were especially active in seeking

4

a place which they might call their homeland. No place fitted this ideals better than Jerusalem. Thus various movements were formed, especially such youth movements as Hashomer, Hashomer Hatsa'ir, Hapo'el Hamizrahi, and others. The national unrelatedness made it necessary to establish these organizations. It is true that the Jews as a people were related to a set of beliefs, but the same blessing which had led to their survival had also denied them the national and social security which members of a culture ordinarily receive. This feeling of unrelatedness intensified itself during the rise of national states in Europe, especially with the rise of Nazi Germany and Italian Fascism. The stronger these national movements became the more limited and restrictive became the security of the Jews, and with the rise of anti-Semitism security gave way to fear.

Under such conditions the youth could not participate in the national movement because an orthodox Jew could not accept this, nor could the local prejudiced communities accept the Jews. The rise of socialism and communism did not improve the situation either. These movements, differentiated merely by the color of their members' shirts and hats, did not deeply affect the attitudes of the people, and left the Jews in an uncertain situation. Zionism and the idea of a return to Israel gained further support as a reaction to the rejection of Jews in Europe. Parenthetically, it was when the European Jews experienced unrelatedness in their communities that Zionism in order to fill the gap actualized itself. Thus, the new movement created an orientation for Jewish youth. They idealized the lost homeland and created an illusionary but intense feeling toward Israel, toward the Jewish people, toward friendship between Israelis and above all toward the reunification and reconstruction of Palestine, based on ideals which had been transferred from generation to generation. These ideals not only reunited Jews outside of

5

Palestine but also stimulated the Israelis within Palestine to become more active. These ideals were not incompatible with the policies of the Allies, although there was some disagreement as to its method of execution. With the establishment of Israel after World War II, the movements which had arisen out of the awareness of Jewish history actualized their first goal—the political existence of an independent state.

The energy which had been created by the group movements was directed toward the establishment of new parties, which varied considerably from socialism and liberalism to restrictive religious doctrinarism which insisted that the Old Testament must become the guide. Nevertheless, all the parties believed in Zionism, and the youth became the potential energy for attaining the reconstruction of Israel. Although they represented various groups, they all scorned idleness, mere talk and bureaucracy; they sought action, constructive effort and particularly group activity in the Kibbutz. The Kibbutz became the representation of a constructive life, and its philosophy became a social philosophy based on relatively just behavior and fair dealings.

Undoubtedly, the enmity between Arabs and Jews strengthened the invisible ties between the youth, and no doubt rivalry stimulated greater achievement. The greatest contribution of these youth groups, especially those concerned with agriculture, was the feeling of relatedness that these youth developed from the cultivation of the land. No one acquires such a relatedness to a new country without first working on the land. This very mechanism made Americans out of the early European settlers. Furthermore, group songs, folklore and group living contributed to their social identity. This was eventually effective and perhaps the only way that Israel could mold the newcomers into Israelis. Coming from various lands, the Jews had already definitely formed their character in terms of the subculture in which they had lived. A Jew from Iran was more Iranian than Jewish, and a Jew from England had his behavior and attitudes formed more by English culture than by Jewish culture. Thus the only way to resolve their inner conflict was to establish a common goal (which already existed) and to increase group activity and meaningful work related to perceived needs. It was such a mechanism which was responsible for creating a new unconscious harmony. And if Israel succeeds in this tremendous task it will offer some theoretical knowledge to the resolution of strong conflicts among diversified groups at the international level. It should also be noted that work, living and recreation in the Kibbutz are directed toward simplicity and the search for achievement rather than material gain.

Organizationally, a youth group was limited to 30 or 40 persons, which in turn was part of a larger group subdivided in terms of age, and each committee sent its representative to the national and international organizations so that they could contribute to the solution of existing problems. On the same basis every district, city and provence had its own organization. While productive work and communial living were the basis of reconstruction, the ideals were continually being reappraised by group discussions based on the principles of Zionism and religious doctrine.

Moreover, it is interesting to note that national feelings which had grown out of a longing to return to Israel and had then become crystallized through group work was further strengthened by the understanding of the historical significance of Palestine in ancient history. However, once the economical aims and a national character were realized, the group aims and ideals became internalized and manifested as the perception of a good personal life. Thus, the second generation of youth in Israel has become more professionally oriented and directed toward a better personal life, in comparison to the intense idealism of the previous generation.

In general then, we can say that this new generation is interested in experiencing life and may even ridicule Zionism. It is my belief that with further economical progress in Israel these youth will become more "fun oriented," like that of the West, rather than being concerned with developing a scientific and humanistic orientation. The reason for this change in attitude is that Israel has attained its limited philosophy, and unless the present "emotional conflict" with Arab nationalism is not solved through a deeper affective mechanism, then the youth will limit their ideals to material comfort. However, if the Jews and Arabs gradually realize that in the past the wise men in both groups transcended religious formalism through Jewish and Islamic mysticism, they may then contribute to the cultivation of a deeper humane feeling, more akin to the rising age of neo-humanism. If these philosophical principles imbue the youth, they will be able to solve their dualism by acquiring a new meaning to life.

Finally, it should be noted that there is a profound difference between the European Jews who migrated to Israel and the Oriental ones. Significantly, the Eastern youth's stronger attachment to his family has led him to participate less in the Kibbutz and youth organizations, and consequently less change is evident in him.[1]

THE CASE OF IRAN

Any understanding of the life of Iranian youth today and their future course requires some familiarity with the historical

---

[1] For further information see R. Arasteh, *Renaissance of Youth... op cit.*

changes in Iranian society during the twentieth century. In fact, the problems of youth—beyond those which naturally occur —are the products of the socio-cultural changes which have been taking place.

I previously mentioned that rapid social change is one of the characteristics of the twentieth century throughout the world, and this itself is a product of cultural contact, resulting in individual, group and national awareness. In certain countries, notably in the Asian and North African nations, the energy arising from this awareness has become a vehicle for political independence and group identification leading to economic prosperity and subsequently to existential awareness. Israel is an example of such a formula, and some other nations, such as Egypt, exemplify the first two stages.

Iran is, however, an exception to this rule. Because of historical prematurity and a series of unpredictable factors, it did not have a chance to fully integrate its philosophy of life so as to fill the social vacuum produced by the cessation of World War II and the disharmony which developed out of the impact of the Allied invasion on the disintegration of government authority. To understand this social phenomenon, which is the cause of the youth problem in Iran, requires further historical facts.

Since the middle of the nineteenth century when Iran began to feel the impact of Western culture, it has produced four generations. The first generation, the rationally rebellious generation, which came in contact with Western social values, was impressed by the mechanism of "social contract" and advocated social justice through laws and representation. Finally with the help of the awakened urban community it allied itself with the courageous tribesmen and brought about a change from a monarchy to a constitutional government in 1906. The conse-

9

quences of World War I produced a further change in the government, best described as a "monarchy with a weak Parliament." The need for unification in the 1930's brought to the fore a submissive generation which lost its power out of fear. The third generation, which came into being immediately after World War II, that is, during the decade of rational decision-making, was a dissident generation which presumed it had the solution. Finally, the fourth generation came into being: it passed its infancy during the 1940's and its adolescence in the decade of trial and error (1950-1960).

An analysis of these four generation reveals that they have been facing innumerable problems, but none has been greater than the problem of the transference of power from one generation to the next. The leadership has lacked continuity, due to the absence of a social philosophy and the pressure of international events, especially those in Europe and America. This discontinuity has prevented Iranian statesmen from acquiring a realistic appraisal of events and the vision "to perceive the end in the mirror of the beginning." Moreover, in periods of crises, such as that following the abdication of Reza Shah, the absence of trained leaders led to a change from ultra-conservatism to radicalism. The same phenomenon has been responsible for weakening the ties between generations, thereby resulting in a generation of youth born during the War, without roots and related neither to their own generation nor to the previous one. Nor does this generation possess the mechanisms which comforted the previous generation—the family and kin congeniality, which in the past was so strong that they gave both emotional and economic security to all the members, even in adulthood.

This change in attitude has not yet permeated the smaller towns and villages, where mere self-identity is identical with homogenious group identity. Moreover, this young generation has lost the mechanism of education, which the previous generation (particularly those who passed their adolescence in the 1930's) used as a vehicle to achieve security. It may be argued that there are more educational facilities now, but the fact is that there was less demand for education from a static society and, in a sense, greater encouragement. When I myself was in the ninth grade there were only ten in my class, whereas now it is virtually impossible to find a class of less than 60. Furthermore, when I entered college, the schools of medicine, dentistry and pharmacy accepted about 200 students a year, and the other schools accepted about 400 more; nor was there much competition. Now, out of 40,000 candidates a year, the universities cannot take more than 4000. In other words, the mechanism of education was, until the 1940's, a comfort-giving system and the college graduate could feel secure that he would find a job waiting for him. This generation has no such security.

I was aware of these general trends when I went to Iran in 1966 at the request of the Prime Minister to make a survey of the problems of youth and to make recommendations for the solution. Although I originally thought of limiting myself to the problem of the young intellectuals, I soon found that the problems of youth are so interwoven with the problems of a changing society that it is impossible to make recommendations without an overall insight into the constructive course of the nation and without understanding the regional differences of Iranian youth.

A third of the population of Iran (approximately 7 million) is between the ages of 12 and 35. Half of the population is below 19 years,[1] and the remark is justified that "Iran is an old land with a youthful population." The absence of research and sta-

---

[1] Iranian Census Report, 1956.

tistics on Iranian youth and their impact on development, and vice versa made it necessary for me to limit my survey to a pilot study.

THE AIM OF THE SURVEY

My primary aim was to contrast the opinions and ideas of 50 influential men and leaders of the youth organizations with those of the youth themselves, taking as a sample a particular articulate group of 69 college students. I sought to find out: (1) How do these leaders and the students perceive the problems of youth? (2) To what extent are these concepts self-projective and to what degree are they due to generalizations? (3) Do the respondents relate the problem to the social issues? (4) Do they see it as a present-day problem or in the context of future trends? (5) What are the common issues and how can constructive forces be utilized for their solution?

In conducting this survey I usually acted as a participant observer and initiated the interviews with a discussion of the organizations to which the respondent belonged. There were often three or four respondents in the group and the situation was purposely unstructured so that they might freely express themselves. These meetings usually took place in my office and continued for two to three hours. I intentionally made it lengthly, for after an hour the subjective ideas and interests of the respondents became apparent, apart from the real issue, that is, the identification of the problems of youth. These sessions were often organized by keymen who knew only my general intention, and in such meetings I could easily observe and evaluate the decision-makers and leaders in action.

However, before beginning these interviews, I had taken two other steps which might be of interest to the readers. I had reviewed the major available sources and writings on Iranian youth. These consisted of books, articles and government surveys, even confidental reports written or prepared by the older leaders—the Senate committee on education, government representatives, religious leaders—as well as by young intellectuals who have unconsciously tried to acquaint the Iranian intelligensia with Western psychological and sociological concepts. Details of the contents of these writings are available in my book.[1] It is sufficient to say here that all these writings and interviews offer only a superficial knowledge of youth, and all share two qualities: they deal only with symptoms and secondly, they are subjective and perhaps objective only in the sense that they provide certain descriptive facts about youth, primarily in terms of formulating the problems of youth, which are basically: the problems of leisure time, acceptance in a group, marriage, divorce, military service, problems at home and in school, dependency, the lack of facilities, the poverty of ideology, work, education, etc.

Although these issues can be of general interest in a well established and secure society, I do not believe that they are the crucial problems, but rather the symptoms of a deeply-rooted condition which the youth of our age, especially those in awakening societies, share, that is, the problem of the diffusion of identity," the search for a new purpose and for identity formation. In such societies as Iran today the search for becoming a socially accepted adult is interwoven with the search for a "meaning to life." This is probably present in other societies too, but more so in Iran where the urge for maturity is intensified. In such a condition youth want to act wholistically, that is, they want to relate to the subject of their desire—blind

---

[1] R. Arasteh, *The Renaissance of Youth... op. cit.*

submission to political movements, sexual urges, group living and various games.

An analysis of the Persian literature on problems of youth reveals that the authors have ignored the basic traits of youth and have taken the symptom of the disease as the disease itself. Just as with ulcers, an operation without a change in the patient's emotional mood offers only a temporary cure, so too the removal of these symptoms in youth today requires a change in the character structure so as to eliminate all the underlying symptoms which produce the illness. However, before giving some suggestions for remedying the actual malady, I would like to summarize the results of my interviews with Iranian youth and officials, and then evaluate it.

How Iranians view youth problems

In general, I interviewed 119 persons, 50 of whom were high-ranking officials administering youth programs dealing with educational, athletic, judicial, recreational matters and the social guidance of youth. There were also several educators, university professors, teachers, writers, ministers and under-secretaries. The youth were college students. Furthermore, I spent two days hiking, where I encountered a large group of young hikers, some of whom I talked to. I also administered an inventory, "Adolescent Reports of Parental Behavior"[1] to 400 senior high-school students. Although all of this material was inadequate in the sense that it was based on a limited and selected sample and did not include any interviews with rural youth and those in the provinces, it did indicate the general trend.

---

[1] A study being prepared for publication.

Several views were expressed by government and business leaders. One prominent leader stated that "aimlessness" was the biggest youth problem. Although he believed that long-range objectives would come about with time, he also emphasized the lack of immediate orientation. An administrator concluded his remarks with the statement that "we are not without guilt; we have not done much, and there is a need for immediate action." He clearly separated personal, group and national problems from one another and believed that opportunities must be provided for the solutions to social problems if self-renewal is to be attained.

Eighty-four per cent of those interviewed believed that youth should be provided with work in order to improve their economic status and thereby solve their problems. The fact that Iranian youth from prosperous families have as much trouble as the needy indicates that the economic aspect although important is not enough. One must also acknowledge that poverty is very apparent and the spokesmen for the youth emphasized the lack of material needs, including even textbooks and clothing. Material satisfaction is obviously necessary for the control of the problem and for the release of greater energy for constructive character reform. Moreover, 90 per cent of the respondents stressed the lack of proper means for recreation, but only three per cent perceived that most youth do not take even the minimum advantage of what is available. A professional colleague —the head of a research unit—stated that all the evidence implies that there is a great difference between establishing an organization and administering it effectively. He believed that good administrators, adept in decision-making could utilize the existing facilities for a number of purposes instead of just one. The same colleague invited me to attend one of the weekly meetings held by leading officials of the youth organizations to discuss their problems and plans. It was interesting to note that they all generally agreed that they were not utilizing present organizational and recreational facilities properly, but when they sought a solution they were blocked by the fear of their superiors, and above all, by their own inner conflicts and varied interests.

This observation made me aware of a greater problem faced by all nations undergoing change, that is, the fact that most of the newer institutions in these societies would have arisen independently without being related to one another. They are now ready to be interrelated and to develop harmoniously toward the goal of reconstruction. This matter is particularly true in regard to the problem of youth. I am also reminded of Margaret Mead's concept[1] that because new institutions have not emerged from the indigenous culture but have been imposed from without, there is also a period of conflict between the traditional and modern institutions. The intensity of such conflict differs because of the role that these traditional and modern institutions play. Where the discrepancy is minimal, as in the case of traditional athletics (the *zurkhana*) in Iran, particularly the wrestling, versus the modern form of wrestling (known in Iran as "foreign wrestling") there is a tendency for the traditional wrestlers to freely borrow the techniques of the other and to participate in international events. But if the discrepancy is great and the ideas are also misinterpreted, then, as in the case of the traditional *madressas* and modern colleges, it may take almost two generations to integrate these institutions for further learning. It is only when the new institution discovers its place within the social structure that it can contribute to the rest of the programs. The point I wish to make here is that youth insti-

---

[1] R. Arasteh, Some problems of education in underdeveloped countries, *Middle East Journal*, Summer 1958.

tutions should function in relative harmony with family morals and within the educational system and developmental planning.

Seventeen per cent of the people whom I interviewed had definite ideas about the changing morals of youth and society, especially in regard to relations between the opposite sexes. There was much support for new legislation which would make people feel sure that the changes occurring would benefit and improve the status of women. However, only 5 per cent of these respondents believed in total freedom in sexual relations. Eighty per cent discussed their personal needs rather than being objective, and the rest were noncommittal. In conclusion then one of the most pressing problems in Iran is that as youth become aware of the importance of a profession in life they delay marriage and when they do marry, divorce often follows because they are deviating from a traditional structure. It is pertinent to note here Robert J. Havighurst's study of youth in Chicago.[1] He found that just as high-school drop-outs may become criminal, those youths who pursue learning may delay their marriage, often until their 30's. This same situation applies to Iranian youth and has led to another problem in Iran, that is, the problem of the bachelor who often fails to socialize with his colleagues who are married.

Sixty-six per cent of the respondents believed that there is a great need for public libraries, clubs, dance studios and athletic societies, although it is obvious that these facilities, with no relationship to work and to learning, may in turn become escape mechanisms rather than useful means of reconstructing Iranian youth. Furthermore, I personally believe that in a country where 80 per cent of the school buildings are inadequate and where there are many schools which have no playground area, efforts

---

[1] R. J. Havighurst, How we postpone youth's coming of age. In R. M. MacIver, (editor) *Dilemmas of Youth in America Today.* N.Y.: Harper, 1961.

should be made to expand these necessary facilities. Similarly, a remedy should be found for increasing the proportion of rural youth going to high school. In Kerman the ratio of rural to urban high-school youth is 1:114; in Tehran 1:17.[1]

Seventy per cent of the respondents considered the present era one of waste for youth. They frequently cited the fact that three-fourths of those who enter high school do not finish, and out of the fourth who do, only 30 per cent attend colleges; the rest remain idle.[2] Another 25 per cent believed that youth must attain a sense of relatedness and an orientation which they not have at present.

EVALUATIONS AND RECOMMENDATIONS

What these interviews reveal is that the government and the people are gradually realizing the problems of youth and accepting them as a reality, but uncoordinated efforts will fall short of a solution. What is needed is a realistic perspective which may yield an aim and utilize the energy of youth.

I personally believe that in its process of modernization Iran should relate the problem of youth to the problem of its national rebirth. Thus the re-evaluation and direction should come from the goal the nation is directing itself toward. Assuming that Iran does not intend to foresake all its humanistic and cultural heritage, I believe that the youth should be divided in terms of age groups, and each age group should be guided according to specific principles. From my knowledge of the third five-year plan for economic and social development and industrialization, I believe that the age group, 12-16 years should be imbued with

---

[1] R. Arasteh, *Education and Social Awakening in Iran, op. cit.*

[2] Based on an interview with the Director, Department of Secondary Education, Ministry of Education, Iran.

18

a new educational philosophy to prepare them to become good citizens and eager for further growth. Those between 16-19 years will be subdivided into three categories: (a) those who do not finish high school will be trained in nearby agricultural centers and work camps; (b) high-school graduates—most of them will be trained further in neighboring industrial centers; (c) high-school graduates who enter college will be encouraged to become independent in their choice of a career rather than merely entering civil service.

The present graduates of the high schools number five times the number that the colleges can accept. Indeed, much of the students' insistence on getting into college comes from the entrance restrictions imposed by authorities as well as from the actual lack of facilities. The colleges in Iran would do well to heed the words of Zoroaster: "Whosoever comes for knowledge, teach him without expectation." Moreover, education in Iran should be modernized so as to provide the type of graduate who will be a dynamic force in the changing society instead of one competing for a desk. I also believe the college years can serve as the years of decision-making in life. Even with inadequate facilities, youths who attend classes will have more direction than those who are adrift without objectives and headed eventually toward withdrawl and delinquency.

At this point I would like to turn to a more select group of Iranians—those educated abroad, chiefly in Europe and America. I have discussed the background of the Western-educated Iranians from the late nineteenth century to the post World War II period in two previous articles.[1] This group, which now

---

[1] R. Arasteh, The education of Iranian leaders in Europe and America, *International Rev. of Educ.*, 8, 444-450 (1963); The role of intellectuals in administrative development and social change in modern Iran, *International Rev. of Educ.*, 9, 326-334 (1963-64).

numbers 20,000, has, as a result of political events, become a matter of concern to the Iranian government, especially when it is measured in terms of "brain drain," for it takes thirty-five years for an Iranian to attain a high level of scientific productivity, and then because of ideological differences and the lack of scientific opportunities he is reluctant to return home. Although the problem requires further investigation, the current reports on Iranians abroad are subjective and naive in their treatment of the problem. This is particularly true of the reports prepared by the Supervisory Office of Iranian Students, newspaper articles, and even the reports issued by the educational committees in the Parliament and Senate. Moreover, university officials who have traveled abroad and reported back to the government have not been without such a bias. Perhaps the most comprehensive studies available in this area are two doctoral theses by Iranian graduates who interviewed Iranian students about their problems and their reasons for remaining in the United States. Since 1953 I myself have been interested in this matter and have published several articles, which are, however, of general interest and deal with students in the United States.[1]

None of the above studies, however, deals with the emotional and unconscious forces which are the most crucial ones. For example, Dr. Bahraini analyzing the factors which led his respondents to remain in the United States rather than to return to Iran, cites such factors as poverty, religion, leaving Iran during the adolescent years, studying in foreign schools in Tehran, marriage to an American, a long stay abroad (more than four years), and specialization in a profession. To many Westerners these factors may appear to be the cause, but I believe they are actually secondary factors and are the symptoms of the

---

[1] R. Arasteh, *Education and Social Awakening, op. cit.*

illness rather than the illness itself. The real problem lies in the ambiguity of the future and in the changing perspective of these youth. In particular, a lack of training within their own cultural heritage has created in them a vacuum which makes mental communication difficult and directs their interest toward their own self-transformation rather than toward others. Moreover, these youth are also the product of the modern age and seek psychological and material comfort in preference to being reformers, particularly if they were born in the post-war period. In terms of their cultural heritage, Iranians are seekers rather than reformers, even if one overlooks the lack of opportunity in Iran.

Thus, at present, Iranian students comprise two generations: one, a generation who participated in the early 1950's national movement and did not succeed in materializing their ideology (regardless of its value); they have turned inwardly to utilize their own energies constructively and participate in political protests occasionally. This group has been misunderstood, for I believe they are a heterogeneous group. The majority of those I have known would sincerely like to participate in the reconstruction of Iran provided they could receive security at home and could trust the authorities. In fact, I consider that their fears are due more to their imaginary ideas about the Iranian government than to the actual situation. Of course, this is to be expected when they are far away from their country and have psychological problems which require an outlet.

The second group are younger students who were born in the late 1930's and who had their elementary training in the decade of trial and error (1940-1950), a time when Iran had lost its old political direction and was searching for a new one. They were in high school during the nation's years of decision making (1950-1960), when Iran was testing its national orientation. These students usually left Iran with a psychological vacuum which has been filled up by ideologies found on college campuses in Europe and America. Separated from a social orientation, weak in their own native tongue, and disdainful of their own literature and system of thought, they have had no other choice than to become, at present, professional and practical men seeking a relatively good life wherever they find it. Can such a person return to Iran without an orientation of some kind? The answer needs further clarification.

To be happy in a foreign country and effective in the course he has chosen requires persistence. If he succeeds in his profession and makes a good marriage he can re-evaluate the sitiuaton in later years and will undoubtedly contribute to a universal way of life. Yet such extraordinary individuals are rare. The majority are constantly encountering problems. Therefore, if we raise the basic question: "Why are Iranian youth attracted by a foreign education?" a number of possible answer come to mind. It is a fashion, arising from an illusionary feeling at home? Is it the high cost of living in Tehran and its social limitations? Is it an esacpe mechanism for youth who cannot stand the traditional life at home? Or is it a real search for knowledge and experience for furthering maturity?

These are all problems which undoubtedly require further research. Yet I am not in error when I state that Iranian youth before going abroad must have realistic aims and objectives to guide them in the new country. Therefore, the greatest contribution that one can make to these youth is to help them clarify their aims, because when they encouter emotional stress that aim can provide a therapeutic anchor. The anxiety that such a youth experiences arises from a series of situations: initially he faces a separation from unconscious defenses and a familiar culture, which can only be cured if the youth acquires mastery in

22

the language of the host country and becomes familiar with its history and social system. When he has not yet overcome this anxiety he must face still another stress, that is, to be accepted by his foreign age-mates. While he is still struggling with the group affilation he must begin to worry about his success or failure in his studies. He is also at an age to be attracted by girls, and if we consider the nature of Iranians and their social deprivation, we can conclude that their unfamiliar behavior will be a major effort directed toward psycho-social harmony and further growth of their individuality. Moreover, in such a transitional period, the youth may fall into a financial crisis and may entirely lose hope, unless he occasionally meets someone who understands his problems; if he does not acquire a sense of belonging to any orientation he eventually adopts reactive mechanisms of revolt and mistrust.

It is in this light that I consider clarity of purpose as the main measure for security and comfort, and it must be supported by some authority or a sense of national relatedness. There have been individuals who have passed through these uncertain years successfully, and their lives should become examples. In fact, many of these individuals did not assume that a diploma was the end of their search. They did not become technicians but searched further until they become reintegrated in a state in which they were able to contribute to their society. These rare individuals have become creators and originators in a way that they have initiated the beginning of a new scientific nation. Iran needs fewer pseudo-Westernized intellectuals but many more originators who can relate technology and modernization to its scientific roots, on the one hand, and to a good life on the other. These individuals are fortunately in the making in terms of the number of prominent Iranians now engaged in the physical and social sciences in Europe and America. Alone and without success, they will not be able to achieve much in Iran unless a community can be established whereby they can share various achievements through scientific means. Such a measure can also serve as a feedback to repay the scientific debt to Western contributions. In short, Iran is badly in need of an Academy of Sciences, a center for scientific research which will relate knowledge to modernization and will also overcome its university inadequacies.

A Theoretical Model of Science, Technology and a Healthy Society in Iran

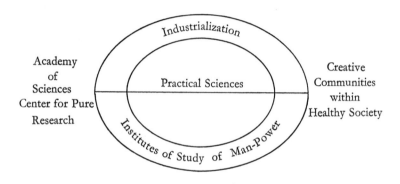

Results

This blueprint brings us to the concluding point: Where are the present youth movements going? The results of my interviews indicate that 90 per cent of the respondents believed that Iranian society and the people, especially the urban youth, have changed, not only in terms of technological advances, but also in regard to value orientation. Yet the general public which still seeks an answer to the meaning of life in terms of religious concepts is not aware of this change, although people are aware of new interests and ideas among their sons and daughters. Twenty-eight per cent of the respondents were aware that measures and values have changed and 17 per cent believed that even the peasants who now come to town have no ethics and are readily losing their moral conscience. There is a general feeling that one cannot trust them. It seems that the inner "guard" of human behavior is losing its ground everywhere, and no professional ethics or sense of legality have yet been established. In other words, the social superego, which controlled behavior in the previous generation, is no longer effective, and no one has yet initiated a new group superego. In fact, I do not believe that a group superego is something that one can create, but it is a phenomenon which can emerge from the consistency of action among people with sane goals and interests.

A re-examination of remarks about this profound human issue and its consequences on growth and maturity yields three different philosophical answers. A respected university professor, who is a good observer and familiar with Persian character and the culture of Iran, told me: "Iranians are at the threshold of the rebirth of reason, which is unfortunately in conflict with unbriddled instinct, on the one hand, and superficial and false Western values, on the other. Luckily, however, this is characteristic only of Tehranis; the people in the provinces have not yet lost their wholistic state, although that state may be in a lower degree of awareness. Therefore, to remedy both these extremes we must look into our own culture and find a period when reason and religion were in harmony, and then strengthen that outlook."[1]

---

[1] For further information see R. Arasteh, *Final Integration, op. cit.* and *Rumi the Persian, op. cit.*

25

According to this well-informed intellectual we must receive revelation from Metazila (a group of Muslims who used reason to interpret Islam) and bring reason and religion into harmony so that we can attain inner security by means of genuine ideas in Islamic religion and external security and modernization by means of reason. This view is somewhat comparable to Arnold Toynbee's idea of "return to genuine Christian ethics" for the West; both thinkers ignore the practical problems of such a philosophy in the midst of an economic and profit-seeking orientation. They overlook the inherent contradiction which exists between these two poles and do not give us the way to resolve them. Moreover, if Iranians seek a group conscience in their past culture, why not delve into a maturer state of their past civilization, that is, the state when genuine thinkers like al-Ghazzali resolved the contradition between logic and faith through an experiential approach, specifically Persian humanistic mysticism. Such a solution requires the "rediscovery of Persia, which is waiting for decipherment.

In contrast to the first respondent, whose thoughts were derived from a Persian cultural base, another young Persian intellectual had views strongly resembling those in the West. He stated that industrialization will gradually develop people's character, and this character will be rooted in self-interest; ultimately profit seeking and specialization will demand professional ethics.

Although one cannot overlook the pressure of such a movement within the social structure, this young intellectual ignores the present trend in the West, that is, people are beginning to realize that "material comfort" is not enough. Man must make his peace with his fellowmen and have confidence in his destiny. Nor can I ignore the fact that great material hardship in this era may attract people more toward this trend, but I do not see how the inquisitive mind of the Iranian can rest at this ideal. On the contrary, I believe Iranian leaders and thinkers must aim at a stage beyond "material comfort," although economics is obviously the infrastructure of the society. Iranians must try to adopt the mechanism of cooperation instead of competition, achievement instead of possession, if they eventually want to obtain "happiness and prosperity" in one breath. This is the only choice which the nineteenth and twentieth centuries have left for Iran and her sister states. The choice is still open, because none of these movements have yet gathered momentum. Otherwise, Iran must struggle for decades to achieve a material state of comfort only to eventually discover that it is a mirage. Furthermore, only men who have distant vision have achieved great goals. A deep vision of the future course of human communities, whether in the East or the West, directs us to "creative communities." Why not aim at such a goal and try to attain it? I believe this analysis applies to the present released state of youth everywhere, and industrialization must become a means of attaining it, not just a goal in itself.

A third group of intellectual respondents believed that time and historical determinism determine the group conscience. Although there may be some truth in this belief, it is still a narrow approach for two reasons: (1) Even admitting that historical determinism is a fact, I believe it is less so in our present age of awareness; (2) Secondly, it is true that group conscience cannot be predicted at present (except if a new prophet arises), but its course and direction can easily be determined. Should it be constructive; should it struggle for the movement; or should it be destructive? It is in the process of action that one of these forces will become dominant, and an individual or a group will develop a healthy character, a neurotic personality, or a criminal attitude, respectively. *Therefore, the most essential factor of all is the*

origin of action and the direction of its progress so as to eventually contri-
bute to the formation of universal inner security and a group conscience.

The milieu for such activities, should most likely be the actualization of agriculture, industrial, developmental, scientific and cultural trends. It is in the process of actualizing these plans that new values emerge and can be strengthened by communication media. The guide line to these values should be a hierarchy which will use laws and justice as an anchor of society to give the greatest value to originators in any field, rather than to those who put into form the pregnant ideas of the originator; to those who transform knowledge to the next generation and administer plans, and finally to live by practical intelligence and impliment these plans. In this process work and love will be the common core of all relationships and will bring youth out of their present transitional period.

Now when we compare the trend of youth in Israel with those in Iran we can conclude that certain national and international circumstances did not permit Iranian youth to fill up their psychological vacuum by political and national movements, to identify with economic changes and to finally seek individual betterment. Yet both Israeli and Iranian youth have reached the same threshold, which requires existential solution. I believe Iran is in a situation whereby youth can benefit from a method which will identify the relationships which exist between socialization and an urge for a *Weltanschauung* and resolve its contradiction by directing its effort toward a society which can produce both internal and external security, inner satisfaction and external productivity.

RAIHANEH

THE TRADITIONAL YOUTH

CHAPTER ONE

THE CHOOPI DANCE

It was late in July. Water from the snow-peaked mountain ran
over the stones through the green meadow down to the valley
and then disappeared in the murmuring stream. Deep in the
valley lay the peaceful village of Khosh Makan (literally "pleasant
place"). It *is* a pleasant place. Mountain brooks join at the base
of the northern slope to form one large stream which runs
through the middle of the village. The mud houses of the
peasants are hidden among walnut trees. When darkness spreads
her chaddor on the ground, the village goes to sleep under the
shadow of the heavy old trees; and when the sun kisses the top
of the Western mountain, then the village comes to life again.
The morning star takes the farmers to their fields and the
evening star guides them back to their families. The air is pure
and one can almost smell the coming of morning. The weather
in summer is pleasant. (In winter the temperature drops below
zero).

There are springs everywhere in the village—in the gardens,
at the foot of the mountains, in the fields and in the courtyards.
These springs serve as meeting places for the women of the
village. Early in the morning they come here with their skirts
full of dishes. News and advice are freely given. Nothing escapes
their observation: it may be the intended arrival of a government official or such natural events as a young village girl

31

getting married or a mother giving birth to a child. As they talk, a woman fills her earthen jug full of clear water, stoops low and deftly lifts it to her head, adjusting it for comfort. She turns and gracefully walks away. The scene is repeated in the evening.

Friday in the village is usually a day of rest. This day was an exception. The morning stillness was broken by gypsy music accompanying a Choopi dance. Choopi dancing is the popular dance in many Iranian villages. It is performed on every festive occasion.

To the bagpipe of the gypsy, a couple began to dance. Their dancing took the form of a mock battle, one took the offensive, the other the defensive. On the sidelines a crowd had begun to gather and they gradually formed a circle around the participants.

In this dance, the man who has the role of the attacker pursues the other around the circle. Both carry sticks. The defender uses his strong stick to ward off the blows of the attacker. The aim of the other is to strike his antagonist on the legs, and if he succeeds the man drops out of the dance. The attacker now takes over his role and a new dancer takes the initiative. In this way, the young men of the village demonstrate their skill to the admiring young girls in the audience.

As the musicians played on their bagpipes and drums, the dancing warriors battled in time to the music. The crack of the whip was like a siren piercing the air. The audience breathed deeply. Another dancer entered the ring. The defeated one slipped back into the audience, hoping that he might get another chance later on. The young danced exuberantly; the old cheered enthusiastically.

It was just about noon when a group of horsemen broke through the circle of dancers and entered the courtyard. The horses were decked with colorful ribbons, and each rider waved a gay handkerchief. There were about a dozen horses in all.

Their clamor and shouting were not enough: they began to shoot bullets in the air. They wanted everyone to know the reason for their gaiety. A wedding was soon to take place.

Excitement was in the air. Loud boisterous shouts and the stamping of feet came from across the fields, mingled with the buzz of voices in the courtyard: enough to drown out the sound of sobbing that came from the house. In one of the backrooms, a thirteen year old girl knelt and prayed alone. It was hard to see Raihaneh's features for her face was buried in her hands. Only her long black hair was evident. It hung down over her shoulders, and seemed to have been arranged with great care for this occasion.

Raihaneh was a source of envy to the other girls in the village. They envied not only her hair and her sparkling eyes but her pale delicate complexion, so much in contrast to their own tough tanned features. Just now her eye lids were weighted down by tears, her eyes hardly visible.

Some of the villagers disliked her and they sometimes said of her, "She thinks herself better than the rest of us, just because she has been to school in Bagh-saba and has finished the fourth grade of elementary school. A girl should be educated at home. Otherwise what kind of wife will she make?"

True, Raihaneh was not like other village girls. The Din Dar family spent most of the year in Bagh-saba, a well known city in southern Iran. During the summer months they spent their time in the village of Khosh-makan where Aga Din Dar owned some property. It was here that the father had arranged the marriage of his daughter to a prosperous middle-aged villager, Dordaneh Barzegar.

This was the wedding day; a day Raihaneh had anticipated with dispair. She could not escape her father's choice of a husband—a man the age of her father.

33

But no one paid any attention to her tears. In the courtyard friends and relatives were singing old village songs, and inside her parents wer busy entertaining guests. The servants were preparing the room for the marriage ceremony. Villagers came with gifts for the bride and groom, and the parents accepted them with many polite thanks. Each gift was recorded in a book, so that when a similar occasion arose, the donor would be repaid in kind, as is the custom in these parts. Most of the gifts were useful ones: some brought rice and sugar; others contributed sheep and goats; and even money was given.

Sometimes the gifts are even used beforehand in the wedding feast itself. What remains is given to the newlyweds to begin housekeeping with.

This wedding was different from most. The groom, Dordaneh had been through the marriage ceremony once before. Now, as a rich and prosperous business man he had everything that he needed, except a son. His first wife had given him only daughters, but because she was a good housekeeper he did not wish to divorce her. For the last few years he had been looking around for a second wife—a young healthy, attractive girl who could give him a son. He had felt a yearning for Raihaneh the moment he saw her; but it had taken him two years to persuade her parents that it would be a good match for their daughter. A second wife does not usually receive the respect and prestige that a first wife gets—neither from her husband, nor from the community. But the parents' reluctance gave way as they became more acquainted with Dordaneh's wealth and received handsome gifts as tokens of his interest in their daughter. In this way he bought their consent.

Dordaneh made most of the arrangements and preparations for the wedding. Included were all the lovely dresses a young girl could desire. He sent three sugar sacks for the ceremony, five rice sacks and ten tins of oil. When the wedding day approached he sent a large silver mirror with two massive silver candelebra. Then he added an illuminated copy of the holy Koran and a big copper tray filled with home-made candies, and several more trays of fruit, as well as boxes of Isfahani jewelry, pieces of art and household items. All of this was carried ceremoniously to the house on the heads of a dozen men. The villagers saw the procession and considered Raihaneh a very lucky girl. Yet there were a few sentimentalists, even among the village folk, who felt there was no substitute for a marriage of true love.

Late in the afternoon of the wedding day, the mirror and the silver candelebra were put in front of the prayer rug and the Koran was placed on it too.

The tearful bride was helped into her wedding dress. The rouge that tinted her cheeks and lips failed to hide the pallor and unhappiness there. The tears on her cheeks heightened the contrast—like pearls in a red velvet case. Her mother tried to console her. There was no need for her to cry. Why, she would be very happy. Had not Dordaneh promised her a home in Bagh-saba with a servant and a maid? She need not live in the village but would be close to her own parents. After all, her parents wanted only the best for their daughter.

Raihaneh's aunt joined them and nodded her agreement. There wasn't any need to worry about the first wife, she told her niece. Dordaneh would stay with her in Bagh-saba.

Their words failed to comfort her. They continued to speak to her in soothing words as they combed her hair and led her from the room. Still her quivering shoulders betrayed her feelings. In the sitting room Raihaneh was led to the prayer rug where she seated herself.

Around her were seated many guests: relatives and friends of

35

her family and of the groom's. There was plenty of gay chatter and merry singing but the melodies failed to reach the heart of the young girl. Silent tears rolled down her cheeks.

It was almost sunset when the religious leader entered the bridal room, accompanied by the groom and witnesses. After reciting a few verses from the Koran which pertained to companionship, the *mullah* (clergyman) stated the customary request for the bride's hand in behalf of the groom, to which Raihaneh had to give words of acceptance. The request was repeated three times by the mullah, and each time the quivering voice of Raihaneh accepted—not from her heart or personal desire but from the demands and fear of her parents. The marriage book was signed by the witnesses and the newly married couple were congratulated by all. In the adjoining rooms a large feast had been prepared for the guests.

In Persian weddings the marriage ceremony is performed some time in advance of the time when the bride begins to live with the groom. In Raihaneh's case, the date was set for the following Friday.

After the marriage feast, the guests departed, along with the groom who left without seeing his wife. It was still difficult for Raihaneh to accept her marriage. She did not sleep that night, nor the next. She lost interest in everything around her. As the days passed she became more depressed and weak from the lack of food. There was no longer any chance for her to escape from a marriage that she was now obligated to consummate.

The following Friday was now at hand. It was late at night when the servants fetched her trousseau and other belongings to take her to her new home. Then the horses appeared—specially decorated ones to take the bride and groom home. The groom handed the reins of the horses to an attendant and went to summon the bride. She dutifully followed him and he helped her mount her horse. A torch bearer ran on ahead of them to lighten the dark alleys. It was not far and they soon arrived. Raihaneh dismounted to bid her parents good-bye, and the tears swelled in her eyes. The groom and his relatives led her gently to her *hajlah* (a room decorated and furnished properly for the honeymoon). Among the relatives who greeted her was Johana, the first wife: but Raihaneh took no notice of her.

The *hajlah* was illuminated with many lights. A bed cover of the palest blue was reflected in the soft light of the chandelier. The pinkness of the mattress cover was visible through the bed spread. The heavy scent of fresh roses in the room was strongly overpowering. As the bride stepped into the room, the relatives gathered in a back adjoining room. They were posted there to see that the marriage was consummated. As is the custom in these regions, the close relatives of the groom are at hand to see that the bride submits herself and that the groom asserts his rights. It is an honor for the groom to accomplish his duties as a husband on the first night; and it is a respected virtue for the bride to be a virgin.

And so the night passed: one prepared in eagerness, the other in reluctance; the groom full of passion, the bride full of despair. Dordaneh vowed again to his bride that he would never let her live in the same house with his first wife. Instead he would take her to Bagh-saba and buy her a fine home there, and she would be able to see her family often. How confident he was that he could make his new wife happy!

CHAPTER TWO

TWO MONTHS LATER

Late in summer, nine weeks after the wedding, the Din Dar family had returned to Bagh-saba, where they awaited news from Dordaneh that he was bringing his young bride there as he had promised. They had no reason to doubt him—was he not a respected member of his village and a man well able to provide for their daughter?

The parents felt the urgency of this matter. For the last two months Raihaneh had visited their home in Khosh-makan every Friday and had told them how much she suffered. With tearful exclamations she described the life she led. Her mother-in-law's house was a big one: it occupied about 1000 square meters. On the first floor were the quarters for the sheep and goats as well as storerooms for food and clothing. On the second floor were many rooms, each one having access to a balcony which circled the house. Many people lived there, and all were related to Masharaf Barzegar, Raihaneh's new mother-in-law. The old woman exercised considerable control over the members of her household; so much so that she had long been called "Khonem Barzegar" (the mistress). And so she was. She had three children of her own: two sons and a daughter; as well as a step-son, Dordaneh, whom she treated as one of her own. All were married and lived with their families in the big old house. Raihaneh related how Khonem Barzegar ignored her and did nothing to make her feel at home; and the others treated her much the same way. Her husband was seldom with her; he was busy with his work, and also spent time with his first wife. Aga Din Dar tried to soothe his daughter. She imagined too many of these things. She should respect her mother-in-law and do as she was told, and in due time everything would be all right.

Khonem Din Dar sided with her daughter. For one thing, Raihaneh had not been trained to live in such a household, run by a domineering matriarch. Khonem Din Dar herself had heard stories from others about the Khonem Barzegar. The old woman not only ran the lives of her children and grandchildren but the lives of the servants and villagers who did business with her. The Barzegar family owned a great deal of property in the neighborhood and people were sufficiently frightened by the old woman's threats to obey her. To defy her orders meant possible loss of employment and certain privileges granted them.

Khonem Barzegar delegated her authority to her three sons. Each one was given certain responsibilities, but always they took orders from her and submitted reports of what they had done.

As Dordaneh was the oldest, he was entrusted with administering the land. Many of the villagers own nothing—neither land, ploughs, water, nor seed. It is customary in these parts for a landlord to value their labor at one-fifth the harvest. Four-fifths of the harvest go to the landlord to pay for the use of land, ploughs, water and seed. Not only this, but at harvest time, a peasant needs fodder for his livestock if he has any. Quite likely he deals directly with the *malek* (landlord) who buys his crops at half the market value.

Thus, it was Dordaneh's job to supervise the peasant labor that harvested crops on his family's property. The crops that the Barzegar family obtained were stored in large storehouses until the winter time when prices were at a peak. Then it was not uncommon for them to sell some of it back to their tenants, but at a much higher price, of course.

Babak, the second son, operated a clothing shop in the bazaar. It was the largest one there. He made regular trips to Bagh-saba to buy material which he sold in turn to the villagers and to the tribesmen. In addition he sold sugar and tea in his shop. These three items were the necessities most in demand by the villagers and tribespeople.

The third son, Bahman, was in charge of buying up the goods that the villagers and tribespeople had; and he took it to Bagh-saba to be sold. From the local people he obtained honey in great amounts, as well as oil, fat, fur, wool and the skins of animals. From Bagh-saba he brought back clothing, tobacco and sugar.

The Barzegar family had built up a large trade with the nomadic tribesmen and these people bought all their household necessities from Babak and Bahman. They often had to buy on credit, which was permitted and no interest charged; but certainly the original price was much higher to begin with.

In the first week of Raihaneh's marriage, she was a guest. She had a special maid, sent by her parents. At the beginning Dordaneh was very attentive to her and tried his best to win her love. But summer was his busiest season, for he had to supervise each harvest and record the profits of his family. The week of his honeymoon was the only time that he was free of work and had the privacy of one of the larger sitting rooms.

The following week, Raihaneh had to join the clan and to work as the others did. She had to follow the orders of Khonem Barzegar if she were to adjust to this strange new life. In this house it was the custom for everyone to arise early at dawn for prayers. Muslim practice prescribes prayers five times a day. Following the morning prayer, the women of the household prepared breakfast for their menfolk and later for themselves and the children. Then Khonem Barzegar gave the day's orders for each of her daughters-in-law and the maids. The girls did as they were told and did not question her authority. But Raihaneh had not been brought up in a village, nor did she feel any kinship or warmth to the old woman. Most of the other young women of the household had been distant cousins of the Barzegar family even before marriage. So they felt it their duty to obey the old woman, and if there were tears they shed them in the privacy of their own rooms. In fact, Khonem Barzegar ranked her daughters-in-law in terms of their obedience and seniority.

It was not easy for Raihaneh to behave like the others. Nor could she easily adjust to their way of life. She was different: she was literate, while the others had received no education at all. She had been brought up in town whereas the others knew only the village. Even her speech was different, as well as her manners in eating, in dressing and in behaving.

Once a week the women of the house baked. Although there was a special maid trained for this task, still Khonem Barzegar expected the young women to supervise the baking themselves. Raihaneh did not know how to bake and even less about supervising a baker. She was only thirteen and her experience was exceedingly limited.

Twice a week a group of the women from the household went to the public baths. Early in the morning the baths were reserved for the men, and the women could use them only in the late morning when the men had left. It was a day's activity: the preparation of going, the bathing and returning home.

Raihaneh tried to make friends with the other wives but she failed. Johana did not encourage the other women to be friends with Raihaneh, for how can two wives live under the same roof? Tension was everywhere. Even the maids recognized the lowly

41

position of Raihaneh, and made little effort to follow her orders. It was Khonem Barzegar who set the tone of the relationship: as long as she refused to accept Raihaneh, the others would too.

On Fridays Raihaneh went to the home of her parents with a new set of complaints. So unhappy was she that there were times when she was reluctant to return, but her parents always advised her to go back. On one visit home she stayed through Saturday and Dordaneh had to go to fetch her. Gradually, what had been hidden in Raihaneh's heart appeared openly in her behavior. The other wives felt pity for her, but to Khonem Barzegar it was a sign of weakness and she disliked the young wife even more. Dordaneh saw the unhappiness of his young wife, but did not know how to ease it.

At last, on one of her visits home, Raihaneh refused to return to the Barzegar household. Dordaneh sent Raihaneh's own maid to bring her back. On her knees, the young girl begged her mother to let her stay, saying that she never wished to return to her husband and his family.

This upset Aga Din Dar very much. He sent the maid back with a message for Dordaneh reminding him of his promise to take Raihaneh to live in Bagh-saba.

Dordaneh received the news sadly, for he had come to love his child-bride and wanted to please her. He recognized the troublesome influence of Khonem Barzegar and the unhappiness of Johana, his first wife. He pondered his misfortunes and wondered what he could do to straighten out the situation. It was his habit when thinking to puff on a "ghelyon" or hookah. (Sometimes it's called a "hubble-bubble" pipe because the smoke from the tobacco passes through water, making a bubbling noise). Several times Dordaneh tried to approach the Din-Dar family to speak of a reconciliation, but without success.

A short time later, Raihaneh left the village with her parents.

He saw them off, and gave his wife a gift of 1500 Rials. The situation was hard for all concerned, but there was no way of changing it.

At home, Dordaneh had a hard time of it. He ate apart from his relatives, although sometimes he discussed his affairs with his brothers. He had a still harder time in the community. Those who had once looked up to him now hardly spoke to him. On one occasion he overheard a relative of Raihaneh discussing him. "He is not a man. What man would forsake everything to marry a second time and then not be able to hang on to her?" These words pierced his heart and he had no answer. There was no one to talk to, either at home or at the market; it was hard to be alone, day and night. Small things upset his temper: on one occasion he struck his wife, and another time he dared to argue with his step-mother. Finally he could stand the situation no longer and he left his home to attend to some business in a village, 30 miles away from Khoshmakan. It was a summer resort called Komer; it is known for its mountain springs, green hills and oil resources.

While in Komer, Dordaneh made an effort to occupy himself with auditing the income of the villagers, for his family owned substantial property here. But again his grief overtook him and reason left. He gazed wistfully at the sky, wondering what Raihaneh was doing at that moment. On the seventh day of his stay in Komer he awoke at four o'clock and lit the oil lamp. He called to Shir Ali, his servant and asked him to prepare breakfast and saddle the horse so that he might have an early start. Within an hour, they were on their way down the rugged mountain road. They stopped about every other hour so that Dordaneh might have some refreshment and a smoke. He sat near the spring and inhaled the smoke and blew it out through his nostrils. Then the two men mounted their horses and went on their way again. Dordaneh seldom spoke, but often sighed to himself. Eight hours later they arrived back a Khosh-makan.

It was already late in the afternoon, but Dordaneh sent his servant to the village square to inquire about transportation to Bagh-saba. There was nothing leaving that evening. In fact a car goes to Bagh-saba only once a week, taking a day to cover 60 miles. This is a great improvement over the old days when it took two days by horse or three days on foot.

The reason why it takes a car a full day to travel 60 miles in these parts is not always the fault of the car. Time is not important. A driver often likes to smoke a little opium before starting, and sometimes the owner of the vehicle joins him in this. It may last several hours. It annoys the passengers, and many don't like to ride in cars driven by opium-smokers. But what can they do? (Beggars can't be choosers.) There are other hazards too. It's not uncommon to have a tire puncture, or the water may freeze in the winter. It's an unusual event if the driver brings his passengers to their destination without mishap. In fact, should this happen they would take the driver to dinner and tip him generously. It's also good policy for a passenger to make friends with the owner of the car, for then he has the first choice of a seat.

Dordaneh did not get started until noon. There were quite a few relatives to see him off, but he paid no attention to them. Instead he chatted with the other passengers, one of whom had never been in an automobile before.

The road to Bagh-saba is rugged and mountainous, and often unsafe—not only because of falling rocks, but because of the tribes who often raid these areas. This is especially true when the tribes pass from Sordesir (a cold place) to Garmesir (a warm place). There have been occasions when the passengers were killed, the drivers robbed and all goods taken. These robberies

44

are most likely to happen when the relationship between the government and the tribal chiefs is weak.

This time no accident happened. They rested at a teahouse along the way. Everyone sat down and spread his handkerchief out and ate his homemade food. Then the car started again.

Dust was everywhere: a layer of it covered the outside of the car and it easily found its way inside onto the occupants. But it was expected and no one really seemed to mind.

There were many turns in the road, for it is a mountainous area. But the driver was not prepared for the sharpness of one which suddenly loomed up before him. The shadow of the mountain in the semi-darkness misled him. Suddenly the car was swallowed in the shadows. The next moment it was in a ditch. The passengers were knocked against the top, then against the door and against the window. When the car came to a final stop, there was a great uproar: no one was really hurt—only a few bruises; but everyone in his own dialect was shouting his gratitude: "Praise be to Allah! Praise be to Muhammad! Praise be to Ali! Praise be to Hossein!" And all the religious saints were thanked in turn.

They continued on their way. By late evening they had reached the suburb of Bagh-saba, a small village called Ghasrodast (castle of the plains). Here the gardens are numerous and the roses are thick in abundance. One sees many people along the way: some on foot, other more fortunate ones travel by car: all are eager to reach the lovely gardens of Ghasrodast, if only to spend the day there.

An inspection post was ahead of them and they stopped to present their papers. The one room office was crowded. The three officers were surrounded by drivers all presenting their credentials. The face of one of the inspectors was inscrutable: a face which masked his thoughts; and yet there were a few who could perceive beneath it. Dordaneh had heard of him from his brothers, and he knew that a few rials would accomplish much. This inspector was known to be easy on passenger cars and strict on trucks.

Dordaneh approached the officer and slipped him twenty rials. He nodded his acceptance, glanced hurridly at their papers and gave their car a swift appraisal; then motioned them on. In Iran laws are made to be broken; for only in this way can money be gained and used for personal benefit. Laws deny, rather than grant, privileges. To obtain many benefits, the poor must necessarily break the laws by bribery. The officer, poorly paid to begin with, accepts the bribe readily.

The car drove on, headed toward the lights of the town. Finally it stopped in front of a garage, and the passengers alighted wearily. Dordaneh, eager to see his wife, was the first to shake hands all around and say good-bye. Seeing some porters near by he called to two of them to assist him. They took his baggage, balanced a piece on their heads and carried a bag in each hand. Dordaneh led the way down the quiet, dimly lit street, turned down a dark alley, and came to an intersection where the houses had been destroyed to make way for a new street, now under construction. After crossing the street, he came to a wide alley into which he turned, and stopped hesitantly before the third door. He knocked with a trembling hand, anxious to see Raihaneh but uncertain of the reception he would receive. He stood waiting—but no one came. He summoned all his strength and knocked again. The door was opened by Jam, Raihaneh's young brother. The porters carried the bags inside and left. Jam called his sister and his parents. They came forward and greeted Dordaneh politely with the customary Persian salutations, "Salam alakam. Halla shuma chetorah?" (Peace be with you. How are you?) But there was no warmth in their words.

46

Dordaneh approached Raihaneh who stood in back of her parents. He took her hands in his own and spoke tenderly. He apologized again and again for his delay and his failure in writing. His eyes begged forgiveness as did his voice.

Aga Din-Dar came forward and motioned his guest toward the fireplace. Raihaneh and her mother went into the kitchen to prepare some supper for Dordaneh, and in no time at all they brought him kabab of roasted lamb and tomatoes. Dordaneh shared his ghalyan with his father-in-law before and after the meal. They puffed in silence, each wondering what the other was thinking. Finally Dordaneh again apologized for his delay in arriving. He said that he had come to make a home for his young wife and that he intended to stay in Bagh-saba. Aga Din Dar was obviously pleased and patted his son-in-law on the back and expressed his pleasure at this turn of events.

They parted for the night. Dordaneh found Raihaneh's room and entered unannounced. She saw him standing in the doorway and began to cry. He took her in his arms and patted her tenderly and told her of his desire to stay in Bagh-saba. He wondered why she cried so. Had she thought that he might never come?

She seemed to read his thoughts, for all at once she told him how lonely she had been. The neighbors had questioned her about her husband and she hadn't known what to tell them. Yet she had been anxious and worried. Perhaps some of them had already suspected her condition and talked about her.

Dordaneh was immediately ashamed of himself and wanted to make it all up to her. Now that she was pregnant she needed him even more. He embraced her warmly and promised with all his heart that he would stay in Bagh-saba and start a new life.

Still Raihaneh felt a need to describe her loneliness these past few months. The neighborhood gossip had been particularly hard to bear, for some of them had found out that she was the second wife of a man thirty years her senior. Imagine how they talked. When she passed by they mimicked the dialect of people from Khosh-makan. She had heard them whispering how her parents had given up their dear daughter to an older married man, just to get her a husband. It had become so bad that she seldom ventured outside. She did not even visit relatives for they talked too.

Dordaneh could only guess how his in-laws felt. He was sure that their honor and prestige in the neighborhood had fallen as a result of his behavior. And no doubt they had believed that he had deserted Raihaneh. Dordaneh's remorse increased as his wife related her experiences.

Even in bed, Raihaneh could not stop talking. She pleaded with him to find some place for them to live, so that their child might have a good start in life. He felt a sudden burst of love and sympathy. He tried to tell her how he felt. He would make amends and behave more properly so as to take good care of his wife. At heart, he knew how deeply he had wronged Raihaneh and her family; and now he looked forward to doing better. The news of his young wife's pregnancy stirred him and brought forth all his longings for a son.

CHAPTER THREE

RAIHANEH IN BAGH-SABA

The bright sunlight of late morning woke up Raihaneh. The autumn leaves glistened in the bright sun. She quickly rolled up the bed, put it in a corner and went to make breakfast. The water in the samovar was still boiling; she put a handful of tea into the teapot on top and poured the boiling water on top of it. The steam of the samovar warmed the teapot.

Then Raihaneh took a handful of warm tobacco, wet it, and pressed it into shape with her hands before placing it on top of her husband's long clay pipe. She went to the small pool in the courtyard to get the wooden parts of the ghalyan: one section was attached to the clay part and in it she put water; the other piece was a thin tube which serves as a mouth piece for inhaling the tobacco which first passes through the water. Finally she put flaming pieces of charcoal on top of the clay pipe next to the tobacco.

For breakfast there was butter, honey and the flat unleavened bread, so characteristic of Iranian meals. As a special treat there were walnuts from Khoshmakan. Raihaneh arranged the breakfast food on a copper tray and carried it up to her room where Dordaneh was awaiting her.

After breakfast, Dordaneh went to speak to his father-in-law. He was anxious to discuss his plans with him. After the few customary words of greeting, Dordaneh told him again of his

49

desire to settle in Bagh-saba and make a home for his young wife. However it would take some time to find a suitable house to buy. In the meantime he needed a house to rent.

Aga Din Dar was obviously pleased with his son-in-law's plans. He offered to help him look for a place to rent. He knew of several men in town who would be able to help them, and suggested that they start out that morning.

After several days of searching they at last found rooms which suited Dordaneh. He had wanted to find a neighborhood similar to that of his own village, where the strangeness of Bagh-saba could not reach him. The house he chose was a large one. Like most Persian houses it was surrounded by a high wall, and the courtyard had a small pool in it. It would be nice for Raihaneh too, for it was close to her parents' home. The arrangement he made with the landlady was that he would rent two rooms upstairs. There were other tenants but they were mostly transients.

This kind of arrangement did not appeal to Raihaneh, but she said nothing; the duty of a Persian wife is to follow and obey. Both Aga Din Dar and Dordaneh had known the owner, Khonem Khorshid ("Sun") in Khosmaken. She was an elderly woman, originally from Khomaken. Besides renting rooms, she operated a distilling shop in her home. In a corner of the courtyard were numerous jars and bottles, and even in the basement she had stored some of her equipment. It is a traditional practice in Iran to take the juice of numerous flowers, like nasturtiums, roses and orange blossoms, as well as wild flowers and prepare scented sweet tasting sherbets. The juices are also used in perfume manufacture.

Khonem Khorshid kept only one large room for herself; the others she rented out. There was a common fireplace which all shared for cooking.

50

A few days later Raihaneh moved into her new home with her husband. Next to her lived the family of a trader from Khosh-makan. It wasn't long before Raihaneh discovered that this house was the same one her husband had stayed in when he visited Bagh-saba before his marriage. In fact, his brothers and other relatives always stayed here when they came to town.

The boarding house was always crowded: at least a dozen different tenants lived there at one time, either on a transient basis or for the year round. And almost all of them came from Khoshmakan and were acquainted with one another. They were here for business—and a few had come here to seek town wives. Sometimes several men shared a single room and cooked their meals in it; or if weather permitted, they cooked in the yard. The few women who lived here had to wear their "chad-hors" (veils) even in the courtyard. On summer nights, the men often slept on the roof. On such nights, both rich and poor share equally in the delights of the heavens: the cool Northern breezes, the starry skies and the perfumed scent of roses.

Then as the sun came up, the men awoke, one by one. Men who had hardly known one another, spoke to their neighbors as long standing acquaintances. They rolled up their thin mattresses and bedding and climbed down. After a hasty breakfast they left the house for their day's work. This was the time for the women to come forth out of their rooms. Of all the tenants, Raihaneh was the favorite with Khonem Khorshid. The land-lady took a motherly interest in the young girl and helped her furnish her rooms, clean them and even helped her cook the kind of food that she thought would suit her husband's taste. Whenever she happened to be distilling flowers, she called Raihaneh to come over and watch. The distilling process was an old one. Into an old pot, the woman put blossoms. The cover had a curved piece of tubing which led to a bottle. Vapors passed from the pot to the bottle. Raihaneh was fascinated by all of this.

Here in Bagh-saba, Dordaneh led a dull life, for there was nothing much that he could do. He usually woke up late, and after a leisurely breakfast he went to the bazaar. Here he chatted with a few business acquaintances. At various times he made deals to sell or buy oil, fat, fur and other commodities for his family which he sent to Khosh-makan.

Occasionly he gave a big dinner for the residents of the house, or he took a few friends home to dinner. Almost every night there was cooked "pollou" (rice) "khoresh" (a meat and vegetable sauce) or chicken or kabab. When he brought guests home he knocked at the door first, so that his wife might cover herself with a chaddhor and keep her beauty properly hidden from others. On these ocacsions, Khonem Korshid shared her sitting room with Dordaneh. None of the other tenants had this privilege, but she recognized Dordaneh's wealth and family background.

Dordaneh's man-servant had been with him a long time. He proved to be a great help to Raihaneh, for he shopped for her everyday. All he had to buy were meat, bread and vegetables. Dordaneh got things like rice, oil, honey, walnuts, beans and cheese from his own storehouses in Khosh-makan.

The days passed by. Dordaneh had little business in Bagh-saba now and he found that his life moved even more slowly than before. And especially in winter there was little to occupy his time. In Khosh-maken, his birthplace, winters are severe. Snow covers everything. If the roofs are not swept clean each day there is danger of cave-ins. Then the yards are piled high with snow from the roofs. The snow in the roads and alleys turns to ice, making travel impossible. Even the bazaar is closed on many days. The villagers lay in a supply of food: sugar, tea, rice, flour, wheat, beans and smoked lamb or chicken for those few families who can afford it. There isn't much to do in wintertime. People prefer to stay at home under the "corsi" to keep warm. A corsi is a low fourlegged square table placed over a deep square box which holds burning charcoal. The table is covered with a blanket under which people put their feet while sitting on cushions around the table. A cozy convenience for wintry days.

During the day, the men spend a few hours cleaning the roof of snow; and the women are constantly busy baking, cooking and preparing nourishing soups of dried vegetables and beans. The young girls help their mothers in the house. For the boys there is nothing to do: they have only to wait for sunshine; and how eagerly they scan the clouds for the first glimpse of the sun on a winter's day! And when the sun peers down on them, they scurry outside and call to their friends to join them in jumping from one roof to another, or from roof to alley, and chase to the fields to play snowballs. Ordinarily there is a telegraph line from Khoshmaken to Bagh-saba, but in winter the heavy snow cuts communication. Rarely does an automobile visit this area in winter, nor is it easy for travelers to approach it otherwise.

So Dordaneh stayed in Bagh-saba and put up with the tediousness of it all. He did so for several reasons. First of all, he had no desire to see his relatives at this point, and he knew that he could never take Raihaneh back to them to live with his first wife and step-mother. Then too, Raihaneh was pregant and she needed his help and sympathy. Also it was winter time, and there was little work for him anywhere, at Khoshmakan or at Bagh-saba. In fact, he had more to do at the latter.

For Raihaneh too, life seemed better now. The rooming house where they lived was quiet in winter time: many of the tenants had left at the first touch of winter, for they preferred to stay with their own families during this season. Raihaneh's friendship with Khonem Khorshid continued, and in addition she was close enough to her family to see them frequently. In this quiet life, Raihaneh saw more of her husband and became better acquainted with him. She took up knitting so that she might knit him a sweater. Her mother helped her make some baby clothes. All together she felt happy and settled at the prospect of becoming a mother: it made her feel grown-up. Now too, she felt more secure in her relationship to her husband. If she could give him a son, he might divorce his first wife.

Dordaneh too wanted a son. Every Thursday night he went to a shrine, lit a candle and prayed. At the door he often gave money to the needy ones standing there. At home, he prayed in the morning, at noon, in the evening and sometimes at night he awoke and called to God to give him a son. No one wishes for the birth of a girl in this part of the world. (But is it really any different in more advanced countries where a girl is equally desired but fights a losing battle from then on?)

Winter passed and the time of "Noo-ruzz" (The New Year) approached. The Persian New Year begins with the advent of spring on March 22nd, when nature itself is re-born. There are many customs associated with this holiday. It is primarily a time to make changes: to paint the house, to buy new clothes; and most of all to receive guests and return their calls. Raihaneh spent a lot of time with her family, helping receive the guests. She took great delight in carrying out the special ceremony of the seven "S's" That is, seven Persian foods, all beginning with the sound of "s" (like "sib" (apple), etc.) are placed on a table-cloth on the floor, along with sweets and fruits of all kinds. There is also a lighted candle, the Koran, an egg and a mirror.

All the family is on hand for the exact moment when the old

54

year passes into the new. They sit on the floor: their gaze is fixed on the tablecloth before them. Each one is actually concious of the start of the new year: some prefer to leave the unhappy memories of the past year to seek happier times in the next.

Noo-ruz is also a time to forget old quarrels and renew acquaintances, especially among relatives. The Barzegar family was anxious to make amends with Dordaneh and his wife. During the winter they had tried several times to send messages to Dordaneh in Bagh-saba, but they got no answer; either because the message failed to reach him or perhaps because he did not choose to answer. At any rate, during the Noo-ruz holidays some of the Barzegar family decided to visit Bagh-saba. Arriving there they went first to Dordaneh's rooming house, but the landlady informed them that the couple were staying with Raihaneh's family during the holidays.

Babak went to call on his brother at the Din-Dar home. The family there greeted him cordially. Dordaneh came forward and the two brothers embraced warmly, kissing each other on both cheeks. For them a few months absence seemed a few years. A servant brought him a cup of tea, and then a fresh ghalyan. The traveler felt somewhat refreshed after his weary journey. The two men had much to talk about. But first, Babak unwrapped the gifts he had brought for Raihaneh and her family. Everyone was pleased and happy with what they received. The family soon retired for the night, leaving Dordaneh and Babak to themselves.

Babak was here to induce his brother to return to Khoshmakan. Family ties are strong in this part of the world. It is not good for a brother to separate himself from the rest of his family for a long period of time. In addition Babak needed Dordaneh to supervise the spring planting and the harvest later

55

on. There was also the problem of Dordaneh's first wife Johana, who had tearfully begged Babak to persuade Dordaneh to return to her. It was not something to be settled in one night.

Babak stayed with the Din-Dar family for a week; and then he returned with Dordaneh and Raihaneh to their dwelling. Raihaneh suspected the purpose of her brother-in-law's visit; and she worried as to what might happen. She sensed her husband's troubled mind. During the day he was away from her, strolling in town with Babak, and only at night when she was alone with him in bed could she make him aware of how much she needed him.

Babak prolonged his visit, but the weeks passed and Dordaneh could make no decision. Finally Babak left without accomplishing what he had come for.

There was much talk in Bagh-saba about Dordaneh and his affairs. The reason for Babak's visit was known, and the townspeople were often fond of quoting an old proverb: "The love that is gained in old age will lead to a bad reputation."

Letters continued to come to Dordaneh from his family and business associates in Khoshmakan, all begging him to return. The management of the land was suffering.

Meanwhile Johana, the first wife, was deeply angered by her husband's absence and disregard for her. Her parents were humiliated and talked of obtaining a divorce for their daughter. In a small Muslim village like Khoshmakan divorce is not an acceptable thing and it brings dishonor to the man.

Late in spring, Babak and Aga Keshtgar, the father of Johana, came to Bagh-saba. After much discussion it was agreed that Dordaneh should return to the village with Raihaneh, provided all behaved kindly to the young wife.

Now Dordaneh had to persuade Raihaneh's parents to accept this move. He went to them with the story that his brother was sick and he was needed in Khosh-makan; and furthermore he told them that his first wife intended to divorce him if he did not return. Aga Din-Dar and his wife were reluctant to send their daughter back with him, even for the summer. But Dordaneh persuaded them that it would be a pleasant change for Raihaneh and he assured them that he and Raihaneh would live apart from the rest of the family. It was agreed, and Raihaneh tearfully packed her belongings once more, wondering what lay in store for her this time.

CHAPTER FOUR

BIRTH OF A BABY

In the orient there is a saying which wives are fond of quoting, "My husband has chained me with a thread of his love, and he pulls me where he wishes." Sometimes the thread is one of fear or need, or a combination of these. In Raihaneh's case, it seemed to be a mixture of love, force and treachery. It was difficult for her to leave her parents and friends, especially Khonem Khorshid to whom she had become strongly attached. But being an obedient wife, she did as her husband suggested and packed her belongings. The most important things she took with her, the rest she left with her parents. The luggage was stored in the old Ford car that served the two communities, and the friends and relatives were kissed good-bye. As the car started up, Raihaneh's mother wept and her father fingered his prayer beads, and with each prayer, asked God to protect them. Their eyes followed the car until it was out of sight. Tearfully, Raihaneh looked back until she could see them no longer.

The sixty miles to Khoshmakan was a full day's journey; late afternoon they reached the village: Dordaneh's brothers and nephews were on hand to greet them. They eyed Raihaneh curiously. Her full blown figure was covered by a chadhor; but even this failed to conceal the fact that she was a town girl. It was obvious that she was wearing Western clothes, not the villager's full skirt and head scarf. As she walked down the street, all eyes followed here: the eyes of the men were on her high heeled shoes, and the women took her appearance in at one glance. At the family home, the first to greet Raihaneh was Khonem Barzegar, followed by the other wives in the family, as well as Johana, Dordaneh's first wife. All the women expressed concern for her condition and insisted that she rest and let them take care of her. This was all very pleasant for Raihaneh. For some time she enjoyed being pampered: her own special maid took care of many of her needs. Her surroundings were pleasant and the rest of the family took special pains to see that she was comfortable. Once a week she went to a near-by shrine to pray for a son and for his safe delivery. A son would insure her husband's love for her; then he might be persuaded to divorce his first wife. Once in a while she asked her husband's permission to visit an old relative, and accompanied by a maid she would spend the afternoon away from home. Every other week, she accompanied the women of the household to the public bath. There she joined in their conversation, but never felt a part of the group. It seemed to her that she was included only because they were afraid of Dordaneh's anger. Johana made a special effort to be friends with Raihaneh: she brough her sweets, and often joined her in knitting things for the coming baby. Dordaneh too gave her extra attention and spent as much time as possible with her.

In the household itself there appeared to be calm, but rage and unkindness lurked beneath the surface. Khonem Barzegar and Johana talked frequently about what would happen if Raihaneh were delivered of a son. The time was fast approaching; but no preparations had been made to help the young wife. There was no hospital or even doctor nearby; in fact it was difficult to find an experienced midwife to assist her. Raihaneh had written to her mother suggesting that she come, but Khonem Din-Dar herself was pregnant. Although they could not be together, they communicated in thought and feeling, sharing a common experience together. The mother had advised her daughter to seek help from the women around her; but Raihaneh felt the hostility of her in-laws; nor did she care to discuss the matter with her husband. In rural Iran, men pay no attention to the details of birth; it is a matter for the woman to attend to: the older women helping the younger ones.

For Raihaneh it seemed a hopeless situation. She had no confidence in the women around her; nor was she at ease in her pregnancy. It was a new and frightening experience for her; and she was in an inhospitable setting. How could she relax? The labor pains began all at once; and she did not know what to expect: she squirmed and cried and wrung her hands in agony. In the last stage of labor, her maid helped her to seat herself on some mud bricks. When the membranes broke she fainted. Then the midwife, who had done nothing till now, came forward and advised her to help the delivery by pushing forward. She did as she was told, but there was no further movement of the baby through the birth canal. Apparently the head of the baby was larger than the opening. Raihaneh was awkward in her efforts to help the birth process, and no one gave her much assistance. The pain was too great: the pupils of her eyes dilated and her skin was hot. She fainted again. Dordaneh's sister and the midwife tugged at the baby's head and succeeded in freeing the child at last. It was a girl. One of the women went back to tell the family. Johana was very pleased with the news: she ordered some village musicians to celebrate the event and inform the community. It was a personal triumph for her as well.

Dordaneh was naturally one of the first to be told of the birth of his daughter. This was his third daughter. He took the news sadly and dejectedly. Raidaneh had been asking for him and he went to her bedside, determined not to show his disappointment. She too was greatly distressed and strongly feared that she had lost her husband as well. Through her tears she asked if he still wanted her as his wife. Dordaneh was touched by her simplicity and sincerity. He held her in his arms and kissed her affectionately. He asured her several times that he wanted both Raihaneh and the new baby. It was not anyone's fault that the baby was born a girl. Rather, one had to accept what God had given. He said the words, and she believed him. If only he could have done the same!

The maid brought the new baby to the father. She had black hair and eyes, and a big melon-like head which was peaked at the back: the sign of a bad delivery and lack of a proper midwife.

For several days Raihaneh rested. Then on the seventh day, as was the custom, female friends and relatives accompanied her to the public bath. A special bath was prepared for her, heralding her safe recovery. Then a big feast was spread out with Raihaneh as the guest of honor. She listened to all the conversation around her. It centered on Dordaneh and what he would do now that his wish for a son was still unfulfilled. The words pierced the young girl's heart; she too wondered what her husband would do.

CHAPTER FIVE

RAIHANEH'S DIVORCE

Raihaneh's daughter was born in the beginning of August, and the infant was named Ma-Monir (meaning "illustrious moon"). The first month after her birth, everything seemed calm and orderly in the big house. But Johana and Khonem Barzegar plotted frequently together. Johana was particularly anxious to be rid of Raihaneh; for Dordaneh had not spent any time with her for more than a year. She was only 10 or 15 years older than her rival, and she still retained some of the beauty of her earlier years. Her bitterness toward Raihaneh took the form of malicious gossip; she told everyone that Dordaneh had only married the young girl in the hope of a son. Her failure to bear a male child was ample proof that Allah was punishing him for a second marriage.

Dordaneh knew of the jealousy of his first wife, and in some ways pitied her; but he was no longer attracted to her. But to divorce her would have meant the loss of his two daughters of whom he was very fond, and a disgrace both to his family and to the community.

Khonem Barzegar decided on a plan to gain her ends and conferred with Johana. Both agreed that much would be gained if Raihaneh could be moved to a small house nearby. Uncertain as to how Dordaneh would take their suggestion, they decided to work through the young girl herself. One day, the old woman went to Raihaneh to see the baby and to visit with the young wife. Raihaneh greeted her courteously, but her suspicions were aroused. What new demands or restrictions was her mother-in-law now preparing to impose on her? But to Raihaneh's surprise her mother-in-law seemed interested and concerned for her and the child. She asked if there was anything she might do to make their accomodations more comfortable and if they had room enough for the maid who was now staying with them. Raihaneh admitted that they were somewhat cramped in their present quarters, but otherwise they were quite comfortable. The old woman wondered if they might like more room, not only for themselves, but for guests when they arrived. The young wife acknowledged that indeed it would be nice to have more space. Now Khonem Barzegar slyly proposed that she might be able to arrange for them to move to Cousin Jaihan's place nearby. Of course it would be up to Raihaneh if she wanted to change, but Khonem would arrange whatever she preferred. With these words she departed.

When Dordaneh came home that evening, Raihaneh immediately discussed it with him. He too liked the idea: they would be away from the tumultuous household of his family and he could spend more time with his young wife and child.

Johana did all she could to help the move. Actually packing was not much of a problem for Raihaneh. Most of the things could be carried directly from their old quarters to their new home. Their most valuable household possessions were a few thick blankets, a jewelry box, a decorated trunk given to Raihaneh for her trousseau, several fine Persian rugs, a small prayer rug, Dordaneh's favorite ghalyan; the Koran and Raihaneh's favorite book of Saadi's poetry.

For a week after they moved, the couple still continued to eat their meals at the big house; for there was no storeroom in Cousin Jaihan's house.

63

It is customary for village houses to have a wooden cupboard in which staples and fresh vegetables are kept, as well as milk and cooked meat; left-overs are sometimes kept overnight. A simple stove to heat the house, as well as an oven are necessities in a village house. Baking provides a unique opportunity for the housewife to demonstrate her skill. Nowhere in the world is there as much variety in bread-making as in Iran. The village of Khoshmakan is known for its own particular kind. The dough is first shaped into a ball (the size of a tennis ball), then rolled out on a smooth surface with the aid of a wooden, spatula-like tool. When it is as thin as a sheet of paper it is lifted up gently with a narrow stick and placed on a circular metal surface, the inside of which is coated with clay, and this is then placed over a very hot oven built up from the ground. Several sheets of bread are baked at one time, and when browned on one side they are turned over on the other. When done, the sheets of bread are piled in a big copper pot. For each meal a few are moistened and folded and placed on the table. In a bakery, there are usually three who bake the bread: one makes the dough; another rolls it out in thin slabs, and the third is responsible for putting the bread on the stove and turning it until done.

After a week, Raihaneh got her own wooden food storage box, but she still did not have baking facilities. Every day her mother-in-law sent over a few pieces, and her husband did the meat purchasing in the bazaar. They had rice, beans and vegetables on hand. Occasionally Raihaneh's family sent them a box of fruit. In her wish to be independent, Raihaneh persuaded her husband to buy bakery equipment so that she might do her own bread making. As a result she stopped seeing her in-laws all together. There was now no one to talk to, except her baby and her faithful servant.

But Dordaneh found many reasons to visit the big house,

sometimes several times a day. He had to talk to his brothers about business matters. Then it was only natural that he stop to see his daughters and their mother. Johana was always very considerate about making him feel comfortable: she fetched him a ghalyan and took tea to him. He felt that he had been unjust to her; and Khonem Barzegar encouraged him to visit Johana more often, telling him that God had witnessed his actions and had condemned his second marriage by giving him a daughter.

Gradually Dordaneh found this new arrangement much to his liking. He took to spending much of his time with Johana: first making love to her, and then returning to Raihaneh. Raihaneh learned of this through her maid, and every time he stayed away for lunch or overnight, she was certain that he was at the big house. More and more she came to realize that she had made a mistake in moving away from her in-laws and recognized it as a trick to separate her from her husband.

Grief-stricken, Raihaneh felt alone and hopeless. The more she was left alone, the more she feared that she would lose her husband. The second winter of her marriage was a cold one, and she spent much of her time indoors. She was obliged to, for to have gone visiting others unaccompanied by her husband, would have invited scandal. There was only one family, acquainted with her own family, who visited the young wife. They found her weak and thin, no doubt heightened by her grief and loneliness. When they wrote to her family, they described her condition. Aga Din-Dar wrote to his son-in-law asking him to take care of his only daughter. He reminded him that he had entrusted Raihaneh to his care, and it was now up to Dordaneh and God to protect her. What else can a father say to a man with two wives?

Johana was still not satisfied with the present arrangement; she wanted to find some way of encouraging Dordaneh to

65

divorce his young wife. One day she saw a young man, a cousin of Dordaneh's come to the door of the little house to see the baby. Being alone so much of the time, Raihaneh found it pleasant to talk to him, but she maintained the proper distance that her position demanded. Johana was quick to circulate the story that the two young people had an interest in one another. Dordaneh heard of it, and questioned Raihaneh thoroughly. Although she protested her innocence, he became angry and hit her for the first time since their marriage. Later repentant, he knew he had been wrong.

Seeing that this plan did not work, Johana went to her mother-in-law to ask her advice. The old woman knew of a villager who had wizard's powers. He was known as a "writer of prayers", skilled at bringing seperated lovers together and furthering love affairs. Perhaps he had some way of solving this problem. It certainly wouldn't hurt to try. An old trusted maid was sent to the next village to fetch Sayd Abrahim, a wizened old man with a black turban and green shawl.

Sayd Abrahim arrived the next day. Khonem Barzegar promised him a substantial reward if he could re-unite Johana with Dordaneh; for as she explained to him, the honor of her family was at stake. A town girl had stolen the love of a man who had rightfully belonged to Johana and to his two children by her. After some bargaining, the wizard agreed to take on the task for 500 rials. First of all, he needed a piece of cloth from one of Raihaneh's garments and one from Dordaneh's. These pieces would be wrapped around a prayer written on a piece of paper and the bundle would be buried in the doorway of a room which Dordaneh often crossed. Then there was another charm he suggested. Some pig's fat should be rubbed on the rival's undergarments but in such a way that it would pass unnoticed; otherwise the charm would fail. Meanwhile if these spells did not work, the sorcerer had a love potion that he was sure would do the trick. The drug "Mehr Gia" (plant of love) was a powder made from the sap of a certain tree. In fact it is a stimulant that affects the nervous system, and may actually be fatal in some cases. After giving his patrons some of it and instructions for its use, he departed, taking with him money and gifts of food.

The next day, Khonem Barzegar invited Raihaneh to tea while Raihaneh's servant was out doing the laundry. During this time, Sina, the trusted maid from the big house, spread pig's fat all over Raihaneh's garments. She also found an old piece of cloth from one of the young girl's dresses, as well as something from Dordaneh's clothes, and she tied these pieces around the paper that had been given her. Then she dug a small hole just in front of the front stoop and buried the charm there, being careful to cover it well.

The two plotters waited a week for their charm to take effect. But nothing happened. Another week passed, and still another. In fact, relations between Dordaneh and Raihaneh seemed much improved: Dordaneh had recovered from his jealousness and realized that he need not fear losing his second wife's affections. His love for her increased. Still he thought it wise to caution her: village people here would gossip if she (a young, pretty girl) were seen talking to a man, even a relative.

Johana and her mother-in-law put their heads together again. Their charms hadn't worked. Should they give "Mehr Gia" to Dordaneh? It might actually harm him. Each woman looked to the other to make the first suggestion. Each one trembled in her heart at what the consequences might be. Finally the old woman took the lead by asking when the best time would be to serve it to him.

They decided that it should be put into his tea on the following day when he visited them. The two women were alone in the

67

room the next afternoon when he came to call. As was their custom, they offered him a cup of tea. He remarked that it was bitter. His stepmother smiled and replied, "Of course, it's just like a man to say that. To a man who has tasted a fresh cup, the old one loses its taste." The reference was obvious.

Dordaneh said nothing, but hastily gulped the rest of the tea, bade them good-bye saying that he had work to do.

Within three days Dordaneh became deathly ill: he developed a high fever and found it difficult to control his limbs. He asked the maid to summon an old friend who had a great knowledge of medicine, although he had received no formal training. The man came, and diagnosed it accurately as poisoning. He was familiar with the tricks and devices these women used to capture their love. He prescribed a diet of milk and certain medicines, and told Dordaneh that in time he would recover.

The news that Dordaneh had been poisoned spread through the village. The suspicion fall on Raihaneh; was she not a city girl, anxious to get rid of her older husband and take a younger one? Hadn't she expressed an interest in one of Dordaneh's cousins? And so the rumors grew, spirited on by Khonem Barzegar and Johana.

At first, Raihaneh acted as nurse to her husband, but as the gossip spread, Khonem Barzegar made arrangements to have her stepson moved to the big house, away from his young wife. The news of these happenings reached the Din-Dar family, and they became very concerned for their daughter, but did not know how best to help her. Raihaneh wrote them describing the hostility her in-laws now showered on her and how there was no way to prove her innocence. Even Dordaneh had been persuaded to suspect her of this crime and he was suspicious of anything she tried to do for him. Nevertheless he had no intention of divorcing her. He was nervous, angry, and had no

wish to see anyone; at times he thought he was going insane.
Raihaneh did not know where to turn for advice and comfort.
In dispair, she felt there was no way out for her but suicide.
Public feeling against Raihaneh had mounted to such an extent
that the mullah (religious leader) of the village wrote Aga Din-
Dar to advise him to fetch his daughter home.

Aga Din-Dar could not face the disgrace of this situation: he
had never expected his son-in-law to go insane and to divorce
his daughter. It was decided that Khonem Din-Dar would go
with his son and cousin to fetch Raihaneh and bring her back
to Bagh-Saba. But it was difficult to arrange for a ride, for few
cars were traveling in the winter time.

Finally Aga Din-Dar contacted a car owner who agreed to
make the trip, provided they got together two other passengers,
all of whom were to pay double the rate, both in going there
and in returning. Two more people were found, and in due time
the party started off. It was an old car—one of the early Ford
models. On the evening of the first day they stopped at a village,
24 miles from Bagh-saba. They spent the night there. By
morning a heavy snow carpeted the ground and all the roads
going out of town. The car had no chains, but still no one
wanted to stay longer in that village; so they proceeded slowly.
After three hours, the car had made it to the top of the next hill;
but going downward the driver lost control and the car hit the
foot of the mountain. Not much damage was done, and there
was still another mountain road to climb. To get to the top of
this one, they ingeniously put carpets under the wheels of the
car and tediously made their way up. The carpets were in shreds
now. They went a few more miles; the car settled in a ditch. All
five passengers pushed and struggled, and at last managed to
free it, and they were on their way again. At the next village the
driver discovered the gas tank was frozen and refused to go

69

further. For three days the group stayed in the village and watched fresh snow come down every day. Their only food was hot tea, bread and cheese. Finally Khonem Din Dar decided to hire donkeys and continue on. She made a deal with a donkey driver to act as guide; and the next morning she started out with her son and cousin. Their progress was slow, made more difficult by the icy winds. Although they were blanketed heavily, still they were cold and their faces and hands were often frostbitten. The wind pierced the heavy scarves that they had wrapped around their faces, and the snow blew into their faces. At the next village they stopped for rest. When the villagers saw a woman travelling they were amazed and admired her courage. They gave the weary travelers hot soup, and wrapped them in warm blankets for the night. The next morning the snow storm was still raging, and the village folk advised them to stay there until the storm abated; but Khonem Din-Dar was determined. Her daughter needed her and she had to go to her.

They had almost reached the next village when the donkey with Khonem on it, lost his footing and slipped and fell in the snow, tossing its rider off. Bravely, Khonem brushed the snow off and helped load the donkey again. Shivering, she mounted; and they continued on their way. Their second night of travel this way was spent in a village, just eight miles from Khosh-makan. The guide had friends there and so another night was spent in a village hut.

The following morning at eleven o'clock the group reached Khosh-makan. By now the villagers here had received reports of the plucky mother and her two companions who had come to rescue Raihaneh. They compared the mother's bravery to that of a lioness; and people began to say that this mother's devotion to her daughter was proof enough of Raihaneh's innocence. It was the Barzegar family that had made all the trouble for others—not only for Raihaneh but for themselves as well.

As soon as Raihaneh heard her mother coming she ran out barefoot in the snow to fall in her arms. The warmth of their embrace melted the cold of their cheeks and left their faces glowing with the brightness of their love. They wept for joy as they made their way into the house. Tearfully Raihaneh told them of her tragedy and begged her mother to rescue her from this wicked place. The Barzegar family was a group of infidels who only wanted to destroy her. And how they had made her suffer! Wouldn't her mother please help her get a divorce?

Sorrowfully the mother agreed with her daughter, but cautioned her about making such a final decision. They would discuss the issue tomorrow. Right now everyone was tired and anxious to get to bed.

The following morning Khonem Din-Dar, resolute and determined to face the situation squarely, went to see her son-in-law. Khonem Barzegar, aud the rest of the family greeted her indifferently. Dordaneh still obviously ill, greeted her suspiciously, wondering why she was there. Raihaneh's mother was quick to state her position. Before them all, she stated that Dordaneh had been a disappointment to her: from the beginning he had acted cowardly; he had made promises but had never fulfilled them. Her voice rose to a high pitch as she shouted: "Dordaneh is not a man, and not fit to be a husband for my daughter. I demand a divorce."

Everyone was now talking at once; most of all Dordaneh who did not want a divorce and was trying to pull Khonem Din Dar to one side so that he could talk to her alone. But his family had already decided for him, and advised him to accept the divorce action. It would be less trouble for him in the end. Hadn't Raihaneh already caused him enough anguish? Too sick to argue, he agreed to their suggestions. The formal arrangements were to be made the next day.

The next day came. It was Friday—the same day of the week that Dordaneh and Raihaneh had been married. The same religious authority who had married them now came to divorce them. Previously he had brought two families together, now he separated them.

According to Islamic custom, in a divorce the husband agrees to return the dowry, which in Raihaneh's case amounted to 3000 rials and a few hundred grams of solid gold.

After the divorce, Raihaneh, her mother, brother and cousin had to wait three weeks for the roads to open before they could return to Bagh-saba. Full of grief they left Khosh-makan.

When Dordaneh recovered from his illness he realized the terrible mistake he had made; he deeply regretted losing Raihaneh and his sweet young daughter. He couldn't bear to continue the life he had known before Raihaneh came to him. His family and community position meant nothing to him now. At the first opportunity he left Khosh-makan and went to live in another village, Kohmer. Here he cultivated a piece of land for himself and lived a simple life. Of his two marriages, one had ended in divorce, and the other in permanent separation.

MA-LANG

THE MODERN YOUTH

CHAPTER SIX

BONFIRE

Circles of dust rose in the air and disappeared like giant balloons. For a few moments they clouded the horizon darkening the bright autumn afternoon. The crowd of people standing about seemed to expect it: the men pulled their coat collars up around their faces and some women clasped their chedhors about them more closely. The wide barren desert of Mehrabad Airport often encourages the mischievous wind, but only temporarily. The sand settled to the ground and the sun wiped the dust off its face and smiled down once more on the crowd.

Faces were pressed against the bars. Small children were boosted to their fathers' shoulders. All eyes turned upward, as the monstrous Pan American Clipper lifted herself up. Defiantly she jeered at the onlookers, and as a parting gesture sent another gust of sand and dust. Eyes burned and voices choaked. No one was spared. They moved back. And when the crowd looked out again, another plane was gently gliding to the earth. This is life at Mehrabad: one plane takes off, another lands. The Pan American freight was still out on the field as the Air France plane began its descent. The on-lookers surged forward again, with an accordian-like motion. Friends and relatives were there to welcome this huge airborn animal which carried in its belly, like some giant kangaroo, an assortment of wanderers returning circled the field, as if it were a buzzard seeking its prey. The throng was excited and impatient.

I was impatient too. This was my first visit to the airport. It was the most exciting place I had ever been to. The wild wind and sand didn't bother me at all. I felt like shouting at the wind, "You can't frighten me and make me turn my back. I've come here to meet my brother who's coming home from America."

Now and then I looked at my family who were standing nearby. They were impatient too. My father's face was turned upward. His glance seemed to pierce and penetrate the hulking bloated monster encircling the field. My mother's eyes were clouded with tears. Perhaps it was the wind and sand, but it might have been longing and eagerness for Hooshi. My older brother, Shapour was checking his watch and I heard him tell Meri his wife, "Hooshi's plane is several minutes overdue."

I looked back at the plane, but I had to turn my glance downward. The plane had landed. The passengers came out one by one. Even though I was smaller than the others, I managed to push out to the front of the crowd. I caught sight of Hooshi first, and I waved to him and then pointed him out to the others. At that moment I had one wish—to be a bird and swoop down on him.

All the passengers had alighted now, and friends and relatives shouted and waved in an effort to attract their attention. But before them stretched the high fence and the formidable custom's office. How agonizing the wait!

Shapour was eager too. He kept glancing at his watch. It was thirty minutes later that we saw Hooshi coming out of customs. Everyone abruptly moved forward at one motion—like a rubber band suddenly let go. Hooshi reached mother first and embraced her affectionately. Then my father quickly stepped forward and kissed him heartily on both cheeks. Shapour was all smiles and no longer worried about time, and he welcomed Hooshi warmly. By this time Hooshi seemed a little tired and embarrassed by all the attention he was getting. He turned all of a sudden to me and asked teasingly, "Is this my sister? I must be mistaken. My sister is 'Ma-lang.' (meaning doll-like baby), and this is some imposter."

I couldn't help but smile, although I felt a little shy too. Like being teased by a stranger. And yet he really wasn't. It was just that he had been away five years. I guess I was just 'ma-lang' when he left, but he couldn't call me that anymore.

He stood waiting for me to answer. So I replied smilingly, "I'm not 'Ma-lang' anymore. I'm Emelia. You've been away five years. Can't you remember?"

Everyone laughed and he did too. Shapour looked at his watch again and suggested that we return to the car. Hooshi's luggage had been checked through so there was no need to stand in the dusty yard of the custom's office.

We all crowded into the car: Hooshi in the back between my parents, and Shapour, Meri and I in the front. On the way to Shemran, where we live, everyone talked excitedly. They all wanted to hear about America. No one in our immediate family had ever been that far before. Several times Hooshi gently kissed mother on the cheek or patted her hand. There were lots of things that I wanted to ask too, but I was too excited to speak.

Shapour said jokingly, "We were all waiting to see if you'd bring back a blonde blue-eyed American. After all, mother likes them. Why didn't you?"

Hooshi looked thoughtfully into space and then answered softly, "It isn't too late."

Prodded by questions about America, Hooshi explained, "It's hard to talk about America, because it's so different. You have

77

to really see it before you can understand. Some day soon I'll show you my slides and then you'll see what I mean."

Several times Hooshi glanced out the window and once he remarked: "Everything looks so small here—the houses, stores, and even the people. They look down-cast and unhappy. And the music on the car radio gives the same feeling." But then he shrugged his shoulders and continued, "It's not for me to judge. After all this is my home. Let the people do as they want: Iran for Iranians."

I didn't quite understand what he meant, but I listened carefully, hoping he would explain more. Instead he looked out the window again. We were in town now, just turning into Shah Reza Avenue, the main street of Tehran. Hooshi looked pleased at the sight of the construction going on: a new pavement was being put in, and on both sides of the street water pipes were being laid. When we stopped for a traffic light, I saw Hooshi scowl and then chuckle. He was looking out the window, and I looked in that direction too. But all I could see were other automobiles mostly. Beside us was a cart filled with lumber and it was being pulled by a man. A horse drawn carriage was just beyond, and on it perched a mother and several children with boxes all around them—probably they were moving. The light changed and we moved on. A bicyclist skirted in and out of the traffic: a pyramid of high yogurt crocks precariously balanced on the back of his bicycle. It all looked very common-place to me: I couldn't understand and I asked him, "What interests you so?"

"All this," he said pointing to the cart, carriage and bicycle, "are the signs of yesterday. They won't be in the picture of tomorrow."

Hooshi looked out the window as he talked, not missing a thing. We passed the site of the university and Shapour pointed out the buildings, "That's the Science School going up there, and that building's going to be a mosque in the center, if they ever get around to finishing it."

"Buildings don't make a university," commented Hooshi thoughtfully. "What is needed are teachers, and good ones at that."

Shapour stopped to make a left hand turn on Pahlevi Avenue, but before he could complete it, a car swung sharply in front of him from a neighboring lane, causing our car to stop suddenly. We all lurched forward. Then we righted ourselves, and now we were headed north on Pahlevi, which goes all the way to Shemran, a suburb of Tehran and located at the foot of the mountains. It's my favorite avenue because there are so many lovely "chenar" (maple) trees on both sides. In the autumn the street is like a path of gold covered by a carpet of yellow leaves. They overflowed the banks, and "jubs" (open sewers) on both sides of the street were coated by them.

As we crossed Avenue Takte-Jamshid, I noticed that my brother turned his gaze eastward. He had not forgotten that Mt. Damavand was waiting to welcome him. A bonnet of white and a blue earthen gown made it so dazzling in the sunlight that the blue sky seemed second best. Hooshi sighed and spoke softly, "It's the sight I've never forgotten. There are some handsome mountains in the West of U.S., but they've always made me homesick for Mt. Damavand."

Shapour asked, "How many photographs did you bring back with you?"

"Oh hundreds," laughed Hooshi. "It'll take me several hours to show them all to you. I've got slides from all over the United States. Just you wait and see."

Father nodded thoughtfully. He hadn't said much up to now, but now he questioned Hooshi, "How does your country look to you today, my son?"

Hooshi looked out the window. "I can see that they're building a lot of houses all along here, and they seem to be very exclusive ones. It's a shame the beauty of Persia is hidden behind walls. In America yards are open for everyone to see."

Shapour interrupted, "You haven's been home long enough yet. Everyone is apathetic and it's a stagnant enrivonment. But perhaps in time, there'll be some changes—economically and socially. At least I hope so."

And so the discussion continued. I had tried to pay close attention, but I grew tired. I felt my head nodding. Then I was awakened by my sister-in-law, Meri. We had come to Shemran and were turning down the narrow *kuchie* that goeds to our house.

The streets were almost diserted at this time of day. Later in the evening, the circle in the middle of town becomes a hub of many activities. The shops, restaurants and cafes open up. People stroll about, stopping to talk to friends or shopkeepers, then eating supper in a nearby restaurant; that is, if they can afford it. There are many who can't. Laborers squat against doorways and walls, making the best out of a few thin slabs of bread and some cheese. I have always felt sorry for them.

Even though our car is a small Europeon one, still my brother had to drive slowly through the twisting *kuchies*. There were obstacles all along the way. Several peddlers were hawking their wares of various kinds of fruits and vegetables; their donkeys trotted on ahead of them. A house was being built a few doors from where we live. Some laborers were carrying dirt our in buckets, others were mixing cement and carrying it into the yard on large wooden trays which took two men to carry. Shapour commented, "These are the things you don't have in America. Those men are all from the villages—mostly peasants. If they're lucky, they find a job for 50 rials a day. Since you've been gone, Hooshi, the situations seems to have steadily gotten worse."

Shahpour was so deep in discussion that he drove right on past our house, and my father had to poke him gently on the back to remind him. Everyone laughed, and Shapour obligingly backed up and we all got out. My grandmother had heard the car drive up and was at the door, welcoming us, and especially Hooshi. She looked at him critically and remarked, "My little grandson, you have gotten taller but thinner."

"Oh, no, Granny," he replied, "It's just my American-made suit that makes me look that way."

Like all the other houses in our neighborhood, a high brick wall surrounds our house and garden. As we passed through the gate, the cry of a lamb greeted us. Everyone looked in its direction. It was tethered to a tree and it would soon be sacrificed in honor of my brother's safe homecoming. It's an old Persian custom that we still keep in our family, although a lot of our friends don't observe it anymore.

I hurried into the house to make some tea. My mother and Meri were already in the kitchen making supper preparations. Outside I could hear the gardener tying up the struggling lamb. Then I heard no more. In a short while he brought the freshly butchered lamb to us. As is our custom, my mother wrapped up some of the meat for our neighbors, and some for the needy people in town and sent the gardener out to deliver it.

When I took the tea upstairs, Hooshi was getting acquainted with our two-year old niece, Nan-a-cee, whom he had never seen. At the same time, my father and some of the guests who had already arrived, were prying Hooshi with questions.

This sort of discussion lasted far into the night, long after supper was finished. I was so tired from the day's excitement that I went to bed early. And so it was for the next two weeks; for friends and relatives continued to call at our house. They brought gifts for Hooshi, and he in turn gave them presents

81

from abroad. Everyone wanted news of America and often times his opinions were sought after, as if he were an oracle, or so it seemed to me. Hooshi had lots to say, but he was also fond of showing his colored slides, and he sometimes let the pictures speak for themselves. There were slides from all over the States—North, South, East and West, even of the Atlantic and Pacific Oceans. Some of the pictures were of people he had met and homes he had visited, along with photos of historical scenes.

These were happy days for us. Once in a while, Hooshi casually taught me some English words and phrases. I was hesitant about trying to speak them, but he patiently repeated them for me.

One evening I looked out the window and saw Hooshi gathering yellow leaves in the yard and putting them on a pile. Then I noticed my mother coming into the yard. She was shocked that he should be doing manual work and told him to let the gardener do it the following day. He smiled and patted her on the back saying, "Mother, the feast is over and the guests have all gone home. It's time to work."

It looked like fun, and I went out and askid him if I might join in the work. We piled the leaves first in several small piles; then we brought them all together in one big stack. Our yard wasn't too large—yet there were lots of leaves. They came from the big maple tree and several fruit trees. There was also a pine tree in one corner and a grape arbor near the garage.

While gathering leaves, Hooshi taught me several English phrases and sentences that were concerned with our job like "falling leaves", "bare trees" and "gathering leaves in piles." He usually showed me what he wanted me to learn. Then he repeated it, and I had to say it after him.

After all the leaves were piled high, we made a bonfire. The

82

leaves were dry and the fire was hungry. The brightness of the fire in the early twilight was like a bright red flower at that time of day. The rest of the family joined us, one by one: first my grandmother, mother and father; then Shapour and Meri. Hooshi pointed to the fire and taught us all to say, "We're having a bonfire." It pleased them all.

Then Hooshi began to question me about school, "What do you want to be when you grow up?"

I looked at him somewhat doubtfully. "I'm only in the seventh grade now, and I have to study many subjects, like mathematics, sciences, Persian, Arabic and also a European language. Perhaps, when I've finished all these courses then I'll know."

"No, no," he replied impatiently, "that's the wrong way to go about it. It's the duty of the school to provide an integrated curriculum which is related to an objective. Otherwise, the school, and it's true of Iranian schools, will create ill-education instead of education."

It still wasn't clear in my wind. "But none of us in high school know why we're studying physics, algebra and chemistry," I said.

Meri was standing near-by and backed me up, "I took all those courses in high school for six years. They were brain cracking courses and now I have no use for them."

"Yes, yes," he agreed. "It's not just a matter of changing the curriculum. There are other things to consider, and it's not so easy in the Iranian educational system, because schools are over-crowded. Nevertheless, teachers can be taught to consider each student as an individual. To do a good job of teaching the teacher may need to use every resource at hand and draw upon experiences in social and family life situations. There are three principles of teaching. One is for the teacher to accept the pupil as he is, another is to give guidance based on the needs of the individual, and finally it is important to give the pupil an opportunity to express himself, and discover the relationships existing in his subject matter."

He paused to see if we all understood. Meri shook her head. "It's hard to think of education in those terms."

I didn't understand it all, and I asked hopefully, "Could you give us an example?"

"Yes, here's an analogy," he answered. "Think of the student as a boat out at sea. The teacher is the sailor guiding it to shore and safety. Whenever there is a favorable wind the sailor doesn't have to row, for the boat is being pushed toward its destination. Just like in teaching—when the teacher sees that the student has discovered the way to solve his problem, then he can relax. But when the wind is unfavorable, just as when there is an obstacle confronting the pupil, then sailor-teacher has to row all the harder to get his load to shore safely."

We nodded. It seemed much clearer. Shapour had joined our group and was listening intently. In his usual jesting manner, he spoke, "If we listen to you much longer, you'll tell us that going to school is a waste of time and makes us less intelligent that before."

"That's exactly what I wanted to say," Hooshi answered him in seriousness. "The school which teaches in a year what can actually be taught in three months is a house of laziness."

My father too had come over to our side of the fire. "Perhaps you can develop your system of education for the needy youngsters of Iran," he suggested hopefully.

Shapour argued, "I don't see how your ideas would work in practice. They're of philosophical interest and you could never teach a student along the lines you suggest."

"But, I'm sure I can. Just find me a student and I'll show you," Hooshi answered.

Hooshi looked around the circle at us. His eyes lighted on me and he smiled slowly. "Emelia, how would you like to be in my school and be its only pupil?" He patted my back affectionately.

I looked at him to see if he were joking. He seemed serious. I thought. It would mean giving up the public school, but it wasn't too important to me. Nor did his suggestion make any impression, one way or the other, on me.

But my family found it an interesting thing to debate. My mother was immediately opposed: she felt all girls my age should be in school with others of the same age. Grandmother was in favor of my staying home, not so much for the sake of being educated by Hooshi, but because she believed I could learn home-making better and could get married sooner. Shapour and my father were curious to see what might come from Hooshi's ideas.

Hooshi explained, "In three months she will look at things and events in a new way. Her thinking will be changed, and she will know enough English to read English text books; because knowing English is the best way of getting acquainted with modern life and science. Then by the end of the year her English will be good enough to enroll her in the only American school here for Persian girls. Not only that, but she will be translating English stories into Persian for all her friends. Most of all she will be able to think for herself and to reason logically."

The idea began to appeal to me. My mother still held out however. "What will she do for friends, if she has to stay at home and study all the time?" she asked.

Hooshi nodded, "You're right there mother. But Emelia can set her up own social group in the neighborhood."

We didn't quite understand what all he meant, and besides we were being called to dinner. Hooshi walked with me across the yard and said, "Think it over. It's a big decision and it will affect your whole life."

I was amazed and somewhat confused. This kind of responsibility for me own education had never occured before. I had been taken to this school and that one without knowing why I was going or why they had been selected for me. Yet in school, I had always been free to choose my own friends and invite them to our home. At 13 years of age, it was certainly a big decision to make and I didn't hnow what to do.

Next day Hooshi called me into his study and asked me if I had made a decision. I nodded and said indifferently, "It's all right with me. Whatever plan you think is best I'll follow."

"Fine," he said briskly. "First of all you should remember that it is the business of the student to learn. The teacher can only guide. Now for your first lesson, I want you to go out into the yard and examine all the trees there. Bring their leaves in and we'll talk about them."

This was Sunday evening, the day after the bon-fire. The following week I withdrew from the public school and looked eagerly forward to a new adventure.

CHAPTER SEVEN

LEARNING ENGLISH

My withdrawal from public school caused considerable comment. Friends at school and at home questioned me as to why I would do such a thing. Pari, my best friend at school, telephoned me and said, "Everyone is talking about what you've done. Even the teachers think it's foolish: you won't be accepted in public school when you return and then you can't get a high school diploma either!"

Some of my neighborhood friends met me on the street and said: "Why did you do such a stupid thing, just because your brother asked you to? You'll be staying at home in seclusion, just like Persian girls did before they were given a chance to go to public school. Your brother must be very old-fashioned."

And so it went on. Their remarks began to worry me. Suppose they were right: suppose I couldn't get a high school diploma, and I had lost all my friends too. But beyond all that, I had a strong desire to learn English—more than learning anything else. And I felt my brother could teach it to me. If he could teach me basic English in three months, than it was well worth the risk.

Looking back on it now, two years later, it is still hard to believe that I learned the basic elements of English in three months. Of course, my brother spent a lot of time with me those first few weeks: we had a leasson for one hour in the morning and another hour in the evening.

In those weeks I learned more than 200 short sentences. The words in the sentences were English words which have the same root as the equivalent Persian word, since both English and Persian are from the Indo-European languages. Hooshi called it "teaching on the basis of philology." For instance, he taught me, "My mother is here," emphasizing "mother" which is similar to the Persian word "madar." And he did the same thing with words like brother ("bradar"), daughter ("dokhtar"), door ("dar"), etc. We made a list of 200 such words, and used them in simple sentences. Everytime, he used the directive method, pointing to objects or indicating action that we were observing, such as "This is a pencil," (holding one up), or "It's raining." (when it was raining outside). At the same time he asked me to listen to English programs on the radio to see if I could imitate their pronounciation and we also went to English and American movies where I paid close attention to the pronunciation of words.

Sometimes my sister-in-law came upon me as I wandered about the house speaking English sentences aloud, "This is the living room," "The dishes are on the table," "The window is open," etc. Meri was highly amused, and said, "You should be studying English from a book. That's the way it's always taught in school."

When I told her that I had not been taught to read—in fact I didn't even know the alphabet, she was even more surprised, and shook her head in disappointment.

Hooshi stressed the importance of learning through the senses, especially in listening. And so I made a list of the American radio programs that were broadcast to Tehran for the benefit of Americans stationed there. Most of the time they spoke so fast that I didn't understand anything they said, but once in a while I caught a word, and I was very pleased when I recognized "Hello friends," at the beginning of a program and "Good-night, friends" at the end with an occasional "and", "today" or "how" in the middle.

In the evening when Hooshi came, we had another lesson. First, I talked to him about the things I had tried to learn during the day and the problems I was having, or things I had forgotten how to pronounce. He always helped me out, and patiently explained things several times if I didn't understand it right away. I remember one of those evenings when he said, "These first few weeks I will have to work especially hard, then it will be your turn."

I didn't know what he meant then, but looking back on it, I understand it now. After the first few weeks, I found that he was placing more and more of the responsibility on me: it became my job to give him a daily report, and he in turn guided me and gave suggestions.

But the first few weeks were different. His procedure was to state an affirmative sentence like, "The book is on the desk." Then he repeated it, and at the same time he pointed to the book. Then it was my turn to say the sentence. Then he made it a question, "Is the book on the table?" and I had to answer, "Yes, it is."

When I learned a new word, it was important for me to associate the sound of the word with the object. I'll never forget the evening that we went shopping for fruit. The shopkeeper was getting ready to close, and he couldn't understand why my brother kept picking up one piece of fruit, then putting it down and going on to another, and another; all the time speaking in a strange language. But as Hooshi picked up a pomegranate, he said to me, "This is a big pomegranate," or with an apple, "The apple is red," and so on and on. When we came out of the store I had all the names of fruit in my mind, and my brother had a bag of cucumbers under his arm. It was good that he did not believe in words, per se. He never taught me a single word; I only learned words in sentences.

When I had learned enough sentences to understand simple statements and requests, my brother introduced a still harder phase to my learning. Now he began to question me, "Where is the book?" "When is lunch?" "Who is downstairs?" I had to repeat the question, then answer it. When I had mastered this phase of learning, I found I could make four to six times as many sentences as before.

About this time, Hooshi suggested that I make a habit of recalling what I had learned during the day, just before going to sleep. On the days when I had a lot to recall, I often fell asleep before I had finished. But it's a very useful habit that I've continued to use.

Sometimes our whole family went out on an outing or to visit friends. Along the way, Hooshi pointed out new things to me. Then it became a sort of game for me to discover things I did not know the English for, and to ask (pointing): "What is that?" and then to repeat after him, "That is a bus." Now I felt less hesitant about speaking out; and Hooshi encouraged me, saying "Only by speaking can you learn to speak."

One day he decided to show me how children learn a language. As his subject he took out two-year old neice, Nan-a-cee. For the next few weeks I was to observe and record all the new Persian words that she was learning. Then one evening, when the bright Persian moon was shining in the sky, Hooshi pointed it to Nan-a-cee, and said "Mah", "Mah." (meaning moon). After several repetitions, she had mastered it, and went to the rest of the family, proudly showing off her accomplishment. Hooshi explained, "This is the natural way in which a child learns his language: by the principle of association. Adults can learn to speak a foreign language in the same way but at an accelerated rate. Just as a child doesn't speak right away, but listens the first two years; so too an adult learning a new language should start with listening. Maybe not two years—but at least two weeks, depending on the individual. Then he gets a feel for the pattern of the language."

"What does he do after that?" I asked.

Hooshi smiled, "What did you do?"

I thought a moment. "I learned sentences about the things around me."

"Yes, and that's the way it should be. Then there's no embarrassment in speaking."

This was the first step to learning to speak English. I learned at home, in the car driving into Tehran; on the street shopping; and when we went walking in the beautiful mountains near our home. I learned whenever there was a new situation and when my brother was with me.

The next step was to talk about my day's activities in English. So, every evening when my brother came home I told him about my day. Sometimes it was hard, and I couldn't find sufficient words to explain, but he helped me out; often by demonstrating how I could make new words, just by adding prefixes, like "in"- to "side" to make "inside" or "out" to make "outside." Or I could add suffixes to words I already knew, such as "hand" became "handful" or "teach" "teacher."

When I had achieved mastery in the present tense, I moved into the past by explaining all my actions in the past tense. In this way I came to learn the past tense of regular and irregular verbs as I needed them. At first I wanted to say, "I go to Tehran today," instead of "I went..." and there were times that I often made the mistake of saying, "My brother teached me a new lesson," rather than "My brother taught me."

But Hooshi never laughed at me. And slowly I made progress; and "graduated" in to the future tense where I could talk about my plans for tomorrow and next week. To illustrate the difference in time, Hooshi drew a horizontal line and divided it into three sections: the middle part he called present, the one to the left was the past, and the one beyond the present was the future.

By the end of the first month, I had mastered the three tenses sufficiently well. About this time I asked him if he would teach me the alphabet. He replied, "I've been waiting for your request. Do you remember when you first started coming to me, you wanted to first learn how to read and write. That's because reading and writing hold more value in Iranian culture. But the person who learns to speak well, will have little trouble learning to write. On the other hand, you know people who read and write English well, but they can't speak it. That's why I've asked you to learn to use your ears first these first few weeks. Now you're ready to use your eyes too. You already know most of the sounds in English and can make them—now you will learn to associate them with their written symbol. But first, let's review the sounds, especially those that are absent in Persian, like "th" as in "thing" and "w" as in "what."

After that he asked me to cut up a large piece of cardboard into small pieces, two inches square. Then on each one he wrote a letter of the alphabet until all the letters, small and capital ones, had been written. And there were duplicates of each. He practiced the sounds with me until I had mastered them. I wondered what he wanted to do with all these letters. Finally, he put together, from the pieces, a sentences which he asked me to read. With some effort I sounded out the words, "I ...wa...nt... to...le...arn......Eng...li...sh." (I want to learn English). I felt excited and happy, and I could see that my brother was pleased too. He put together another sentence, "This is my book." Then a third, "Where is my pencil?" I caught on to what he was doing, and I began to assemble the answer to his question, "It is on your desk." He laughed, and we began to play a question and answer game, spelling out our sentences on the floor. Often I had trouble spelling the words, but he helped me. My assignment for the next few days was to construct my own sentences using these cardboard letters. When he came home he checked what I had done and pointed out my errors.

My efforts grew, and the desk was seldom long enough to hold all my sentences. They spread to the floor. One evening Shapour stepped inside the door and unintentionally disarranged my sentences. I was very upset and cried, "You've ruined my whole day's work. Just see what you've done."

Shapour looked down bewildered at the mass of letters on the floor and tried to help me, by arranging them alphabetically. He apologized and remarked. "There are much easier ways to learn the alphabet than this."

I had to smile. Then I showed Shapour the sentences I could make. He soon caught on and started helping me, although there were quite a few things I had to help him with. Hooshi was surprised to see the two of us that evening making up sentences. Shapour said to him, "Your Emelia seems to be making progress. She's even taught me a few things, and I studied English in college."

Hooshi looked at the sentences we had assembled, and pointed to several places where we had made mistakes. Some of the mistakes were mine, especially spelling. English is a peculiar language when it comes to spelling, because it's often very different from the way in which it's pronounced. My brother also helped me to put capital letters, commas, and periods in the right places in the sentences.

When Hooshi thought I was ready, he brought me thirty

small books written in English, and they concerned different aspects of nature study. He had gotten them from the Laboratory School at the University of Chicago and they had been prepared by Ruth Parker. The first book was called "Winter is Here." It was winter, appropriately enough. There were different scenes of winter with very simple descriptions. There were also books about such things, as electricity, food, etc. I could read whatever interested me. At the same time I was to continue giving my oral reports of my activities.

My skill in reading and speaking improved rapidly. One day Hooshi took me to the United States Information Agency Library to become a member. The clerk asked me to write my name and address in English. It was very difficult, because I had had no practice in it. The woman wanted to take the card away, saying, "It's become the fashion to become a library member here, even when they can't sign their name."

Hooshi spoke up, "Maybe she can't write her name yet, but she can read." And he proceeded to show her my ability.

I got the library card. Then I checked out some children's books on history and geography; I used them only as references for some projects that I was carrying out. I'll talk about them in the next chapter.

About this time, Hooshi introduced me to the dictionary. At first I used a large Persian-English dictionary; later, when I knew more words I used Webster's English-English dictionary. He also told me to always check the pronunciation when I looked up a word and to be sure of what I knew, as well as what I didn't know. To facilitate my learning, he let me use his typewriter. As I finished each book, I typed a summary of it. It was slow typing, because Hooshi also wanted me to learn the correct way to type. Sometimes I was impatient to get the words down on paper and I resorted to typing with my two index fingers. Later I wrote a summary of my learning to type.

Sometimes I finished a book in a day; other times it took me several says, a week or even several weeks. The books were of different kinds. My brother had brought mostly science books with him from the States, a few in the field of social sciences. One of the science books that I enjoyed was on food, and I typed a summary of it and made a report of it to my family. I talked about food value in terms of vitamins, minerals and calories. My sister-in-law and mother were especially interested in this, and we tried to determine what vitamins and minerals were in the foods that we were eating.

Two of my favorite books were gotten from the USIA Library. One was called *A Child's History of the World* and a similar one *A Child's Geography of the World*. *Treasure Island* fascinated me, although I didn't understand all the nautical terms or all the actions of the characters. Later on, when I saw the movie it became clearer. Then there was Helen Keller's *Autobiography*. It was such a charming story that I read it twice and started to translate it into Persian.

A little later I began to read *Anne Frank's Diary*, and my brother helped me through it. It interested me very much and because it had been written by a girl my own age, it encouraged me to do some writing too. And so I thought about becoming a writer. But how does one become a writer? My brother suggested I read the story of a writer's life, and be brought me Tolstoy's story of his own childhood. And the same time I was reading short stories, written for American school students.

One day my brother took me to visit an American family whom he knew. The American man had a fatherly attitude toward everyone. Later I learned that he was the chief of UNESCO Technical Assistance in Iran. He spoke to me in a

95

kindly way and asked me some questions in English. I answered him, and he asked me to read. I read to him and he questioned me about it. He remarked that I had learned at least one thing: "to comprehend before proceeding further."

In my reading, I encountered different forms that words take in sentences. I wanted to know how sentences are formed. Hooshi gave me a simple lesson in grammar. First he taught me simple definitions of parts of speech: for example he defined adverb as "add verb" meaning something that can be added to a verb. As an example he said, "The man walked slowly." After he had talked about nouns, verbs, adjectives, adverbs and prepositions, etc. he told me to take some colored pencils and use a different color for each part of speech. I underlined a page of words a day. In a few days I knew the relationship of words to one another.

Hooshi repeatedly emphasized the use of the dictionary, and I learned much about words by exploring there. At the end of nine months, I had progressed well in reading and speaking, and typing summaries. My handwriting was still poor, but in time that improved too.

Learning English wasn't all that I learned from Hooshi. From the very beginning we had lessons several times a week in reading and writing Persian. Hooshi had given me a short test to see how much I had learned in an Iranian public school, and I think he had been quite disappointed; for I remember he said, "Emelia, if you want to be proud of being an Iranian you should know your own language well. Otherwise how can you communicate with those around you."

He prepared a list of Persian books that I was to read and discuss with him. One of the books was the "Golestan of Saadi" a classical book of Persian literature and considered a masterpiece. Then I read a famous book on speaking. The author,

M. A. Foroghi was an Iranian statesman who wrote on the best method of public speaking. He gave many examples, especially from Greek and Roman orations. I also read, in Persian, the translation of Homer's *Illiad*.

Hooshi asked me to make a daily schedule for studying Persian. The best plan seemed to me to read several pages each morning right after our morning prayers, when everyone was still sitting around. Thus they could help me correct my mistakes.

Still I needed practice in writing Persian. It takes a lot of skill and training to develop good penmanship and the ability to express oneself in writing. Hooshi devised another plan for me. He put me in charge of writing letters to our relatives in the provinces. Of course, he always looked them over to see that they were free of errors. He encouraged me to write in short clear sentences. Thus at the same time both my Persian and my English were improving.

CHAPTER EIGHT

LEARNING IS FUN

No longer was I disappointed that I had left public school. For the first time in my life I realized that learning could be fun. Previously school work had made little impression on me. It was not directed toward any goal. School had been primarily a means of seeing friends, talking to them and playing games together. Our games were often boring. Studying at home had only one drawback. I felt lonesome for my friends.

Hooshi sensed my loneliness and asked me to invite a few of my friends to visit me. Among all my friends, I liked Pari best. She often came to visit me, and I visited her in return. She had three sisters, and they along with two other neighborhood girls became my chums. We made up our own group. Later Pari became my student and I taught her English. In fact, her older sister, who had already finished high school, also came to me for help with her English.

Learning English at home with my brother was not just a simple learning situation. It became a way of life. Hooshi's method gave me confidence and a way of approaching new situations, such that I felt I could master other things. Not only that, but he showed me how all of my environment could become a subject of learning. One of the things that convinced me of this was reading a book on the history of mankind. Things I had taken for granted, the customs and habits of my country, as well as those of others, could be studied. Previously in school, I had learned things only from books—things that I had to memorize and recite. In arithmetic, problems dealt with abstractions that had nothing to do with reality or my life at hand.

Now I was encountering a new kind of learning: learning by observing and making experiments. It was all new to me, and I wasn't always sure how I should proceed. In school, everything had been arranged for me, step by step. Our lessons followed the same procedure, day after day. And every one's work was expected to be almost identical.

Very early in my learning experience, Hooshi said to me: "The things you see every day and take for granted can teach you a lot. Just look out the window now."

I did as he suggested, but nothing attracted my attention particularly. Like any other yard, there were trees, flowers and a pool in the center of it.

"Your first lesson in nature study," he announced, "will be to collect leaves from the different trees in our neighborhood. Be sure to examine the tree carefully so that you can describe it and distinguish it from other trees. Try to organize your observations systematically."

I felt mystified. How could trees teach me anything in themselves. Wasn't it first necessary to go to a book and read about them; then go out and collect specimens? I shrugged my shoulders.

In a week or so, I had collected many leaves and had made notes about the arrangement of the leaves on the branches and the shape of the tree. Each leaf was put between the pages of a thick book—in fact one of my old school text books. (This was the only use I had for it now!) I brought it into Hooshi's study and he looked at it carefully, along with the notes I had made on each page.

99

"You've done a good job, but you're not finished. The leaves you've collected plus your observations will help you to find the name of the tree. Here, I'll show you how."

He pulled a book down from his book-shelf. It was written in English, and Hooshi opened it to a section which was outlined in great detail. "It's a kind of key that helps you unlock the secret of the tree," he explained.

He took one of the leaves from my book, and helped me locate the exact description of the tree. At the beginning of the outline, the trees were divided into general categories, but further on in the outline, the classification narrowed down until it described just one tree. Hooshi did the first one, and I did all the rest. It was lots of fun—just like unraveling a mystery.

The next day my brother gave me a book picturing how plants grow and the things that they need in order to live. In the next few weeks, we planted bean seeds under different conditions to see how they would grow. Some grew well, others did not. The ones that got water, soil, air and sunlight prospered.

It was just ten weeks after starting my *new* school that I paid a visit to my *old* school. My friends welcomed me heartily, and the teachers greeted me cordially. One of the teachers asked me to speak before the class and talk about what I had learned. I described how I was learning English, as well as the experiments and observations I had made on plant life. Many of them seemed envious of my progress, and several asked if my brother was planning to open a school soon. To this, I laughed and explained, "My brother doesn't believe in schools and text books the way you do. He often says, "All of nature is a school, and the student must write his own textbook."

On another occasion I learned about our world and the United States in a most unique way: by collecting and mounting stamps. When my brother was in the United States, I saved all the stamps from the letters he sent home. Many of the stamps had been issued for special occasions: American holidays, historical events or for important people. In addition, he himself collected many stamps from his fellow foreign students in the United States. He brought these home with him and gave them to me, along with the stamp album. "Your job," he directed "is to sort and classify the stamps according to the country, then look at the numbers on the stamps and determine their value. Put all the stamps of one country together, in order of increasing value. I would suggest that you divide your book into different sections, as many as there are continents. Then under each continent, put the countries that belong there."

It sounded like an easy job, for I had had geography in the fifth grade. But it wasn't that simple. With all the stamps spread out in front of me, it wasn't always easy to decide to which country they belonged: the pictures were often very different for one country. Then I had to try and remember in which continent the country belonged. Fortunately, I had borrowed a geography book from the American library, and it helped. But the biggest help was a small globe of the world that my brother had in his study. I really "circled" the globe, time and time again, in an effort to locate an unfamiliar country. I'd never realized that so many countries existed. There were some countries that I didn't have stamps for, but I'm keeping a place for them in my stamp album. Who knows? Perhaps I'll be able to visit those countries one of these days. Nowadays when I read about some far distant place in the newspaper I can easily picture it in my mind's eye, or rather on the mental image of the world globe that I have in my mind.

When I first began to study with my brother, I thought it would be easy. No classes to attend and lots of time to myself. I must confess that I am inclined to be lazy, or so it was until I started Hooshi's class. But how things changed! In fact, I got so interested in my projects and experiments that I didn't want to stop studying, even when my friends came to call.

One Friday morning I was busy assembling stamps in my album. It was the morning that I had set aside to finish this project. But Hooshi interrupted my plans. He poked his head in my room and announced authoratively, "We're going for a walk in the mountains this morning. Be ready in half an hour."

I nodded indifferently. Why did he have to pick today? Just when I was getting ready to finish off this project in fine style. Little did I realize that this casual hike was to turn into a classroom session. But then I shouldn't have been surprised. Hasn't Hooshi always said, "Your classroom is anywhere you choose to be."

And on this particular Friday we went hiking in the mountain valley, not too far from our home; although I had never been there. Not only my knowledge, but my horizons had been hemmed in before. Now I was being given a chance to explore my own surroundings and those beyond. More and more, as time goes on, I find myself moving beyond my own little world. Like a pebble thrown in the water, my circle is ever enlarging.

Hooshi is very fond of hiking. In fact he has a special photographic album just filled with pictures of hiking groups that he has known. He did a lot of hiking when he was in college in Tehran. Now having returned from the States, he was eager to resume his old program. He phoned a few friends and the plans were made. One of his friends was a man quite a bit older than Hooshi, but he was fond of hiking. Mr. Firuz brought along his grown daughter and his two sons, who were near my age. There were several others of Hooshi's friends who came.

The valley that we explored that day was very beautiful. I had never seen so many beautiful and different kinds of wild flowers.

While the others were resting under a near-by tree, I began to pick some of the different flowers. I brought them over to where Hooshi was sitting. Innocently I asked, "What are the names of these flowers?"

"Now you see, you've already found the subject for your next project," he replied. "How are you going to go about it?"

A project to study wild flowers. I had never thought about it before. How should I plan to study them. Perhaps like the way I had studied trees. First I would need a notebook.

We hiked a lot that day, and I'm sure the mountains were lovely, but I don't remember much of what we did. My mind was on the next study project, and how I would study wild flowers.

The following day my brother came home from work with a small book under his arm. He remarked, "It seems I am learning a few things too." He smiled and presented me with the book.

I opened it. Inside were many drawings of flowers and the names of the parts that make up a flower. Descriptions of different flowers followed. Everything was written in English.

"You see," Hooshi explained, "I don't know much about wild flowers, but I expect you to find out all about them and teach me. This morning I talked to Dr. Seena at the University, and he gave me a simple book for you to follow."

In the next few weeks, I became fully acquainted with that small book, and some others that I found in the American Library. Classifying wild flowers was similar to studying trees. First I had to put them into general classes, then find their more precise category. To do all this, I had to examine their petals, carpels, stamens and sepals. Often I had to use a magnifying glass. Every evening I told Hooshi what I had learned and showed him the flowers I had mounted and classified.

One morning Hooshi asked me, "Would you like to come to

the University with me today? I think you will learn something."

Although I had passed by the gates of the University many times, I had never been inside them. My eagerness to go must have been evident. "Oh, yes," I blurted, "I'll get ready now."

There were many students on the university grounds. I was puzzled by their appearance, and I questioned my brother, "Why do they all walk with their heads down, reading from a book? None of them seem to be aware of what is going on around him and they don't even seem to know where they are going."

Hooshi replied, "You are an intelligent observer. You are right about these students. The kind of education they receive does not make them aware of what is happening about them. Nor does it guide them to find their goal."

He continued, "These students are preparing for their final examinations, and they must memorize their subject matter. Understanding is not important, but repetition is."

I looked at the people on the walks. One student was pacing back and forth, reciting to himself. I could see him peering at his book, then glancing up, his lips moving rapidly. A boy and girl were walking together, and he was reading to her. Under a tree I saw a student sitting with half closed eyes, his book beside him. Others were sitting on the steps of buildings, probably trying to predict what the possible questions might be.

The human scene in front of me was monotonous. I turned my gaze to the garden in the center lane. The flowers were lovely there. My feet followed my gaze. I looked at each flower, carefully noting the arrangements of its stamens, petals and carpels; and then tried to think of what family it belonged to. It was fun—just like opening a box and discovering a lovely gift inside.

Hooshi saw that I had discovered my lesson for that day, and he left me in the garden while he attended to his business. I made

104

many notes about the flowers, and he came back all too soon. To me, the garden was the university. Perhaps that's the way I'll always think of it.

Some friends of my brother offered to drive us home. They were Americans and lived in Shemran, not far from us. Hooshi introduced me to them, "This is my sister, Emelia, Mr. and Mrs. Smith. She understands only English."

They laughed and shook hands with me saying, "We've heard a lot about you from your brother. It's nice to meet you now. What have you done today?"

"I've been at the University observing the students and the flowers," I replied.

"Well," laughed Mr. Smith, "Which did you find most interesting?"

"Oh, the flowers naturally," I replied smilingly.

It was everyone's turn to smile. Mrs. Smith commented, "Your brother has not only taught you to speak English but to observe too."

They were very much interested in hearing about my wild flower project and also about hiking in the mountains. Mr. Smith suggested to my brother, "Why don't you and your sister join us this Sunday. We're driving to the village of Damavand so that we can get a good view of Mt. Damavand. We want to see Iran's highest mountain before we leave next month."

The following Sunday turned out to be a beautiful spring day. The Smiths picked us up in their car and we drove to the village of Damavand. We found a shady spot near the side of the road, and we parked the car there. Near-by was a small wooded area and we ate our lunch there, next to a small stream. Just by looking up we could see Mt. Damavand. For lunch we made kababs, first building the fire, then roasting the meat and vegetables. It was delicious. Mrs. Smith remarked, "This is one of

105

the Persian foods that I'm going to remember to cook in the States when I go home."

I was curious about American food, and asked her, "What kinds of food do you eat in America that we don't eat here?"

She described to me America's two most popular dishes: "hamburgers" and "hot-dogs." My brother laughed at her remarks. I didn't understand what shee mant by "hot-dogs." Later at home I questioned Hooshi about this, and he kidded me, "Silly, you should have asked Mrs. Smith to explain more about the food. Hot dogs are really sausages, and not made from dog's meat."

Another day, my brother arranged for me to take a tour of Parliament, the palaces and Tehran museums. The tour was sponsored by the Iran-America Society, and most of the people who went on it were Americans. The Persian guide spoke English, and I had to listen carefully to what he was saying. Not many school children are able to visit these places, and I felt very privileged to be there. I also knew that, as part of my lesson, I would have to explain to my brother everything that I had seen that day.

There were other American activities that helped my education along. The USIA sponsored American movies weekly. Of course, I had seen American movies in the local theaters, but always with Persian translations. Now, my brother began to take me to movies at the USIA auditorium, along with some of his American friends. Often, there were no Persian translations, and I had to listen carefully to understand what was going on. Sometimes the movie characters spoke in a kind of American accent that I was not familiar with. Then I would lose the meaning of the story; but Hooshi usually sensed my difficulty and translated some of it for me. There were many excellent movies that I saw at USIA, and often I learned a little about American history too.

Looking back on this phase of my education, I wonder if I realized the full significance of it then. It was thrilling, of course. Every day I discovered something new that added to the previous day's knowledge; like finding pearls one by one, and at the end a necklace.

Equally important, I acquired a method to collect and organize knowledge, and make it my own. First of all, before starting a project, Hooshi and I always sat down before and made a plan of what I should observe and how. Then, when I returned home, I made an oral report to my brother and later gave him a written report; in English of course. This was our usual arrangement. It wasn't always easy, especially at the beginning. But he helped me to express myself—not by telling me what to say or write, but by asking simple questions. Then in answering his questions, I discovered the way to say it. With experience I found many different ways to to express an idea, and I needed less and less help.

Movies were seldom merely entertainment for me. Hooshi usually selected educational and historical films for me to see. I especially remember "Seven Brides for Seven Brothers", and "Gone With the Wind." I hope to read that book some day.

So far, I have described several of my projects to you. But the one that I enjoyed the most was called "Persian Games for American Girls." It all began at picnic that I attended with my brother. There were two American girls there, and to entertain them I asked them to play a game with me. It is called "Ughol-Do-Ghaul." (one stone, two stones...") After explaining the rules and demonstrating how it is done, one of them remarked "Oh, it's very similar to one of our games. You play with pebbles, while we play with star-shaped pieces of metal. We call it 'jacks'."

When I related the day's adventures to my brother, he suggested, "Why don't you make a project out of Persian games. If you collect enough, and do a good job of recording them in English, perhaps I can get it published for you."

The idea appealed to me. I decided to start first with the games that I knew myself, then find others from my friends. I recorded them all in a large notebook. When I had collected quite a large number, I showed my results to Hooshi. As my final effort, I typed them all. Hooshi took them to an American family and they enjoyed reading about them and even tried to play some of them. I still collect these games and I wish there was some way of presenting them to American girls.

CHAPTER NINE

ADVENTURES IN TRAVELING

It was June. Summer was approaching. The trees were fully clothed in green now. Some flowers were already in bloom. The open windows of my room welcomed the fragrant scent of lilacs, and other flowers. There were times when I wanted to leave my books and walk in the garden. I felt somewhat restless: perhaps a case of spring fever.

For almost nine months I had been studying diligently. My English was steadily improving. I seldom used the giant two volume English-Persian dictionary now. Instead I looked up unfamiliar words in an English-English dictionary. There were many projects and experiments that I had planned and carried out under my brother's guidance. Along with these there were written summaries and reports of books I had read and activities I had taken part in. The floor of my room was carpeted with neat bundles of these manuscripts. Each activity had been an adventure. It was like climbing a mountain: sometimes difficult to ascend, but never dull, and always the rewarding sense of accomplishment on reaching the summit.

Yet now I felt a little tierd, and I silently wished I might have more chance to enjoy the out-of-doors. About this time my brother suggested that we all go North to the resort area around the Caspian Sea. It was just the kind of vacation I had been dreaming of.

In a few weeks we had made our plans. It was a busy time of the year for my brothers, and they decided that my parents and I should go ahead; then they and Meri with Nan-a-cee would join us later.

My excitement mounted. I made lists of the things I wanted to see and do. Right then and there I decided to keep a journal of my trip. I had always wanted to keep a diary, especially after reading *Anne Frank's Diary*, and now it seemed a good opportunity to start. Of course, all my impressions would be written in English.

The plan was that my parents and I would take a train to Shahee. In a few days time the rest of our family would join us there. I had never been on a train before, nor had I visited the Caspian.

My brother drove us to the railway station one Friday morning. Besides our luggage we had brought some fruit, seeds and nuts to nibble on during the trip. I don't know if you eat seeds in America, the same way we do in Iran. We had brought a large box of dried salted pumpkin and water-mellon seeds. In eating them it's necessary to crack them between your two upper middle teeth in such a way that the seed comes out intact, and then it's easy to spit out the shell. When I was a small child it took me a lot of practice to acquire this skill.

As much as I love eating seeds, I almost forgot about them. I was too busy looking out the train window to bother about anything else. From Tehran to Shahee it is about a day's travel by train, and one arrives in the early evening. The farther one goes, the more mountaneous it becomes: I tried to count the tunnels that we passed through, but I soon lost track. My father said he thought there were about 60 tunnels that the train had to pass through. We seemed to be continually climbing mountains and traversing valleys. The contrast startled me: first there

110

were the bleak gray mountaneous rocks, and then the brilliant emerald green fields of rice and tea. The scenery was further enhanced by the costumes of the women working in the fields: their bright ruby red tunics topped coal-black trousers.

In all too short a time the train came to the end of the line. It does not not go beyond Shahee. It's too bad—I would have liked to continue traveling by train. At the same time I was tired from all the excitement and activity of the day's adventure. We took a taxi to a small hotel that had been recommended to us. Our plan was to stay here until the rest of the family arrived Sunday evening.

Shahee is a small, city, best known for its textile mills. The next day we decide to visit one of them. The factory building was very ugly on the outside, and seemed somewhat dark in the inside. The first room that we were taken to was a very large one: many women sat or stood in front of looms that were weaving cotton cloth of many colors. In another room there were large tanks of water with chemicals of all kinds; this was the place were some of the cloth was being dyed. I was quite interested in watching the fabric being dyed, not only into plain colors but patterns as well.

The following evening the rest of the family arrived: Shahpour, Meri, Nan-a-cee and Hooshi. They were obviously tired from the car trip. Hooshi remarked, "The roads in Iran are like footpaths compared to the super-highways that I've seen in the U.S."

We spent the night at Shahee and started out early the next day. There was some discussion as to where we should go next. After looking at our map, it seemed that our next stop should be Cha-loose. In a few hours we were in Cha-loose, a city famous for its silk factories. We stopped to visit one. The building reminded me of the textile factory at Shahee. Are all factories built the same? A guide took us from room to room, explaining how the silkworms are cared for and how the silk fibers are spun into threads and later woven into cloth. There were many young girls working at the looms—some of them seemed younger than me, and they all looked quite pale and thin. I felt sorry for them, and wished that I could have spoken to them.

In the afternoon we were on our way again. By evening we were at Ramsar, where we planned to stay a few days. It was a busy season of the year, and we had some difficulty in finding a hotel that had rooms free. Finally, we found one on the edge of town. Everyone was tired, especially my niece Nan-a-cee who had slept on my lap ever since leaving Cha-loose. Next morning we did a little sightseeing in the town before going to lunch at Hotel Ramsar. At first I thought it must be a hotel out of some American movie, because there was nothing in it to remind me of Iran. Even the people looked different: I didn't see any woman with a *chador* (veil) and the people all around us were speaking foreign languages, French, English and occasionally German. In fact, I wondered if we would have to order our food in French, because the menu I had was only written in French; but the waiter spoke to us in Persian. From the windows of the hotel we looked out in three directions: on one side there was the endless sea stretching as far out as one could see, in the other direction were the magnificent forests, perched on high mountaneous rocks. Then there was the lovely garden of the hotel. I couldn't believe it. I turned my head from side to side, and back again, until my neck ached and I had to stop.

As we left the hotel, Hooshi asked, "Do you know why this resort is called "Ramsar" (which means tamed or obedient)?"
"Ramsar."

I had no idea of how it got its name. My brother continued, "Some years ago when Reza Shah (the father of the present king) was visiting the region around the Caspian Sea, it is said that

112

his car got stuck in the mud here and he was delayed for several hours. They say he became angry and took his cane finally and struck the ground shouting 'I'll make your unyielding ways obey my will.' In 1930 he ordered the construction of this modern city, and four years later it was completed. So he named it "Ramsar."

While my brother had been telling me this story, we had all been walking toward the beach. In Iran, where lakes are scarce, I had never seen so much water before. The waves fascinated me. I took off my shoes and waded cautiously. With each pulsation I felt myself pushed back a little. Nan-a-cee wanted to try it too, but we all felt that the waves were too strong for her. So I came out of the water and persuaded her to walk along the beach with me. It was soon time for us to return back to our hotel, and I followed the others somewhat reluctantly, although my parents had promised that I could return the next day.

True enough, I spent all of the following day at the beach. We packed our lunch and ate it there. For several hours I lay in the sand staring out at the wide expanse of sea. At other times I strolled up and down the beach looking at the people. They interested me. Some were obviously European or American with thier fair skin and features. But of course there were also many Iranians: their behavior was so Westernized that I wondered if perhaps they weren't Europeans too. I picked up many unusual shells on the beach and kept them. It would be an interesting project to study next in school.

Like all Iranians, our family is fond of the sun, Hooshi most of all. At the beach the sun was very intense and bright, and we all stayed under a beach umbrella, except for Hooshi. He put a blanket in the sun, and stretched out to read. Shapour called to him: "You'd better join us under the umbrella, or else your skin will be as red as a pomogranate."

113

Hooshi laughed and replied, "I am a warm-blooded Shira zee, and they never burn from the sun, the sun burns from them."

We all laughed, half-believing what he said. A while later I looked over toward him and saw that he was asleep. At five o'clock we packed our things and prepared to leave. I went over to tell Hooshi that we were going. It was difficult to recognize him: his skin was a bright red, like fresh cherries in late summer. He pulled himself up, first on his knees and then slowly to his legs, lik an aged man. I put out my hand to take his arm and he drew back as if in pain. "It's better that you don't touch me, I am on fire and you might get burnt."

Everyone sympathized with his condition, although Shapour could not help but remark, "It seems the sun challenged you to a duel and you obviously lost."

Our stay at Ramsar was at an end. I felt as if I could have spent my life there. The city of Bandar Pahlavi (port of Pahlavi) was next on our list. It took just a few hours to get there. We stayed with some friends of my parents, Agha and Khonem Javan. They were eager to show us the fishing that goes on there. We drove to the seashore. There were many small boats at anchor there, and the water looked rougher than it had at Ramsar. We could see several fishermen wading out into the water. They wore high rubber boots. Our host explained, "Those large nets that they have are for catching the fish. They leave the net overnight, and in the morning there are thousands of fish, mostly sturgeon."

"Is it the sturgeon fish that are caught for cavier?" I asked my father.

Agha Javan replied, "Yes, their eggs are the cavier. It seems that most of the sturgeon prefer our side of the Caspian Sea, rather than the Russian side. In fact, the Russians used to have

114

a contract to fish on our side of the sea for sturgeon. The contract ended in 1952.

Shapour asked, "Are we near the fishery?"

Mr. Javan answered, "Yes, it's within walking distance. If you like we can go through it now.

We all walked in the direction of a large building he pointed out to us. A guide took us through, and explained how cavier is prepared for shipment to Tehran and many places throughout the world. He also pointed out one large sturgeon that they had recently caught. It weighed about 1000 pounds and in its abdomen were several hundred pounds of cavier.

Returning to Agha Javan's home, we spent a pleasant evening with them and their family. It seemed too soon to leave, but tomorrow we had to get an early start so that we could reach Tehran by nightfall. In the morning we said our good-byes and departed. I took one last look at the sea, and waved good-bye to it from the car window. I settled back in my seat to think about all the wonderful things I had seen and done. For the past week, I had made notes of what had happened, but I was eager to get home. There my typewriter was waiting and it would be easy to type up my impressions, enlarging on the descriptions in my journal.

Our family tends to enjoy conversation, especially when we are all together. All the way home, we talked and sang and joked. But at times I paid no attention to what was going on in the car; the outside was more interesting. Sometimes there was lots of greenery, as when we passed through the rice and tea fields; other times only the barren mountains were in view. And always the road: round and down, then round and up. We had to caution Shapour to drive more slowly, as it was beginning to make a few of us nausated. And then the unexpected happened. We had a tire puncture and had to stop. Shapour and Hooshi

115

set about trying to change the tire. Fortunately for us, the next vehicle on the road was a truck. The driver stopped and offered to help. In no time the tires were changed and we were on our way again.

Soon Tehran was in sight. Granny with her sharp ears heard the breaks squeak and rushed out to greet us. We were home again.

CHAPTER TEN

A NEW SCHOOL

The end of August. It had been intensely hot for several weeks. The wind sometimes whipped up the sand and tossed it about on the streets, or in the yard. I preferred to spend most of the day indoors where it was cool, for our house was surrounded by trees. In the evening I often took a walk in Shemran with my brother, or occasionally we went to Tehran to see a movie. After returning from the Caspian, I spent some time writing down my impressions of the trip. I also became interested in geography and history. One day Hooshi brought home a new book, *A Glimpse of World History*: it was by Pandit Nehru. We read the introduction together and discovered that Nehru had written it to his 13-year-old daughter in the form of letters when he was in prison. My brother suggested that we read a letter every night together. Although difficult reading I enjoyed it.

Several times in the past few weeks, Hooshi had said mysteriously: "In another week or two, I will have a pleasant surprise for you. I suggest that you try to improve your handwriting. Using the typewriter doesn't give you any practice in writing."

So I spent more of my time writing summaries and book reviews by hand, rather than with the typewriter. I wondered what surprise my brother had in store for me. And what did it have to do with handwriting?

Many of my girl friends had gone away for the summer, and I

sometimes felt a little lonely. They'd soon be coming back, but then they'd be busy getting ready for school, and I wouldn't see much of them anyway. Many of my friends still didn't understand why I wasn't attending school. Maybe they felt that I was trying to be superior to them or that I didn't care for their company. But that wasn't the case. I enjoyed my brother's school very much, but I often wished that several of my friends could have joined me in my work. I wanted to share my experiences with others.

One evening, Hooshi asked smilingly, "How is your handwriting? Do you think other people could read it? What would a teacher think of it?"

I replied seriously, "I think my handwriting has improved; and since you're my teacher, I'll give it to you to read."

He read one of my recent summaries and nodded his head several times. Finally he said, "You've made progreess. And as a reward, I'm going to take you on a special trip to town tomorrow."

He didn't say anything more, and I wondered what he meant.

In the morning as we drove into town my brother started to explain: "I'm taking you to visit an interesting school. It is an American school for Iranian girls. All the classes are conducted in English, and the subjects are very similar to those in American schools. Would you like to be a student there?"

I could hardly speak. This certainly was a surprise. It was more exciting than anything I could have imagined. "Oh, yes," I answered, not having words to express my obvious pleasure.

We went to see the principal, Mrs. Jenkins. She was a pleasant elderly American woman who spoke to us very kindly. Hooshi explained to her about my interest in enrolling in her school. She replied hesitantly, "Many Iranian girls are interested in attending our school, but they do not have enough knowledge of

English to keep up with the curriculum. You see, all our books are American ones that are used in American schools. We cannot take all the girls who apply, and naturally we must select those who have a ninth grade diploma and whose English is the best."

I listened carefully to what she said, and then without waiting for my brother to explain, I said in English, "My brother has been my teacher for almost a year, and in that time I have studied many American books. I would be glad to read to you from one of your books."

Mrs. Jenkins smiled and took a book down from her shelf, and handed it to me. I read some passages about the old stone age, which I was not too familiar with; but the sentences themselves were not difficult.

She seemed pleased with my pronounciation and replied hesitantly to Hooshi, "It's seldom that we take a girl from the Iranian public schools. Iranian schools teach a little about a lot and as a result their students are poorly equipped to study here. But your sister speaks enough English, and I don't think she'll have any trouble. She can register now in Section C, the beginning section of the Second Grade."

The following day I started school. On the first day, the teacher asked us all to introduce ourselves and announce our names out loud. Then after that, she asked if anyone could talk to the class in English about some happening. I volunteered to describe a movie I had just seen. It was "Three Coins in a Fountain." The teacher said I had done well. The lessons that day were very easy for me.

The following week, after a faculty meeting, another girl and I were promoted to the next class: Section B of the Second Grade. The English lessons were still very easy for me, but arithmetic caused me some difficulty. I had never had arithmetic

119

in English and so I decided to put most of my effort into that subject.

We were asked to buy six books. I looked through them, and decided that I would most enjoy reading the two that were called *Old Ways and New Ways* and *Then and Now*. The first talked about how man developed tools and ways of doing things; the second book contrasted earlier developments of man with the most recent ones. I enjoyed making reports of them for the class.

Classes were given only in the morning. We had the afternoon free, although there were various social activities planned for three afternoons in the week. I wanted to do well in my classes, even those that were easy for me; so I spent much of my free time in preparing my assignments. Somehow I found time to study Persian too, which Hooshi helped me with.

Handwriting and arithmetic caused me a little difficulty the first few months, but I worked hard at them. When we reached our first marking, I was above average in everything, but I resolved to bring up my handwriting and arithmetic to equal my ability in English. This I did, and I then directed my interest toward grammar and phonetics, which I found very helpful in improving my pronounciation.

The girls in my classes were very friendly to me. Many of them had started together in the first year and were now together for the second year. They welcomed me like an old friend, and they were very interseted to learn that I had never studied English in a school before. In fact, it amazed them to see me write compositions so easily—but then I had had an intensive year's practice of it.

Even the girls in my neighborhood seemed to want my friendship more, now that I was in school again, especially the American school. They consulted me as the final word whenever they had compositions to write. On one occasion I wrote an

120

English composition for a girl who was taking an entrance examination for the University. She memorized it, in case she was asked to write an essay.

My daily schedule had changed somewhat now that I had to go into town each day. But I still got up at sunrise, as was my habit. I guess I must be one of those people who never need alarm clocks to awaken. The sun is my awakener. The early morning air in Shemran is refreshing and I like to poke my head out the window in the morning and breathe it in, like a fish coming to the surface of the pond for oxygen. After a breakfast of bread, honey, butter and tea, I got a ride into town with my brother, Shapour. At noon, I went to the taxi stand, near the school, where there are station-wagons that load up passengers for Sherman.

School wasn't all study, far from it. We had a school council, just as they do in American schools. Each class elected two representatives and these two girls would help plan the school parties or represent the class on special occasions. At one election I was chosen as a representative. I also took part in a play that our class put on for the rest of the school.

In the morning at ten o'clock there was an assembly for all the students in the school, about 300 in all. At this time general announcements were made. There was group-singing, and one of the teachers played the piano for us. Sometimes educational movies were presented. One day I suggested to my teacher that my brother might be interested in showing his slides of America to the group. The following day the principal asked my brother if he would come the following week and talk to the girls at assembly. He did, and showed his slides. Everyone liked the pictures and the interesting things he had to say. I felt very proud of him.

In the afternoon, many of the girls stayed after to play ping-pong or volley ball. There was a special athletic group in school and they arranged the times for all to play. Our class played twice a week.

At the end of the first semester, I felt that I had accomplished a great deal and I had also acquired many new friends. My composition writing was improving, and one of my best ones was called "A Blind Girl." The girls in my class thought I had copied it from a book, and I was secretly pleased at the compliment.

CHAPTER ELEVEN

WRITING AND MONEY MAKING

Going to school in town opened many new doors for me. It also encouraged me to try new things. Let me tell you one example of this. As I explained to you previously, I was accustomed to going into town every morning with my brother who drove to work. At noon it was my responsibility to get home myself; this was something new to me. School had always been within walking distance from my home, and I had rarely used public transportation—and then only if accompanied by an older person.

For a while it seemed strange and a bit lonely for me to go to the taxi station and climb into a station wagon with other passangers, bound for Sherman alone. Then one day, I met one of my teachers going to Shemran; and another day several girls from school. Gradually the other girls and I made arrangements to go home together at noon.

There were even times in the morning when my brother couldn't take me into town. It was necessary for me to go by station-wagon; but after the first time the newness had worn off, and I felt no concern about going into town alone.

Living in Shemran, in the suburbs of Tehran, is a pleasant experience for me and my family. There are many people who say, "It's too difficult to live that far away. Transporation is bad, and in winter when there's snow and ice, you can't get to work."

To this, I always reply, "Transportation is much better than it used to be. It takes only 20-30 minutes to get to town. In fact I've heard people say it takes them sometimes that long to go across town in the morning or evening when traffic is particularly snarled up."

And of course, I always cinch the argument by saying, "Just think of all the hot summer days in Tehran, when just a short distance away in Shemran you can have cool weather, a beautiful view of the mountains and a quiet place to enjoy life."

Living in Shemran now presented no problem to me. Of course, I preferred going with my brother in the morning, but I could just as well go alone in the station-wagon. When I went with Hooshi, we spoke only English and I talked about my activities at school. I was happy in school and at home, and I had many friends.

Yet with all this I sometimes wondered what use was it to know English. What value was anything I was learning? What use would it be to me in the future? Of course, I had learned typing by typing summaries of books I had read, and later I did some typing for my brother in his work. But this was not enough. Where did it all lead? Even, as much as I loved reading books, I asked myself, "What is the good of reading all this?" And another time I dreamed of myself as a writer, but then I pondered, "What can a writer do?"

The answer soon came to me. One day some of my friends in the neighborhood were visiting me. They were all from the public school I had once attended. Pari picked up my copy of *Old Ways and New Ways* and asked, "What kind of book is this? The pictures look interesting."

I told my friends about a few of the chapters in it, and they wanted to know more.

Later that evening when Hooshi came home, I mentioned

what had happened during the afternoon. He asked, "Would you like to translate the book into Persian so that your friends can read it?"

"Well, I would like to do it, but it will take me a long time," I said.

Hooshi smiled and remarked, "You won't have to do it all at once, and you might even earn some money, he added mysteriously."

"How is that," I asked?

"Oh, I have some friends who could publish it in a weekly children's magazine," he answered, "and of course they would pay you for each page they print. You just start translating now, and I'll see what kind of arrangements we can make."

The following day was an American holiday at school, and so I decided to use the morning for translating some of my text. It was an interesting project; I hadn't done much translating of English into Persian. In fact, in teaching me English, Hooshi had always stressed the fact that I should think in English and never translate a Persian word into English, or vice versa. But at the same time he had not neglected to teach more Persian. As I explained to you before, I spent part of the day in studying Persian, and I had considerable practice in writing to our relatives, for our family is a large one.

The task was not difficult, for my brother had taught me to write Persian in short simple sentences. However I had some difficulty with the first chapter. When I read my translation of it to Hooshi that evening he was not pleased: it needed many changes. He pointed out my errors and helped me rewrite it. He remarked, "You are lucky to be a student during these times. When I was your age there were no children's magazines. If we wanted to read anything, it was adult literature and usually we read it only to pass our examinations. Therefore you ought to

125

do a good job in translating. The children reading it will appreciate it."

When I had translated the first chapter, Hooshi took it to the editor of a children's magazine. They liked the story very much and agreed to publish it in serial form. However, they thought the book was too long and should be condensed in some way. But what can one do, when the story of mankind is very long and its beginning is not known to us, nor is its end predictable?

Writing for children was fun. I realized that the vocabulary and style should be simple; yet I had certain ideas I wanted to communicate. Then the editors of the magazine asked me to translate *Moby Dick*. I had never read it in English before, but I enjoyed reading the children's simplified edition of it so much that I knew other Persian children would like it. Persians like heroic stories. Every week I translated two pages. The story was successfully received.

For the first time in my life I was earning money. Looking back on it now, a few dollars a week doesn't seem like much. But to me, it was to be the first step in accumulating my worldly fortune. It was a success. Friends at school and in the neighborhood congratulated me; they read my stories with interest. Some at school were a bit envious and remarked, "I wish I had thought of doing that," or "I wish I had someone like your brother to help me."

My fame spread. One day Hooshi said to me, "The principal of an elementary school in Tehran has asked me if you would speak before her pupils. Are you interested?"

"Of course, I would like to," I answered. "Do you think they would like to hear about how I collected my wild flowers? I could show them the dried specimens I have mounted."

"That sounds like a good idea," Hooshi replied.

One afternoon that week, my brother picked me up at school

126

and we drove to a near-by private elementary school. The building was quite attractive on the outside, much more so than the school I had gone to. The teachers smiled and spoke to us, as we passed through the halls. The corridors themselves were attractive and cheerful: all along were children's drawings, and also displays of children's wood-work. We entered the principal's office, and she greeted us graciously. My brother wanted to know more about the school program, and so she explained, "This is a new school where modern teaching methods are employed. The classes are small, 30 pupils in each class, and we have other activities like music, art and dancing. We have a fine lunchroom, as well as a gym, and a playground outside."

I marveled at all the fine facilities this school had. How different from the elementary school that I had attended.

The principal took us to one classroom that was in session and we observed the children discussing their lessons. The next hour the teacher introduced us to the class, and I gave them a short talk on how I learned about wild flowers, showing them my collection. The students asked many questions, and some of them mentioned that they would like to do the same thing. The teacher volunteered to help them get started.

Hooshi and I were interested in seeing how English was taught, and the principal led us to another classroom, where an English lesson was in progress. When I went to elementary school, foreign languages were generally studied in high school only; but nowadays many parents want their children to learn a second language early. For these reasons private elementary schools teach English in the lower grades. Of course they charge tuition, but I know many parents who are willing to pay to have their children receive better instruction. I compared this elementary school to some of the public ones that my younger friends attend. In public school there are about 40-60 children per classroom; some of the first graders go to school for only half a day because there are no facilities for them.

The English class seemed to be making some progress; the students were conversing about their daily activities. I joined in occasionally, and asked one or another a question. It was lots of fun.

It was soon time to leave. I had had a pleasant time and promised to come again.

All these experiences: going to the American school, writing for the children's magazine, and talking to others, strengthened my inner self. It gave me confidence to realize that I could use my knowledge in the process of acquiring it. It wasn't necessary to wait until I had graduated from school. I was happy in my new surroundings, and my family reflected my feelings. I think they were beginning to understand Hooshi's often spoken saying, "There is a difference between school and education." Schooling was merely knowledge gotten from a formal school system. Education could be gotten from anything and anywhere, provided there was some guidance.

My writing activities continued. One day Hooshi remarked, "How would you like to explain to a lot of teachers how you learned English?"

"How would I do that?" I asked.

Hooshi showed me a Persian educational journal, and explained that teachers and educators contributed to it. If I wrote my explanation in simple Persian, he would help me edit it and submit it in my name.

I was pleased to do it, and my brother sent it in for me. In about a month he presented me with an envelope. Inside were about fifteen dollars for the five pages that I had written. It pleased me to learn sometime later that a distant relative had seriously read my article and began to study English intensively by this method.

There were times when I thought about becoming a teacher. So many of my friends came to ask for help with their lessons, and Hooshi encouraged me to help them as much as I had time for. He said, "The easiest way to learn is to try to teach others what you know."

At the same time writing appealed to me. I began to make a translation of *Helen Keller's Life*. It has been one of the most fascinating stories I have ever read, and I read it twice. I would like all Iranian girls to be able to read it. At the present time I'm still working on it and I hope that my translation will in some way measure up to the English original.

CHAPTER TWELVE

MY FUTURE WORLD

The school year is coming to an end. Examinations have been announced. There's still much to be done. Yet one afternoon last week I paused in the midst of my studying to look out the window at the trees in the yard. I wanted to say to them, "What is your future? Don't you ever think about what you'll be in the next few years?" But of course not. Trees are rooted to one place and they are content with very little—sunshine, and food from the soil. I reflected. Well, there are many people whose lives and ambitions resemble that of trees. I asked myself, "Do you want to be a tree?" I laughed aloud. It was a funny question, but what I meant to imply was "Are you content to let your life be determined for you?"

My question remained unanswered for several days. A few days later I had a chance to answer it. The occasion was a letter my family received from one of our relatives. It was passed around from one to another, but no one gave it to me. Most every one seemed amused by it, except for Granny who kept saying to the others, "It's no laughing matter. She's 14 by now, and it's time we started preparing for her future."

They must have been talking about me. But what did they have planned for my future? And what did it have to do with the letter? Finally I became impatient and demanded, "Isn't anyone going to tell me? Am I too young to know, even though it concerns me?"

My mother turned to me and explained, "We received a letter today from our cousins, the Orang family. Perhaps you remember Ahshan who is now twenty. His family wants to make plans for his marriage. They would like to have you for their daughter-in-law and they have written to ask our permission. Of course it's rediculous. Some day I want you to get married and have a family but it's too soon now."

Shapour interrupted, "But mother, perhaps Emelia wants to get married now", he teased.

He was joking and I knew it. But the whole idea made me blush. I blurted out, "Why did they choose me? They have seen me only a few times, and that was when I was a young child. I don't even remember what Ahshan looks like."

My father said soothingly, "It's all right. The matter is already solved. We'll write and explain that she's too young to make a decision in this matter now."

Our discussion stopped, but my thinking has continued. This might have been my future world: an early marriage, life with Ahshan and the start of family life. But I want more out of life; later on I can marry and raise a family. Then too, my thinking has been influenced by the girls at school. They are all opposed to pre-arranged and early marriages. There was one girl in the upper class at school who dropped out a short time ago. She was just 16, but her family had arranged her marriage for her. One of my class-mates went to the wedding and reported that the wedding party had been given at the University Club and had followed the Western practice of dancing and then the Persian custom of serving fruit and cake, sweets and Persian nuts.

There is no use thinking about weddings for some years yet. I feel that I have to develop myself. There are still many things that I don't know about the world or about myself.

Yesterday I was reviewing the text, *Old Ways and New Ways*.

All at once, I got a new perspective of man's existence: starting from individualized forest and sea life to when man discovered the art of cultivation and the art of husbandry and began to set up villages. The communities grew and spread all over the world. In the old communities the women cooked and sewed and reared children. In the new community it's important that everyone be educated, girls as well as boys. Both can contribute to improving the world and making a better life for themselves.

But now as I write the final chapter of my experiences these last two years, I wonder what the chapter beyond contains. Certainly, I'm going to finish my schooling at the American school if at all possible. Then I want to see some more of the world, and see how other people are living and building their future. Someone once said, "It's better to see the world and go hungry, than to see nothing and be satiated." That's the way I feel now.

Although I can't do much traveling in the next few years, I have found a kind of substitute for it. I write "traveling" letters. That is, I have two pen-pals, one in Germany and another in the United States. My German girl friend, Hilda, writes often from Hamburg; she is in the ninth grade of a gymnasium. Since I don't know German, she writes in English. Nancy, my American friend, was in Iran with her parents last year. Now she's back in Philadelphia and writes me about her school and the social activities there. I've been reading American history in school and we've much to talk about.

Here I am at the end of my journal. It's up to-date, but it's not really an end. It's just a beginning, an introduction to "my future world."

CYRUS

IN SEARCH OF SELF

CHAPTER THIRTEEN

CYRUS: A SEARCH FOR SELF IDENTITY

O joyous and gay is the new year's day, and
  Shiraz most of all;
Even the stranger forget his home and
  becomes its willing thrall.
O'er the garden's Egypt, Joseph-like
  the fair red rose is king,
And the Zephyr, e'en to the heart of the
  town, doth the scent of his rainment
  bring.

These few lines written by Sa'di (1194-1291) seven centuries
ago still describe Shiraz well. Today on the outskirts of town,
Sa'di's magnificent tomb, along with Hafiz's mausoleum stand
as two everlasting memorials to the glory of Shiraz. Sa'di's
Gulistan and the lyrics of Hafiz offer comfort and solace to
Persians in the same way as the Bible does to a needy Christian.
Their melodies and universal themes touch everyone's heart and
are quoted frequently in daily conversation. Again and again
their ideas are sought and reinterpreted. In the evenings and on
holidays people frequently go to the monuments to contemplate
the ideas of these sages and discuss their philosophy. By continually reciting the works and discussing them, Persians seek
to discover a new answer to life or to regain their hopes, secure

their status and satisfy themselves. Thus poetry, especially the verses of Sa'di and Hafiz, are a frequent topic of conversation in the homes of Shirazis.

Another favorite topic of conversation is religion, with the emphasis on the philosophical. The practice of it is secondary. Yet the men of wealth fully acknowledge the power of the "mullahs" (clergymen) in the community.

The mullahs belong to the second class. They tend to keep to themselves and their income is dependent upon the generosity of the faithful. Also in the same class are the big, successful business people, the nouveau riche. Equal in social standing are the governmental and local officials whose salaries are all too low, and in order to support themselves they both tax and accept bribes from the lower classes.

In a class apart and below are the independent artisans of the city, who work with silver and bronze in ceramics and textiles, in caligraphy and illustrative work. To the same class belong the smaller traders and shopkeepers.

Factory workers and peasants constitute the fourth class. Their standard of living is very low. Wages are almost negligible because of the surplus of cheap labor. The situation is further accentuated by a lack of child labor legislation and the presence of women competing for the same jobs.

The shopkeepers and artisans, laborers and peasants form the greatest bulk of the city's population. They work hard, produce a little and have their own pleasures. They live by three principles: "Live for today;" "Trust in God," and "Let fate decide."

Whatever little money they save during the six days of hard work, they spend on the week-end. Their common attitude to life is "Work six days a week in order to enjoy the seventh." Friday is the Persian "Sunday." Groups of people meet early in the morning in the public square, at street corners in front of the mosques, at the gates of bazaars and at homes. Then they set out for a picnic on foot, by carriage, or by car.

Some go to the nearby gardens, many of which are open to all to enjoy on Friday. Others have their picnics behind the rows of cypress tress in the south of the city. Some go to the green hills toward the north and others to the green meadows of the lima-bean plantations in the north-east. Wherever they go for a picnic, they find pleasure and relaxation reciting poetry. Even the poorest laborer is acquanted with many verses from Sa 'di and Hafiz[1] the two great poets especially revered by Shirazis.

"Trust in God" is a strong guiding principle among the lower classes. Even though many of them are illiterate, they practice their religion faithfully and follow the authority of their religious leaders. Various religious leaders have their followers, but much of the religious participation in the city is centered on one religious group, "The enlightened ones"; a group which concerns itself with the religious instruction of every Moslem in the city, especially the large number of people who are active members of their organization. Its appeal is largely with

---

[1] Hafiz was born in the early part of the fourteenth century and is considered one of the greatest poets of all time. Although he was born in Shiraz he belongs to all and stands beyond time and space. Hafiz loved his native city passionately just as Shriazis continue to love his lyrics. Even outside of Iran, Hafiz has been admired by such people as Goethe of Germany, Tagore of India, and Iqbal of Pakistan. Because every reader can find a statement to express his mood of the moment in Hafiz's writings, he is regarded as a mystic. Consequently his book of lyrics is used for telling fortunes.

The magnificant tomb of Hafiz is situated not far to the northwest of Sa'di's tomb. It is an elegant garden, surrounded by tall cypress trees. Tourists visit his garden the year round. Everyone takes pleasure in reading the various quotations engraved on his tomb stone and on the surrounding walls.

the bazaar merchants and the older generation, for the youth show little interest in it. The party derives its support from the wealthy and the business men of the community as well as from the shopkeepers.

The leaders of this religious group teach classes in reading and is Islamic doctrine early in the morning and late at night by means of a monitor system. Their common devotion to the faith unites all classes; but also teaches, on the one hand, fear, obedience and reverence, and on the other, kindness, endurance and patience. Underlying their teachings is the respect for the family and its importance as the core of society.

The third principle functioning in the lower classes is that of fate. A member of the poorest class usually finds the reason for his misery, misfortune or illness in a short phrase: "It is Gods' will." The majority of the laboring class has no idea of social justice or injustice. The dignity of human beings is guaranteed both by religion and the national constitution, but to the leaders, the rich, this is just a phrase in the holy book and in the constitution.

The common people may be "led by the nose" by authority and ground down by business, but they still remain faithful to authority as has been their practice again and again. They are content with very little, as long as they are not starving and have shelter; but their homes lack all modern sanitation and their diet is substandard.

The one meeting place for all classes is the bazaar. Here one sees all kinds of people—some veiled, some in Western dress, others in patched suits or robes or turbans. The bazaar in Shiraz is an old one with a noble history. It is called Vikil's bazaar after Vilik-Al-Roaya.[1]

---

[1] Karim-Khan Vikil-Al-Roaya rose to power in 1750 to make Shiraz the capital of Persia. Before that Shiraz had been the capital of a province ruled

Vikil's bazaar consists of covered avenues, arched at the top with bricks, one about half a mile in length meeting a somewhat shorter one at right angles to form a rotunda. Beautifully arched, the bazaar is cool in summer and a good shelter on rainy days. It is the biggest center for the sale of clothing. There are rows of shops on both sides. The ceiling of the arches is decorated in oriental designs with colored tiles. Both sides of its upper windows open and throw sun beams on sets of colorful pieces of fabric of many textures and imported from various foreign countries.

In addition to the shops there are also itinerant fruit peddlers who advertise the quality of their products in a high sing-song voice. Their donkeys are loaded with baskets of apricots, peaches, apples, pears and grapes.

Late in May the bazaar of Vikil is thronged with schoolboys. Some schools have closed already and others are about to adjourn. The youth of the city find the bazaar a natural haven from the sun's penetrating rays. It is a good way to pass the time of day—loafing about, visiting old friends as well as making new ones.

Among the groups of school boys is Cyrus's gang. Cyrus Amin is sixteen, under-weight but of normal height. He usually meets his friends at ten in the morning. There are four of them and the oldest is Hormuz who wears glasses and gives the appearance of being a salesman. However he is four years behind in school, and for a while Cyrus tutored him in English and mathematics. Though academically retarded, he is socially

by various princes. Although he was entitled to use the term "king of kings" he preferred to be known as Vikil-Al-Roaya meaning "deputy to the common man." He is remembered in history as a brave soldier, a just ruler and a public-spirited citizen. He contributed to the welfare of the people of Shiraz through the construction of a mosque, common baths, a better water supply, a citadel, streets and the bazaar which bears his name.

mature, talks about sex, about his fights with his brothers and sisters at home and sometimes about his experiences with girls. Cyrus is not too much interested in his talk and tries to influence him to change his social behavior. Yet Cyrus sympathizes with Hormuz's intellectual inaptitude and Hormuz in turn admires Cyrus's ability. The two boys have known one another for about a year.

The next member of Cyrus's clique, walking to his right, is Farad. Farad is broad-shouldered and taller than the rest of the gang. He seems strong and is a year behind in the tenth grade. While walking, Farad plays with a piece of chain, hits every boy with it, and sometimes holds it in his teeth. He is a member of the soccer team of the school and plays halfback well; and it was at a soccer game eight months ago that Cyrus first met him. Cyrus considers him a friend with a good heart and harmless.

The next one of Cyrus's gang is Baram, walking to Cyrus's left. Baram is about seventeen. He is athletic, thin and muscular and is one of the best runners in the school. He seems darker than the rest and that is why the members of the gang sometimes call him by the nick-name of "Seeah" meaning black. He is the same height as Cyrus and probably underweight too.

Cyrus and his friends are all from middle-class homes in the community. They do not have much responsibility at home. The women are in charge of house-keeping. The men are busy, and there is no work available for adolescents during summer vacations.

At this time of day, Cyrus and his friends walk up and down the bazaar. It is considerably cooler than outside, but the boys find little to occupy themselves except to walk and talk. They encounter other groups of boys, other classmates, all similarly occupied. Some of Cyrus's classmates point him out as one of the luckiest boys, for he has passed every test and has nothing to worry about. Yet Cyrus is not satisfied with the results of the tests, and would have liked very much to be the first student in his class.

Cyrus studies diligently and he has a lot of school work. In the tenth grade he had twenty-two subjects, all compulsory. Classes meet six hours a day and almost six days a week. During the school year and several times a week, Cyrus takes his favorite books and reads and walks to Sa'di's tomb. Then he takes a bath in the underground spring there, and studies as he walks back home. He generally takes these outings about 7:30 in the morning before breakfast. Sometimes his brother, Dariush or Barum join him.

Cyprus is full of energy, works hard and uses his energy to memorize dry course material in order to be the top pupil in his class, for this is the only way that he feels he can continue his studies. Still he manages to find time for an hour or more of recreation a day in playing soccer or basketball.

Cyrus gets along with most of his class-mates, except those who make a practice of being friendly with the teachers. The rumor goes that they have social weekly meetings, and a few of the students from the upper class invite teachers to their homes. This group has never been particularly cordial to Cyrus, nor has he made any effort to know them. In fact he considers the boys of this group as corrupt and feels that the teachers are partial to them. Cyrus is especially bitter because one of the youths of this group was ranked as first in the class and he is not as good as Cyrus in mathematics nor does he study as hard.

Cyrus is accustomed to meeting his teachers only in class, and he has never spoken to them socially. He only answers them when he is asked questions, and the teachers in turn have never had a chance to really understand Cyrus. Perhaps that is why they sometimes misjudge him. Cyrus was shocked when one day

141

one of his teachers mistakenly found him guilty, slapped his face and asked him to leave the class. "Sir, you are mistaken. I did not imitate your voice, believe me," said Cyrus. But the teacher furiously ordered him to be quiet while he was almost pushed out of the room.

This kind of injustice received from the teacher depresses Cyrus and it discourages him from expressing himself. There is no room for criticism in the classroom. Sheepishly, one has to follow what is written in the textbooks or what the teacher says. This does not fit Cyrus's ability and character and dissatisfies him. However there is no other way to get an education.

As the boys walk past the shops in the bazaar, Cyrus reminisces about the past school year, and wants to discuss his school impressions, interests and hopes with his companions, but they want none of it. They are only glad that school is over and there are no more tests. School scenes of many kinds enter Cyrus's mind: they annoy him, plague him and trouble him greatly. How can he be a top student when he does not own the textbooks and has to consume many hours late at night and early in the dawn copying others' textbooks? Why do the teachers seem to prefer other students? How can he go on to college except by scholarship and when there are so many applicants? Then there are the tests at the end of the school year. No matter how well prepared one is, the scoring rests entirely with the teacher and much depends on how the teacher feels about the student. Many of the pupils do not ask to see their papers because if someone asks a question he is considered impolite. Cyrus gripes to his friends, "Why did I become the fourth from the top this year in school? If my father were an officer or landlord, I could have asked to see my paper; but my father isn't and the principal doesn't have to worry that my father will cause trouble for him."

Baram, Hormuz and Farah are silent. They can't understand why Cyrus should complain. Being fourth from the top is something to be proud of. At the same time they agree with Cyrus that the teachers are greatly influenced by the wealthy people in the community. If their children are failing, they call up the local director of education and insist that he speak to the principals and teachers. As a result conflict arises and cooperation between teachers and principals even becomes impossible. Finally Baram remarks to Cyrus, "Oh, forget the whole thing. Let's be glad that we haven't failed any examinations and that there's no school for several months."

It is now noon. At many shops in the bazaar either the owner or the apprentice works as a muezzin. Everybody who feels like crying out can be a muezzin. Therefore, at once a few dozen of them stand and call all men to pray in the following words:

> God is great! there is no God but one!
> Mohammed is the prophet of God! Come to
> pray! Come to salvation! Come to good
> deeds! There is no other God but God!

Cyrus bids everyone good-bye and hurries off to meet his father and brother for noon prayers at Masjed Vikil. Masjed Vikil borrows its name from the same great ruler of the eighteenth century. It is built exactly in the center of the city and is close to the bazaar. The arch and door-way are made of stone and its pulpit, made out of a single piece of marble, is famous. The long stone pool is situated in the center of the mosque and around the sides are gracefull arches with the pulpit at the southern end of the long, beautiful hall.

On reaching the mosque, Cyrus sees his father and Dariush his brother at the pool preparing for prayer: washing their hands,

143

face and feet. They greet one another and join the others as the muezzin calls for prayer. In the eyes of God everyone is an equal and there is no pre-designated position for prayer. Sa'id Nouri of the Englistened Ones leads the prayers. Afterwards he preaches on such topics as religious enlightenment, politics and social, economical and moral situations.

After prayer service the Amin family start for home. They hurry because they know the rest of the family is waiting for them. In addition Mr. Amin has to return to his fabric shop in the afternoon. It is a small business and Mr. Amin works hard to support his family in a modest way. He buys goods from wholesalers and sells it to individual customers. Everyone considers him an honest and trustworthy business man.

Dariush helps his father in the store. Four years older than Cyrus, he left school in the tenth grade to teach the children in a nearby tribe. He became seriously ill with malaria and returned home. Now he works with his father.

At the gate to their house, Mrs. Amin greets her husband and chides him, "Why must you always go to the mosque before eating? You could just as well go later."

But Mr. Amin is not concerned by her remarks. For him, God's duty comes first.

Cyrus greets his mother and oldest sister, Ferri who is standing in the door-way. Ferri finished elementary school and now stays at home to help with the housework. Cyrus's younger sister, Nazi is outside playing; she is nine years of age and will be in the fourth grade.

As Cyrus walks across the yard he comes to a room with three doors. They are completely made of wood, and there is a hole in one of them. The walls of this room are dark black in color, and there are numerous examples of this kind of wall in the city. The black color is a cheap and natural paint. It is not

144

painted by man or women—it is just done by smoke, rising out of the open fire place on which they cook and which in winter heats the room. This room has several different functions. It is a kitchen, and in cold weather a sleeping room. It serves as a dining room, and it is also a room for prayer.

The main part of the floor of the room is covered by an old Persian carpet. Once a year this carpet is washed. In one corner there is a pile of beds, covered by a cotton carpet, that is a "gilim." In the next corner is a trough built up with bricks. It serves as a fireplace, and everything is cooked here, rice, stew, and other things. To the east of the fireplace is a prayer rug. Everybody in turn prays a few times daily on this carpet. In the front of the entrance to the room is an uncovered space for leaving shoes. Everybody who enters the room first takes off his shoes at the door, then goes and sits down on the carpet.

After the table cloth has been laid and all have washed their hands, the family sits down to a simple meal. It consists of stew with lots of potatoes and tomatoes and a very small amount of meat. There is cheese and bread too.

It is the custom for everyone to take a nap after lunch. Cyrus takes a towel and sheet and beckons Nazi to follow him. He asks her, "How is your reading coming along?"

"I didn't read at all this morning. I spent all the time helping mother," she confesses. "Maybe I'll read my book this afternoon."

Cyrus pats her and says, "Be a good girl and do your lessons."

Just at the edge of the small pool in the center of the yard, he stops and asks Nazi to hold the towel. After putting his head under water several times, he remarks, "Now I feel better."

Nearby is the well which furnishes the water for the house. There is no fan or cooler in the house and Cyrus prefers to make a shelter at the well. He covers it with two old broken doors,

145

lies down and asks his sister to read her book aloud to him. She begins and Cyrus corrects her from time to time.

However within minutes he is fast asleep. The flies that buzz around him seem not to disturb him. He sleeps peacefully on, perhaps dreaming of what the summer may bring.

CHAPTER FOURTEEN

A DAY GOES BY

It is late afternoon. The temperature has risen to an unexpected high of 80 degrees, and the lack of satisfactory accommodations or facilities makes the heat seem unbearable. A dreadful dream accentuated by innumerable mosquitoes and flies awakens Cyrus. Rubbing his sleepy eyes, he pulls himself up to a sitting position, stretches himself, then rises. He takes a towel and wipes the perspiration from his face and body.

Next he goes to the well which provides the water supply for the house. Stooping down he lowers a bucket into the well, then hoists it up, emptying it into a pipe which carries the water into a small pool in the middle of the yard. Bucket after bucket, he lowers and lifts; his legs and arms working rhythmically. After twenty such buckets he is exhausted—the muscles in his back, arms and legs ache, and he gasps for breath. He pauses to admire the effects of his labors. Cyrus gets a sense of satisfaction in seeing the pool filled, and it also seems to fulfill the need of his body for activity.

The pause has refreshed him. There is still the garden to water, and he does this more from a sense of duty than for enjoyment. In Iran even a small patch of lettuce and radishes such as this one requires a lot of attention. It almost never rains and the sun shows no sympathy for green vegetation. To Cyrus it seems as if his watering produces no effect—the plants continue to look tiny and delicate; whereas in filling the pool he can immediately see the result of his efforts.

It is time for afternoon prayers and it is a welcome relief from his duties. He washes his hands and feet, his forearms and prepares himself. Cyrus takes his prayers seriously and never neglects to pray the prescribed five times a day.

Feeling a need for refreshment, he goes into the kitchen for a cup of tea. His mother and Nazi are there, and Nazi teases him for having fallen asleep after lunch—just when she was reading to him. He apologizes. Mrs. Amin gives him a cup of tea; it is served in a simple way—everyone drinks from the same cup. Cyrus is thirsty and asks for another. Raised as a good Moslem, Cyrus is accustomed to drinking only tea and milk. He has never tasted any alcoholic drinks.

Not quite knowing what to do now, Cyrus wanders about the yard kicking fallen leaves about. He grows tired of this and returns to the house and resolutely puts on his jacket. It is still early to meet his friends, but he is bored and somewhat fed up with the emptiness of his home life. Outside on the street he feels better—no one need to know that this is the house he lives in. In fact, Cyrus generally arranges to meet his friends on the street corner, for he does not want them to see where he lives. If by some chance, a friend does come to his house, he always rushes to the door, opens it half way or goes out of the house to talk to him.

On the main street close to Cyrus's house there is a museum named Pars.[1] In the center of a large garden stands the main building and in front of it is a long pool which mirrors the reflection of the beautiful cypresses and colorful flowers sur-

---

[1] This museum houses many relics found at Persepolis. Persepolis is considered to be the cradle of Iranian civilization and is located about 35 miles from Shiraz.

rounding it. A high iron fence encloses the grounds, and Cyrus often pauses and looks through the railings. Although he has passed the museum almost every day, he's never had an opportunity to go inside. It only seems to be open at times when he must be in school.

The only objects that Cyrus can see from where he stands are the winged figure, the bas-reliefs and the bases of large cylindrical columns. They excite him and arouse his curiosity. All the dry ancient history of Iran that he has had to memorize seem to come to life on looking at these objects. Curiosity turns to longing and longing disappears in the air. His attention shifts to the garden plots; and from time to time he turns his head to see if his friends are coming.

At last the gang appears: Baram is in the lead with Farad and Hormuz somewhat behind him. They greet Cyrus and pair off: Baram and Cyrus; Farad and Hormuz. They walk along the main street toward the public square. The main street in Shiraz is a broad avenue. It is adorned on both sides by growing trees, and new modern buildings. Its wide pavements are of concrete and tree leaves dance on it when stirred by the north wind. Trucks, buses, cars and carriages as well as horses and a few loaded donkeys pass back and forth. In the evening the principal vehicles in the street are carriages which take the people out of town to public gardens where they can enjoy the cool crisp air.

Slowly the members of Cyrus's gang stroll up the street. Once in a while Baram teases a carriage driver by calling to him and then paying no attention to him. The driver becomes angry and shouts threats at them. Hormuz and Farad laugh boisterously and even Cyrus has to grin. At their leisurely pace it takes them an hour to reach the public square.

It is in a modern part of the city and nearby are beautiful houses all equipped with the luxuries of running water and electricity. Cyrus and Baram watch a pretty girl who comes out of one of the houses. It is Liali. Her big brown eyes have captured at least a dozen boys, her long dark hair has beguiled a second dozen and the third dozen are intrigued by her superb figure fashionably gowned in the latest Paris mode. The boys stand in rapt attention as she passes by, tossing her smile to the right and left.

Baram is by nature highly excitable and competes with his other rivals for Liali's attention. He often composes poetry about Liali, writes to her and occasionally talks to her.

Cyrus admires this romantic fervor in his older friend. He himself finds it hard to express his feelings for girls. Even with his sisters he is somewhat aloof and not so likely to be talkative in their presence. In childhood he always played with boys; in preadolescence he attended a boys' elementary school. His junior high-school was also only for boys, but it was close to two girls' high schools. He met the girls several times a day but by that time his shyness was already deeply rooted. Cyrus has quite a number of feminine age-mates among his relatives but always stays clear of them. When they visit his home, he is usually busy outside, and when he encounters them in the street he greets them without stopping. Once a year at New Year's time he visits their homes but he does not stay very long either.

Cyrus's feeling for Liali is somewhat different: he admires her from afar but senses the futility of the situation. She doesn't seem to know that he even exists. Once in a while when the boys enjoy talking among themselves about her, Cyrus is fond of remarking, "Our hands are short and the palm dates are hanging at the top of the high palm tree." Although Liali has gone, the boys remain in the public square and talk about sex in general and the beautiful girl specifically. When the conversation becomes somewhat waring to Cyrus, he quotes a proverb: "The description of love is itself half of love affairs."

150

The sun has kissed the top of the Eastern mountains and set. Twilight is at hand. Tired from endless discussions on sex, Cyrus suggests to the others that they go home. The boys are reluctant to accept his suggestion, but finally everyone agrees to buy some plums first and eat them in the public garden.

Cyrus carries them in his handkerchief until they find a comfortable spot. Away from the public at the bank of a stream, they sit in some straw and eat the fruit in the silence of the evening. Soon music from neighboring private gardens livens the air. Cyrus likes to listen to instrumental music and beautiful songs, but he really knows little about music. He's had little training in it and can't even sing a song. Dancing, singing and playing instruments have no place in his school or home. Dariush, his brother, used to play a musical instrument and he is the only one in the family who can carry a tune.

In elementary school Cyrus had a course in music, but he was lost in finding where different notes should be placed—what comes on the fourth line, where *sol* is, and the number of notes in a scale. These things confused and puzzled him. Yet he made a good grade in the course, but has had no practical use for the material. He doesn't own any musical instrument and, in fact, can only recognize the violin, drum and flute. For a few years the state carried out an order that the national song should be sung by the pupils every morning before their lessons. This however was a formality and pure ceremony. The elementary school that Cyrus attended, considered the best in the city, possessed no music room and owned no musical instruments. Occasionally, one of the teachers played the national song on his own violin in front of standing rows of pupils, and it seemed to Cyrus just like the sound of the water wheel in the well at his home.

The boys saunter down the street headed for home. Farad and

Hormuz are the slowest and Cyrus repeatedly calls to them to walk faster. They pass through a few narrow alleys to reach the main street again. Evening has given way to night and in the darkness a few women pass by and brush up against the boys. Strolling up and down the street they exhibit their charms and smile at passers-by. The other boys joke and laugh about it, particularly Hormuz who seems to enjoy the situation, but Cyrus loathes the sight of such women. His strict religious upbringing has much to do with these attitudes to sex, and he shuns those who lead such corrupted lives. His sense of values, fostered by a sense of an ever watchful God, keep him away from such temptation.

In a teasing manner, Baram sometimes makes as if to follow one of the women and instinctively Cyrus pulls him back. Their faces are serious and a scuffle ensues; but it is all part of the game between them and a harmless way of utilizing their pent-up energy.

There is actually little outlet for the boys' outbursts of physical energy. Cyrus is fond of sports, but there is no club that he can join and he cannot afford to buy his own sports equipment. Baram owns a pair of boxing gloves, but since nobody else has any, he puts them aside and fights with his bare fists as do the other boys. Baram has discovered that the quickest way to start a fight is to tease Cyrus, particularly about his serious attitude to life. Cyrus flares up easily and the two boys slug it out. There are few injuries, although once Cyrus got a nose bleed and on another occasion Baram got a black eye.

Close to the museum the boys part and go their separate ways. In the middle of the alley, just opposite his house door, Cyrus sees a drunken soldier and a girl whose face is somewhat familiar to him. He looks the other way in disgust and hastily shuts the door of his gate, muttering again and again to himself, "Now it's starting all over."

152

He sees his mother and continues angrily, "*Those* girls have returned."

"Which girls?"

"Don't you remember the two girls who used to live in the Jew's house. They're beginning their business all over again. I'll tell Father when he comes home—he'll do something about it. Last year he convinced the Police Department to act, but now they're back. I'd like to move every single stone of this house and cover the whole of their house."

"Cyrus, calm down!" His mother puts her hand on his shoulder, but Cyrus goes on, "The first thing father should do is to see Mr. Vazir and ask him to help in moving them. After all, he lives next door to them. It's worse for his family than for us."

His mother pleads, "Don't get so excited. It's not such an easy matter. Remember that even Father didn't succeed in getting rid of them. And maybe a lot of people stand to gain by having them in the community. Of course the Jew wants to earn a living, and so to make money he rents his empty rooms to the one who pays more, regardless of his or her business. To make his business more profitable, he invites the best looking prostitutes to his home and also sells liquor there. He trains his young daughter to serve drinks and his good-looking son to sing. Now *you* want to go and ask help from our neighbor, Mr. Vazir whose son was a commissioner to the girls and blackmailed the Jew. Don't forget that policemen also like money. It isn't only the Jews who live without principles; many people behave in the same way—even officers of the law. The police talk to us openly and connive with them secretly. They always promise us that they'll do something—but that's all. They obviously make money out of them and want money from us too. If we pay more they'll be moved, but if they offer more the police will help them settle in another alley, maybe even in the next house. Please, Cyrus, don't make trouble—we have enough headaches—don't add to them."

Cyrus listens to what his mother has been saying. He can't accept her complacient attitude and yet he doesn't know what to do about it himself. He feels thoroughly disgusted with the whole situation. Almost at the same moment his father appears at the gate, having just come from evening prayers. He inquires if Cyrus has prayed yet and he replies that he is about to. He goes to prepare himself.

Cyrus puts aside his cares and washes himself. Always at this time of day he feels a certain serenity: the day is coming to an end, and he gets a sense of satisfaction in having done his best to live according to the principles of his faith.

Supper is usually a simple meal in the Amin household. Cyrus joins the rest of the family and eats in silence, already thinking ahead to what he'll do after supper.

Finishing hurridly, he takes an oil lamp and goes out of the room, and in passing tells the others that he is going to read to Mr. Khan. The light from oil lamps is never much good and in addition soot from it covers the walls of the room making it even darker. Cyrus carries the lamp gingerly, trying not to inhale the noxious smoke from it.

He enters an adjoining room which is really part of an old shop. A bookshelf holds several dusty volumes, one of which he selects and carefully wipes the dust off. The title reads, "Shahnameh."[1]

---

[1] Shahnameh means literally "Letters of the kings." It was written in the tenth century by a great Persian poet, Ferdowsi. In this immense epic (60,000 lines) he depicts the legendary history of Iran in pre-Islamic times. Each of the 50 chapters is devoted to one king, but the author in addition, describes the emotions, opinions and personal lives of many more people —good and bad, old and young, happy and unhappy.

154

With the book in one hand and the lamp in the other, Cyrus makes his way upstairs to a small room in the west end of the house. The light here is much better and the walls actually appear to be white. It is a guest room. In fact, Cyrus and his family believe that the best food and light should be reserved for guests.

Mr. Khan has been waiting for Cyrus. A business man and old friend of Cyrus's father, he lives among the tribes and comes to town only when he has lamb-fur to market. However, this time he is in Shiraz to obtain medical treatment for his cataracts.

Cyrus greets him warmly, "I promised to read Shahnameh to you tonight and here I am."

Taking a cup of tea, Cyrus sits in the corner on a Persian carpet. He opens the book to the story of "Suhrab Rostam," a tragedy in which a father kills his son.

Cyrus reads well for his grade level and he enjoys reciting the colorful lines of Shahnameh. Yet he is not able to recite it in the heroic manner that Khan expects. Several times he interrupts Cyrus and vividly recites the lines from memory. Khan is, in fact, illiterate, but he has committed to memory much Persian poetry.

Now again he asks Cyrus to stop, but this time he compliments the youth on his reading ability, and asks, "Wouldn't you like to live among the tribes-people as a teacher? It doesn't matter that you haven't finished school; you can read and write and that's all that's important."

"Well, I am looking for a job for the summer, but I..."

Khan interrupts, "Cyrus, let's make a deal. I'll provide you with your own personal tent and I'll help you get a horse. In fact, I can even arrange for you to marry a beautiful girl from the tribe. You teach the boys of the tribe how to read, and the families will pay you in cattle. If you want to wait and discuss it with your family you can let me know before next Wednesday."

155

Cyrus nods his head but says nothing. He continues to read the fascinating story of Suhrab—Rostam and is eager to see the result of the tale. However, before he can finish, Khan has fallen asleep. Cyrus silently closes the book without finishing; Khan's proposal is on his mind.

"It would be a good job," reflects Cyrus. "I can be independent and know that I'm doing something for people. Of course, I'd like to finish school and go on to college if I could, but our family doesn't have the money to send me. Well, I think I'll talk it over with the family first."

Cyrus tip-toes out of the room and goes in search of Dariush. Together they take their bedding and climb to the top of the roof of the house.

Next to the Amin house on the right is the home of Mr. and Mrs. Issac, a prosperous Jewish merchant of lambs-fur. Mr. Amin is tolerant of other people's views and believes that everybody must be allowed to choose his own faith and worship God in the manner he thinks right. Mr. Amin has won the friendship of this neighbor and the two families have become acquainted. On many a Friday night when the Jews do not touch fire, Cyrus has helped the Issac family by lighting their lamps. The family has many modern conveniences including a radio.

Cyrus likes to listen to the news from the radio, but he is too shy to ask others for favors. Instead he and Dariush have become accustomed to lying on the roof in the open air listening to the radio reports from next door.

The news is about World War II. There are reports from Germany, England and Tehran. The boys hear them all but they become increasingly confused as each side claims the same victory. On some points Cyrus argues with Dariush but neither seems to have enough facts to convince the other.

The night is cool, clear and bright after a miserably hot and dis-

156

agreeable day. It is typical of Shiraz weather. Furthermore, there is no factory smoke to cloud the sky, and all the stars are visible. As he lies there on his mattress, Cyrus gazes upward. From the Milky Way he turns to the Big Bear and then the Small Bear and finally finds the North Star. His mind wanders to the evening's conversation with Khan. It would certainly be an exciting job working with the tribes-people and far different from his monotonous daily routine of living. And then too, summer jobs are not so easy to find. Most everyone takes his own son as apprentice—if he is a businessman he takes him into his shop or if a landlord he establishes him in the village and even the gardener trains his son. At times, Cyrus has thought of selling ice-cream, but he's afraid of being teased by his friends. Only professional or governmental work is deemed desirable by Iranian youth.

Cyrus conjures up a picture of his life with the tribes. He imagines himself in a spacious tent surrounded by several small boys who gaze admiringly at him as he reads from a book. Outside there are sheep, goats and a horse—all his. "And to top it all off, I'll marry a beautiful tribes-girl," Cyrus jokes with himself. He can't help smiling, for a story comes to his mind at this moment, "I'm just like the man who had only a jar of butter, and started to think about his future. He then decided he would buy an ewe: she would bear him a lamb. In a few years he would have his own herd of sheep. He would then sell some and in return would build his castle, marry the noblest girl in the city, hire maids to wait on her and servants to serve her. If anybody should disobey her, he would punish him with a stick... Meanwhile the stick struck the jar and the butter ran on the floor and the poor farmer paid for his day dreaming. Well, it seems just like that when I hear that I shall marry the daughter of a noble tribesman."

157

No, there's no sense to it. I can't take the job. I have to finish my studies even though I haven't any money or a job."

Cyrus pulls the sheet, up over him and concentrates on falling asleep, but memories crowd up on him. Khan's proposal reminds him of a similar incident several years ago when Dariush was in the tenth grade. The same man had come to his father and they had made an agreement. His brother left school and accompanied Khan. Khan's hospitality helped him until he got malaria. Cyrus even recalls the day his brother opened the house door and his mother did not recognize his face. He vividly recalls the day when he had to hold his brother's arm, prepare him for the doctor's injection of quinine and then support him so that he wouldn't faint. Cyrus feels himself shake as he remembers the trembling body of his sick brother. It's too much for him. and he protests aloud, "No, no, I'ill never listen to that tribesman even if he offers me all his property."

Distraught and upset, Cyrus sits up and struggles to compose himself and erase the memories of his brother's illness and Khan's suggestion. At that moment his eyes are attracted by a scene being enacted on the opposite roof. Glasses of liquor are being drunk, one after another: everyone is drinking to the other's health. The Jew's daughter fills the empty glasses: his wife plays the lute and his son sings in a low sensuous tone. The black hair of the girls on the white shoulders of the men blows in the wind and is highlighted by the beams of light. Hypnotized by the scene, Cyrus feels disgust for the neighborhood his father loves so well. He cannot pull his eyes away from what he sees—it is distasteful yet somehow compelling. He watches for some time until finally the lamps are blown out and only shadows remain.

CHAPTER FIFTEEN

A SUDDEN DEPARTURE

The mid-morning sun bears down unmercifully on the small group in the corner of the theological school. They are theological students and Cyrus listens to their endless discussions of religion attentively. Their ideas are not new to him, and although he is sometimes tempted to raise some new issue with them, he keeps silent and reflects inwardly. There are also times when he becomes more absorbed in the activities of the ants on the ground or the birds that fly by.

Half way through the discussion Cyrus looks up to see Baram hurrying toward him. He gets up and goes to meet him. Baram is the first to speak, "Come on, I want you to meet one of my old schoolmates. Hurry up! He's got lots to tell us about his work with the Americans."

Cyrus can't see what all the rush is about, but he comes willingly for he has grown tired of sitting and listening. Outside the theological grounds, Hormuz and Farad stand in rapt attention listening to a youth with dark browneyes, black hair, tanned skin and good physique. He is introduced to Cyrus as Shushi and the two shake hands.

There are some benches nearby and the boys go over and sit down. Cyrus says to Shushi, "Baram says you are working with Americans. Are you a spy for them?"

"Don't be ridiculous, Cyrus," scoffs Baram. "Nobody spies on anyone."

"Just let him talk, won't you? Come on, tell me then what you really do," asks Cyrus for a second time.

Shushi explains that he is an interpreter. He is now on vacation, but in a few days he'll return to his job in Andimeshk. There many Iranian semi-skilled workers, employed by Americans, cannot speak English nor can their employers communicate with them. Consequently there is a need for someone who can interpret and who speaks both Persian and English.

"So you're an interpreter," remarks Cyrus. "You must be able to speak excellent English."

From out of his pocket Shushi takes a pack of cigarettes, a well known American brand, and offers some to Cyrus.

He refuses politely, and Shushi lights his own, holding it smartly between his fingers, as if perhaps to display his maturity. After inhaling a mouthful of smoke, Shushi goes on to explain that he doesn't have to be proficient in English. All he needs to know are the common daily expressions and the essentials of conversational English. He relates how he sits beside an American sergeant on the trip from Andimashk to Khoram-Abad.[1] Accompanying him are Iranian truck drivers, ranging in age from forty to sixty. In the event a truck driver gets into trouble, Shushi listens to their complaints and translates it into English. In turn he takes the orders and commands of the sergeants and repeats them in Persian to the truck-drivers.

On some occasions there are inexperienced truck drivers who have accidents; some are injured and even die. Shushi helps the sergeant take the injured to the hospital and the dead to their homes and then to the cemetary. Baram interrupts and remarks enviously, "Your job sounds very exciting."

---

[1] Two cities in southwest Iran.

Shushi is the center of attention and speaks with authority on the matter of working with Americans. He explains that anyone who has passed the tenth grade should know enough English to carry on a conversation. If any of them are interested in working with Americans, Shuchi would be glad to take them with him when he returns to Andimeshk. Cyrus modestly remarks, "I've had that much English but I don't understand English enough to converse. Baram speaks better than I do."

Actually Batam attends the Anglo-Iranian Institute three times a week. There he has good native teachers of English from England who are far superior to those in the public school. Cyrus has a great desire to be a student there, but he has never been able to save five dollars for the summer course. On the other hand, once in a while during the week he asks Baram about his lessons in order to catch up with him. Shushi turns to Cyrus and Baram and says, "The American organizations in the southwest of Iran need people like you." He talks about his brother's work there, his friends, the amount of money they all make, the cost of living, and other things. Seeing that they are interested, Shushi suggests that the following day, Friday, they go on a picnic for the whole day and that they speak only English. In that way, Shushi might be able to tell them whether they could get a good job with the Americans.

Hormuz protests emphatically, "Not me!" He and Farad are actually the poorest in English and do not wish to try it. It would be a very waring experience for both to try to speak English and they are glad to withdraw. Baram however accepts the proposal eagerly. Cyrus wouldn't mind practicing his English but he doesn't think it's good enough for the job requirement. All along he has wanted to converse with Baram in English so that he might improve his speaking ability. The matter is settled and they decide on a meeting place and time for

161

the next day's activities. Cyrus rushes off to noon prayers and the others go home for lunch.

The following morning at nine o'clock Cyrus meets Baram and Shushi at Pars Museum. They greet one another in English and start down the street. They leave the houses behind and set foot on a dusty unpaved road. For once the boys are silent. Nobody talks, everyone is waiting to hear the others. In the quietness their steps raise dust, and the dust turns to nothingness in the air. Finally Cyrus breaks the silence and says in Persian that Shushi's proposal was a good idea. This helps them get started and Shushi suggests that it might be the easiest if everyone begins with his daily routine. For instance everybody can mention what he does from early in the morning until he goes to bed.

They all participate in the conversation. Shushi tries to correct Cyrus's conversation. He points out his errors, such as his usage of the wrong tense, forgetting to put "s" on the third person singular, and not remembering to use "ed" for the past tense of regular verbs. Although Cyrus knows the rules, he is not really aware of them for he has had little practice in speaking and so has not gotten the habit of correct speech. He speaks slowly and hesitantly, but he explains his daily routine fairly well. Shushi remarks that these slight errors are not too important. After a few days practice he will be all right. In school, Cyrus has always been very interested in English; but he started with the wrong teacher and in the wrong way. His first teacher apparently knew little English and pronounced it badly, and was only interested in having his pupils memorize English words through repetition. He would never read for them but insisted that one of the better students read the new lesson aloud to the class. Then Cyrus and his classmates were required to copy the new words an infinite number of times; and after this came spelling. For hours Cyrus

162

would sit among the group and in a loud voice repeat the letters of the words. Even though Cyrus has always been taught to respect his teachers, he disliked this particular teacher very much. At that time this English teacher was also the principal of the junior high school which Cyrus attended; and as he was the principal and the authority of the school no one could object to him. Yet his poor methods developed in Cyrus the false idea that a foreign language was nothing more than the accumulation of words. He was thus stimulated to memorize the sequential lists of words in the small vocabulary list attached to the first book of English. So now he has a relatively good vocabulary but no knowledge of how to use it. Cyrus's second and third teachers of English were not much different from the first one, and he strengthened the bad habits he had acquired in his first English class.

Half way between the city and their picnicing site, Cyrus discovers a mulberry tree. He calls out "Mulberries!" The others repeat it. Mulberries are cheap in the market and cost even less in the garden or on the tree. Cyrus is eager to have some before going further. At the foot of the tree he takes off his shoes and climbs up, throwing down handfuls of the fruit to his friends. Between mouthfuls Shushi remarks, "Delicious."

"Delicious," repeats Cyrus.

"Delicious," choruses Baram.

Finally they are on their way again. Occasionally they encounter barefoot women carrying their dairy products to town in order to exchange them for other foods. There are also some donkeys loaded with grapes trotting in front of their owners. Cyrus sympathizes with all of them. The road is dusty, the weather quite warm, the sun shines brightly and there is no shade at all. But the sight of Sa'di's tomb spurs them on. In a few minutes they are in the elegant garden of the tomb. Cyrus is thirsty.

Just in front of the tomb he climbs down about twenty-five steps to an underground section where there is a running stream. Its sourse is at the foot of a mountain nearly sixteen miles out of Shiraz, but Sa'di's tomb is the first place where it comes to the surface. Throughout the year its water is continuously lukewarm. After washing his hands, Cyrus borrows a bowl from a young woman sitting on the platform and filling up her jars. Washing the bowl, he drinks; then waits a while until the woman has left. He takes off his clothing and goes into the water. Being modest Cyrus usually bathes beyond the arched part of the stream. He enjoys playing with innumerable fish which swim back and forth in the stream. Actually this part of the brook is named '*hoze mahi*', because of the fish and means "a pool full of fish."

Meanwhile Shushi and Baram have returned from visiting Sa'di's tomb. Cyrus gets dressed and tells his friends that after a good lunch he will be ready for a long hike. The boys walk to a nearby village and buy home-made wheat bread, onions and yogurt.

Out of sight of Sa'di's tomb, they go through a vineyard and up a short path toward the mountainside. At the bank of a small brook they decide to have their picnic. After eating their simple yet wholesome meal, Shushi suggests that they tell Persian stories in English.

It is a lot of fun. One story after another they tell. Cyrus feels himself progressing in English conversation just since the morning, exactly as Shushi had said.

Shushi encourages Cyrus to speak, for he now realizes that Cyrus's vocabulary is as good as his own. In this way the boys spend the day. When they are tired of telling stories, Shushi talks. He tells them more about his job with the Americans and gives them an idea of how much money they can except to earn.

164

He tells Cyrus that many of his co-workers are not as good in English as Cyrus seems to be. In addition there are other jobs that the boys could apply for: for example, checking the goods coming in and going out, working as a clerk or even as a driver. Shushi explains that in case they don't like the job they are free to leave at any time. These jobs are not permanent: when the war slows down, unemployment will increase. It would be a good experience even for summer vacation and would certainly be more interesting than killing time by walking aimlessly in the bazaar.

Baram is all for it: he enjoys traveling and looks forward to an exciting experience. He asks Shushi what his plans are for leaving. How much money do they need to go there and how will they go—by car, train or bus? Shushi replies that he plans to go through Esfahan[1] and Iraq[2] by truck. At Iraq he will take a train to Andimenshk. Baram agrees to the plans and he knows he has money for the fare. His parents will raise no objection to his going. Baram turns to Cyrus and says excitedly, "Aren't you going to go too Cyrus? It would be more fun if the three of us went together."

Cyrus is undecided: he can't make up his mind. In spite of his quietness he is just as eager as Baram to go but there are many problems involved. At the same time it is an opportunity not to be passed up lightly. He could learn more about his country; and traveling by train would be something he has never done before, although he has read a lot about the construction of the magnificant railway which connects the Persian Gulf to the Caspian Sea. Cyrus knows exactly how many tunnels there are along the way without ever having seen one.

---

[1] Esfahan is the second largest city in Iran.
[2] Iraq is a city in Iran and should not be confused with the country of the same name.

Still it would be difficult for Cyrus to be ready in five days. At Baram's insistence, Cyrus says that he will make preparations on the assumption that he is going; but he emphasizes that the matter be kept secret from Hormuz and Farad, especially Hormuz whom Cyrus has been planning to tutor during the summer months. Even though Cyrus has indicated his willingness to go with them, he would still like to think over the plan and if he should change his mind, he promises to let Baram know within a few days. Now Cyrus turns to Shushi and jokes, "Well teacher, it seems we've passed the test. If we're going to visit Hafiz's tomb we'd better leave now. It's almost four o'clock."

On Friday evenings it is customary for many of the people of Shiraz to take a walk and visit the tomb of Hafiz. Baram, Shushi and Cyrus decide to take a longer way by passing the vineyard at the foot of the north side of the mountain and then going to Hafezieh (where Hafiz rests). Just as they are about to leave the picnic site, Baram disappears in the shade of the vines and comes back with a few bunches of grapes.

Cyrus is dismayed, "Aren't you ashamed of yourself? Do you think it's right to rob a poor peasant?"

Baram merely laughs at his words and offers him some grapes. Cyrus refuses, and Baram brags, "I didn't take very much. Why, if the gardener had been there, he himself would have given me twice as much."

Cyrus shrugs his shoulders. He has become accustomed to Baram's blasé attitude and he still respects him as a friend. Yet Cyrus could never bring himself to such behavior: it would be unthinkable. As a very young child he was taught not to take things that did not belong to him. This attitude persists.

The boys make their way along the mountain range threading their way between the green vineyards. At last they reach Hafiz's tomb. Cyrus is very fond of reading the sublime lyrics of Hafiz inscribed on the memorial stone tomb and walls of the building. The boys take turns reading the lines aloud.

Not far away is a graveyard in which forty saints are buried. The graves are shaded by tall cypresses, and Cyrus pauses to rest under the shade of one of the trees. He contemplates the remarkable lives of the men buried here. From this point there is a fine view of the city and Cyrus gazes out beyond, contemplating his future and life in general. And again he comes back to the forty saints: why had they isolated themselves from unfriendly people, from harm and worldly turmoil? He does not understand the reasons behind their mystic lives but he appreciates the serenity of the place.

Baram and Shushi cannot understand why he seems to enjoy sitting in such a morbid place. They are eager to leave and Cyrus follows reluctantly.

In a few minutes they come to the soccer field. This field is the only stadium in the city and its equipment is not good. Cyrus plays soccer fairly well and his favorite position is that of forward. Occasionally on Friday evenings when the best city teams compete against one another, Cyrus admiringly observes three of the best players and sometimes gives them shouts of praise.

As the sun begins to set, Cyrus starts out toward home. There are clusters of people walking home along the dusty road; a few traveling by carriage or car. The pedestrians inhale the dust which rises from the vehicles of those who ride. On Friday everyone tries to put on a neat suit, but the concept of "neat" is relative: a product of the culture of the people, for some are obliged to go barefoot. Walking home Cyrus is conscious of the poverty of some of the people, and if he finds a few pennies in his pocket he gives them gladly. When they are in the center of town, Shushi asks his companions if they would like to go to a movie with him. Cyrus isn't too keen on going. The two movie theaters in town show only cheap foreign films. These pictures are not based on the demands of this society and consequently the movie business is a poor business venture even though tickets are very cheap. Despite this Cyrus is not able to afford the price of a ticket and in his whole life he has only gone twice. He did not find them objectionable; in fact he thought them both educational and interesting, but lack of money prevents him from developing the habit of going to movies.

Cyrus bids Shushi and Baram good-bye and starts home. When he is with his friends Cyrus's personal problems often occupy his thoughts, but when he is alone it is even more true. So now he ponders the events of the last two days. Before meeting Shushi he had worried about getting a temporary job; and now that a job seems certain he worries about getting there. How can he go when he has no money at all? Where could he get 1500 rials for the fare? He is not accustomed to borrowing money and he feels sure his family hardly can give him that much. He is too proud to let his friends or family know of the situation: he keeps his misfortunes locked in his own heart. Perhaps for the first time Cyrus realizes how happy he could be if he had money for the trip.

At home that evening Cyrus is unusually quiet. He views his parents, brother and sisters through half-veiled eyes. What would they say if he knew he were contemplating a long trip? They would certainly be upset to think that he was leaving them —even just for the summer. Cyrus has never been separated from them for such a long period of time. But still the desire to have the experience of taking the trip, sitting in a jeep and working as interpreter prods Cyrus on. He must find a way of going. Now, as he thinks about it, his parents might agree to his going with Baram and Shushi if he could find some way of getting the money himself.

168

Cyrus prepares for bed. One of the things he does is to wash his teeth with a mixture of coal and salt. It is earlier than when he usually goes to bed and Cyrus is not tired either. He wants to lie down and think of a plan for getting some money. Should he ask Shushi for money? He probably has some, but Cyrus decides it is not a good idea—he has only known Shushi two days. "Baram might lend it to me," he thinks, "but no—he has to get 1500 rials himself." He continues in the same line of thought, "Hormuz could lend me that much, but I don't want to discuss with him my plans for going."

Cyrus tosses about in bed. Tired from the long day's hike he still cannot sleep. He turns from one side to the other, lies on his back, then on his stomach. In a moment he is on his feet, drinks a glass of water and then goes back to bed. He fixes his eyes on the stary sky. A new thought enters his mind. He might approach the department of education for the 1200 rials they owe him for his last four months allowance. But it doesn't seem possible that he could obtain it in the next few days.

A year ago he was the second best student in the ninth grade. One day the principal said to him, "Cyrus, you're in second place."

And Cyrus replied, "If I had the textbooks, no one could beat me; so I suppose I should be thankful that I'm second best."

This statement deeply impressed the principal and he looked about for some way to assist the young student. He hadn't been aware that Cyrus was too poor to buy books. The principal recommended Cyrus for a grant of 300 rials per month from the department of education. In spite of the fact that there is a law for compulsory education it does not make provisions for extending educational facilities to every one.

At first Cyrus was reluctant to accept the principal's proposal. It meant publicizing his poverty and might tend to make the teachers discriminate in his favor. But the principal wisely advised him to accept it, and he did, although the allowance never came on time. Always, in winter, he got the autumn stipend, in spring the winter amount and in summer the spring allowance.

Thinking about it now, Cyrus feels the hopelessness of trying to get his back allowance in just five days' time. Still it would be worth a try. Content with this idea Cyrus falls asleep.

Next day Cyrus dresses neatly, puts on his only silk shirt and goes to the department of education early so that he may be the first one to see the director of the finance department. Arriving there he finds no one in the office except the old doorman. Cyrus asks him when the director will appear and the man replies indifferently, "How would I know!"

Cyrus waits and waits. It is ten o'clock when the director appears followed by his assistant. They go immediately into an inner office and close the door behind them, only to open it a moment later and call for tea. The waiter hurries off to fetch it, and Cyrus has a chance to sit down for a few minutes in the waiter's chair. The servant returns and Cyrus begs him to tell his boss that he has been waiting several hours to see him. After some hesitation the man agrees to take Cyrus's message. He says what Cyrus has asked him, but the director doesn't look up from his reading. Finally he dismisses the waiter, "Don't bother me. Tell the boy to come back next week. Can't you see how busy I am!"

Cyrus receives the message discouragingly. He feels he has a right to meet this man and he stubbornly waits. It is almost twelve noon when the director emerges from his office. He hurries out of the room and Cyrus follows him until the man notices him and stops. Cyrus tells him that he is badly in need of his allowance. The director curtly refers him to one of his staff assistants at a nearby desk. The clerk recognizes Cyrus from previous times, "Oh, it's you again. Why are you here this time? Do you think someone owes you something? I told you before that the student allowance is always paid the middle of the month. Come back in three weeks."

His rudeness surpasses that of the director. He refuses to let Cyrus explain. Disheartened completely, Cyrus leaves the educational office. He walks down the street slowly with his hands in his pockets and his eyes on the ground. His one hope of getting money is gone. It came and left as quickly as snow melts when it falls on the swift river. Cyrus's pride is hurt and he feels very depressed. In such a mood he passes several of his friends without greeting them.

Close to his home is a shop which Cyrus visits almost daily. One of the shopkeepers is Daad, a young boy Cyrus's age. He is a happy, good looking youth whom Cyrus has known since elementary school. When Daad was in the fourth grade his father died and he subsequently had to leave school. The two boys were inseparable companions in the third and fourth grade, and even now they see one another almost daily. But today Cyrus is so upset that he passes Daad without greeting him. Daad is taken aback. He follows his friend, grasps his hand and says, "I missed you today."

Cyrus apologizes and starts to walk away quietly. Daad calls to him and asks if he'd like to go to the mosque with him. Cyrus accepts and the two make their way to a nearby mosque. The two wash their hands and face, their feet and forearms and stand together in prayer. It soothes Cyrus's injured feelings and helps him develop a more positive attitude toward his surroundings. Even the psychological effect of repeating the short verses of prayer helps Cyrus forget his troubles and encourages him to forgive the injustice of those around him and to strive for self-betterment.

After prayers Cyrus tries to assume a somewhat casual indifferent attitude to what has happened, but Daad perceives the grief written so clearly on his friend's face. He questions him, and Cyrus in turn is touched by Daad's concern and interest in his affairs. He relates what has happened in the last few days and the experiences of the morning. Daad sympathizes with him and shares his friend's unhappiness.

Daad pulls 200 rials from his pocket and offers it to Cyrus, saying that he can pay it back when he receives his allowance from the Department of Education. Cyrus looks down at the ground and accepts his friend's offer. Daad is sure that he can get another 1000 rials from his brother for Cyrus. Cyrus offers to pay 100 rials interest on the money that Daad and his brother are loaning him. Daad is astonished at this and tells Cyrus that he feels it his duty to help a friend in need, and furthermore it is against his religion to accept interest from anyone. Cyrus repeats his thanks again and again, not knowing how else to express his gratitude. They bid one another good-bye and Cyrus goes on home.

In less than two hours, Daad comes to the Amin home and gives Cyrus the 1000 rials he has obtained from his brother. Cyrus writes a note for Daad to take to the Ministry of Education to collect his allowance.

No sooner has Daad left than Baram arrives. He tells Cyrus that he is already to go: he has gotten permission from his family, his suitcases are packed, he has the money and he wants to leave as soon as possible. In fact Shushi has told Baram to be ready to leave Wednesday morning. If Cyrus is still interested in going with them he should have everything packed by Tuesday. Cyrus replies that he will do his best to be ready then.

Cyrus now has 1200 rials, but he still needs 300 more. He decides to ask Hormuz for a loan. He is sure that Hormuz has that much money and will not let him down. Full of hope Cyrus starts out Monday evening to borrow the 300 rials from Hormuz. On the way to his home, Cyrus realizes that borrowing money and being in debt have always been against his principles. There have been times when he has gone hungry rather than borrow. He becomes anxious, starts to sweat and wonders if his friend will ask him why he needs the money. Borrowing 300 rials from Hormuz seems more dreadful than borrowing 1200 from Daad and his brother. Perhaps it is because he has known the former only eight months and his other friends eight years. Now he goes to a washing place, bathes his wet face, sits down, tries to compose himself and begins to think of returning home.

Cyrus does not like to borrow money, probably because he evaluates borrowing thus: "In asking for a loan, one faces shame. If one accepts money, shame blackens the outside of the borrower's face, and if he cannot pay it back, shame shows on his whole face."

Hesitantly Cyrus starts to walk back home, but remembers the last sentence of Baram. They are expecting to see him tomorrow. The memories of the past few days crowd upon him: the scene at the Finance Department and all his ideas to make money for the next school year. These thoughts seem to pull him toward Hormuz's home. He finds himself at the door and knocks gently several times. The door opens and Cyrus faces his friend. Hormuz kindly invites him in and tells him his family has been looking forward to meeting him. His family and relatives are just now having a party for him because he has successfully passed the tenth grade. Hormuz can't find words enough to express his thanks to Cyrus for helping him with his courses. He pushes Cyrus toward the living room, but Cyrus protests saying he must return home quickly. This is the time to ask Hormuz for the loan but his courage fails him. Instead

173

he lets himself be led forward to meet Hormuz's relatives. Everyone is happy to know Cyrus and congratulates him on having been such a good tutor for Hormuz. He modestly replies that Hormuz has exaggerated his ability as a teacher—he is just an ordinary student and he was glad to study with Hormuz. Cyrus accepts a sherbet but stays only a few minutes. He gets up and apologizes for having to leave immediately. He offers no excuse and Hormuz is somewhat taken aback, but he sees Cyrus to the door and presses his hand warmly to express his gratitude. In turn Cyrus gives him a heartly hand-shake; it gives Hormuz more the impression of farewell than of good-bye.

Cyrus goes home wondering what to say to his family. He has always been a straight-forward boy and never kept anything from them. Yet what can he say to his parents now? It is Monday night and tomorrow he is scheduled to go. To go without saying good-bye would hurt them and they'd be unhappy for the whole summer.

He is at home earlier than usual. There is a need for two jars of drinking water and Cyrus takes the jars and walks out of the house. He generally tries to fill the jugs at the time of day when his friends are not likely to be on the street. If Cyrus were seen doing such menial tasks other people would think he is poor. It is the custom for those who can afford it to hire a porter to carry water to their home daily. Tonight Cyrus is indifferent about whether he is seen or not. He goes through an alley to a short street where the local water-supply is located.

This water-supply was built nearly three hundred years ago. Constructed firmly, it has the appearance of a large covered pool. It is made of cement and unusually large bricks. Thirty steps down is the pump. Here, Cyrus fills the jars and goes back up the steps. He is almost out of breath and pauses a moment before continuing. At home he leaves the jugs in the open air to cool.

It is supper time. Cyrus approaches the table with some foreboding. This is the one opportunity he has to speak to his family about the trip. Yet he waits, hoping for some opening that will make it easier. By chance, Mr. Amin asks Cyrus, "And how are your plans coming along for the summer?"

Cyrus replies slowly and hesitantly, "Well, I have a chance to do some translating for Americans."

Everyone is immediately interested and Dariush remarks, "I didn't think there were many Americans in Shiraz."

Cyrus finds it difficult to continue. "The job isn't in Shiraz —it's in Andimeshk."

"Andimeshk!" exclaims Mrs. Amin. "How can you even think of leaving home—and so far way." She begins to cry in protest.

Cyrus is visibly upset too. His sisters, Ferri and Nazi begin to sniffle, and Cyrus looks to Dariush for support.

"If I knew English as well as Cyrus, I wouldn't mind going with him. It's a wonderful opportunity for him, and he'll only be gone for the summer," Dariush remarks.

Mrs. Amin dries her face and says, "But it's such a long way and he doesn't know anyone there."

"Oh, but Baram is going too. And Shushi who was Baram's classmate a few years ago, is working for the Americans and he'll take us with him," explains Cyrus quickly.

Up till now, Mr. Amin has said nothing, merely following the conversation with great thought. Now he says, "None of our children have ever been away from home, and it's not easy to let one of them go even for the summer, but if it'll add to Cyrus's education, and I think it will, then he should go."

Mrs. Amin takes the verdict quietly. Ferri and Nazi are still perturbed at the though of his leaving, but Dariush beams approvingly. Cyrus is inwardly pleased, but his happiness is some-

175

what shattered by his mother's next remark, "Of course it'll still be a few weeks before you leave and we can talk more about the matter later. You don't really have to decide about going right away."

Cyrus is silent and Dariush asks him, "When do you have to be in Andimeshk?"

Cyrus replies in almost a whisper, "We're supposed to leave tomorrow."

"Tomorrow!" everyone echoes in dismay.

"How can you leave tomorrow?" questions Mrs. Amin. And she begins to cry anew.

Ferri gently leads her from the room and Nazi follows.

Mr. Amin pats his son on the arm. "Well, if that's the plan then we must accept it. Cyrus, how much money do you think you need for the trip?"

Cyrus swallows and finds it hard to begin. He circumvents the question and says evasively, "Well, the Department of Education owes me 1200 rials and I've borrowed that much from Daad and his brother until they can get my allowance from the Ministry of Education."

Mr. Amin's face reveals disappointment. "But why didn't you come to your family and arrange it with us. I would have been glad to have given you that much for your trip."

Cyrus hangs his head in shame. Mr. Amin takes some money out of his pocket and says kindly, "Here's 500 rials to add to the money you borrowed. If you need more, write us."

Cyrus is deeply touched by his father's actions. Never before has he appreciated him as much as now. He almost wishes he weren't going after all.

Dinner has not been much of a success. Dariush, Cyrus and Mr. Amin discuss some of the details of Cyrus's trip, and finally all adjourn for bed.

176

Next morning Cyrus meets Baram and Shushi outside the Pars Museum. Shushi informs them that it is necessary to make reservations for Wednesday morning. The cheapest way of going is to find a truck going in that direction. After searching the different garages for several hours the boys finally locate a truck driver who is loading his truck with figs and sugar and leaving for Esfahan the next morning. He says that one of the three boys can ride on the seat with him and the other two will have to sit on the load. Cyrus and Baram decide to sit on the load and give Shushi the more comfortable place with the driver. The driver insists that they bring their baggage to the truck in three hours time, and in addition he suggests that they spend the night sleeping on the roof of the garage so that they will be ready to leave at five in the morning. More important, the driver cannot let two of them ride on the load when they are driving through the city, for it is against the law. Because of many accidents, the office of transportation does not permit any truck driver to have passengers on his load. But still it happens that the drivers do pick up quite a number of needy people going out from the city. So the driver tells Cyrus and Baram that they should go ahead of the truck and wait outside the city until he gets there. The distance between the garage and the appointed place is about five miles. Baram and Cyrus decide to walk there early in the morning so as to arrive at five. They pay the driver a deposit and go for their luggage.

Cyrus returns home. It is noon time and his mother and sister are busy preparing lunch. Without telling them that he is home he goes to his room and quietly packs his things for the trip. There is an old wooden box that will serve as a suitcase and in it he puts a blanket, an old cotton rug and a small pillow; as well as a few favorite books such as a prayer book and an English grammar. He puts the box behind a

177

door where it is not too visible and prepares himself for lunch. In a short time the family have all assembled for the noon day meal. Mr. Amin has just gotten a new shipment of goods in the store and he talks about his new merchandise. At one point Dariush starts to ask Cyrus about his plans for leaving, but Cyrus motions him to remain silent. Dariush is puzzled but says nothing. It almost seems as if the family has forgotten about Cyrus's plans for departure—nothing more has been said about it. In truth it seems impossible to all of them that he could actually be ready to leave today. Surely it takes at least a week to make preparations for such a long trip.

Throughout the meal Cyrus says little. He is busy absorbing the features of those about him: the tired yet patient loving eyes of his mother, his father's graying hair, the dark beautiful features of Ferri's face, Dariush's thoughtful expression and Nazi's impish smile. He can hardly swallow his food and several times chokes on it. He stands up and says quietly, "I must leave now."

They look at him, wondering what he means—waiting for a fuller explanation. But words are difficult and Cyrus can hardly hold back his tears. He embraces his mother warmly and his cheeks are wet; he fondly kisses each in turn. Everyone is tearful but still too surprised by the suddenness to fully show their grief.

Cyrus gets his box and goes out the door. Ferri holds a holy book for him to walk under. It is a sign for God to protect him. Nazi takes a bowl of water in which there are a few green leaves and throws it behind the traveler as a sign of anticipating a pleasant trip.

Dariush and Mr. Amin insist on going to the garage with Cyrus. Darius takes the box and they depart amid much weeping from Mrs. Amin and the girls. Cyrus directs his gaze to the ground to hide the tears that have gathered in his eyes.

178

On the way Cyrus explains what took place that morning. It is some distance to the garage and by the time they arrive Dariush and Mr. Amin know all about Cyrus's plans.

Baram and Shushi are waiting and Baram greets Dariush and Mr. Amin. Cyrus introduces Shushi. After stowing away their baggage the group decides to take one last walk around the town Mr. Amin and Dariush accompany them as far as their store. Cyrus is again faced with saying goodby. Knowing that Baram and Shushi are standing nearby he does his best to assume a manly pose but his voice visibly betrays him and he lowers his head in confusion.

The boys continue on their walk. About seven in the evening they return to the garage and spread cotton rugs out on the roof. Shushi and Baram have wrist watches and they agree to wake up at 3:30 so that Barum and Cyrus can be at the appointed place at 5 A.M.

The boys arise on time and the two of them start out with instructions to Shushi where the truck is to pick them up. After an hour's walk they are at the appointed site. Baram looks at his watch—it is a little before five.

They look carefully at every truck that passes by hoping that it is Shushi. They wait and wait. At six-thirty their truck has not appeared. Cyrus is impatient and aggravated; he wonders if he should go back to see what has happened, for he is beginning to suspect that the driver has told them a lie. However, Baram who has had previous experience with such drivers tells him that they usually arrive late. He reminds Cyrus that this is what he told him at three thirty. "But no, you were so sure that the driver would be on time," grumbles Baram. He takes a friendly poke at Cyrus and the other returns it. They fail to see the occupants of a truck that is passing by. It passes and stops over the hill. The boys hear the screech of the brakes and run toward

179

it. Cyrus is annoyed with the driver and complains to him about the delay. He retorts, "Just be glad I'm taking you boys with me. Don't forget it's a big risk for me."

Cyrus doesn't say any more but climbs up on the load and lies down next to Baram on sacks of figs and sugar. The truck starts up and they leave the city behind. The view of the city disappears and all that remains are mountains, hills and the blue sky.

From Shiraz to Esfahan the distance is some three hundred miles, over an unpaved road. With a good truck it is possible to make it in one day, but with a heavily loaded one it varies. It might take two days, and then there is no guarantee that it will arrive.

Cyrus lies on the sugar sacks, repeating his favorite verses of poetry and sometimes a prayer. The noise of the truck finally lulls him to sleep. It is almost 11 o'clock when Cyrus opens his eyes and sees the famous Persepolis nearby. The truck driver stops to have his breakfast, and the boys jump down and join Shushi to eat also. They discover that the inn is expensive and unsanitary. Shushi notices some black tents not far away and he goes to the tribesmen and asks if they have any home-made bread and fresh cheese. At this time of year the tribespeople have the best dairy products. Baram and Cyrus have gotten three glasses of tea from the tea shop and they carry them to a shady spot. Shushi joins them and the boys eat hungrily.

The driver calls to them and they are on their way again. The highway becomes troublesome— a series of valleys and mountain ridges of desolate beauty. Cyrus observes the curves, the way the wheels go along the edge of the narrow road and the accidents they see in passing. It is all new to Cyrus and somewhat frightening. What are their chances of having an accident? Their safety is in God's hands and Cyrus submits himself to God. He tries not to look at the road and prefers to rid himself of worry by sleeping. Once he wakes up and feels that the truck is moving backwards. It is a slippery section and the truck is heavy and the driver somewhat careless. The truck slides all the way down the hill until it stops at the foot of the mountain. It is late at night—almost midnight and the driver is obviously tired. The truck has stopped at a safe place and the driver tells them he is going to rest at a small inn nearby until morning. The boys follow him there. The whole inn is merely one big hall connected to a small dirty kitchen. Along the sides of the main room are platforms and in the center a few benches. Some trucks are parked outside and the drivers and passengers are all spending the night at the inn. A few have covered themselves with blankets, others are in sleeping bags and some are sleeping on the platform. A few are sitting together drinking tea and smoking. The boys hear them discussing some of the recent robberies that have taken place at the inn.

Cyrus remarks to his companions that it doesn't seem to be a respectable place to spend the night. Baram and Shushi motion for him to be quiet and are too tired to think about such matters. They find an empty corner to sleep in. Cyrus carefully puts his money in his shirt pocket and keeps his shirt jacket on. The boys share a blanket between them.

The inn is filled to capacity and the inn-keeper now boards up the door and puts a few benches against it as an extra safety measure. Cyrus finds it hard to sleep and now and then he peers out into the room to see what is happening. His anxiety about the money keeps him awake but in time the fatigue of the day's adventures overcomes him and he sleeps soundly. As is his habit he arises early. A walk outside refreshes him and he observes the scenic view from the inn. In the early morning silence he repeats his prayers and joins his friends.

Late in the afternoon of that day the truck reaches Esfahan, one of the most beautiful cities of Iran and once called "half of the world." It is known for the beauty of its buildings and it is typical of Iranian artistry in architecture, painting and the richly ornamented tiles in the interiors of some of the buildings.

The boys would like to spend a day or more in sight-seeing about Esfahan, but there is no time. They take a few minutes to write messages to their families. Cyrus discovers that in his haste he has left his police identification card at home. Shushi suggest that he have his family send it to him at Andimeshk.

In Esfahan the boys bid goodbye to the truck driver and look for a new vehicle going toward Irak.[1] Shushi suggests they go on a tanker truck from Esfahan to Irak and then a train from Iraq to Andimeshk. There are a good many of these tankers which transfer oil from Abadan to the central parts of Iran. On their way south they are empty and travel fast. Shushi describes the tankers as being able to seat two persons comfortably, three if necessary, besides the driver. He convinces the other two that this will be the best way to travel and the fastest: they could leave Esfahan late at night, cover a distance of one hundred fifty miles and take the train the next day in Iraq.

Without much trouble the boys locate a tanker going to Irak. The driver wants to know what their final destination is, and when he hears that thay are going to Andimeshk he is vehement in voicing his dislike for Americans. He is openly critical of their plans but agrees to take them to Irak. The boys are angered by his remarks and say nothing to him for the rest of the trip.

The tanker arrives in Irak about one o'clock the following afternoon. Cyrus carries his wooden box on his head; it makes

---

[1] A city in Iran.

a good umbrella against the sun for the weather is very warm. The road is dusty and the walk to the station is a good five miles. Once of Cyrus's shoes is worn thin and his wooden box seems three times heavier than it really is. He sweats but continues walking. They reach the station tired, thirsty and hungry. When they inquire about tickets they learn that first class tickets are exclusively for the allied forces, and no on except members of the three great powers, Russia, England and the U.S. can use first class carriages. Furthermore, they are too expensive. So are second class tickets, and the third class ones are all sold out. Further inquiry reveals that it is possible for them to go by freight car, and they make arrangements with the man in charge.

At four thirty in the afternoon the train pulls into the station. Cyrus awakens to new excitement—his first train ride. After examining several of the freight cars, the boys find an empty one and stow their baggage in it. They spread a blanket in a clean corner and sit on it.

The final lap of their journey is now under way. Through the door of the car they watch the meadows, valleys, hills and wheat farms now turning yellow in the heat of the last days of spring. At every station the train stops five to fifteen minutes depending on the size of the station. It doesn't matter to Cyrus—he sleeps soundly through it all. Finally the train crosses the mountain range and slows down as it approaches the province of Kuzestan. The heat of the sun awakens Cyrus and he recalls what people have said about the intensity of the sun in this part of Iran. He feels the train coming to a halt. They must have arrived at their destination. It is Andimeshk.

CHAPTER SIXTEEN

AN EXCITING JOB

A hundred fifty miles from the Persian Gulf and situated in the flat costal low lands lies Andimeshk, now a sprawling city of some 20,000 inhabitants. World War II has accentuated its growth for in 1943 it is an important link in the chain of railway transport from Shah-pur on the Persian Gulf to the port of Shah on the Caspian Sea, close to the Russian border. In fact, the expansion of the city has paralleled the growth of transportation, both of the railroad and the roads, most of which have just been paved with the advent of the Allied troops. Large awkward wooden buildings have been hastily constructed to accomodate the goings-on of Russian, American, Arab, Iranian, and British personnel stationed there.

Camps have been built for American soldiers, officers and advisors at the extreme north end of the city. Close to their living quarters are temporary buildings which serve their administrative personnel and all the activities connected with providing supplies for a war. There are American ration depots, an American school for driver-training, an American truck drivers organization, an American interpreter group, American technicians and various American administrative offices. There are Iranian translators, interpreters, drivers, semi-skilled laborers, laborers and mechanics, checkers, crane-drivers, managers and clerks—all employed by the Americans.

The Russian section is housed in an area far to the south of the city. The Russian agencies help in the administrative aspect of transporting American goods to their country.

The British in Andimeshk are mostly concerned with the ever-important oil pipelines. They do not participate in transporting goods to Russia, although they are engaged in war activity to the extent that their troops occupy the western part of Iran which the Allies have set aside as neutral territory.

The main section of Andimeshk consists of a series of shops selling such things as are necessary for day-to-day living. Here there are also some restaurants and houses. In another section of the sity there are a number of brothels. The women there are of many nationalities and their number has increased with the large influx of foreign visitors. Although these women live off the male employees of the town, they must pay certain taxes to the police department. In fact, the city has a large police department, and the police are strict about enforcing their laws. If people resist them they are taken in. Many can testify that they've been locked up for failing to pay their fines.

There is little to do in Andimeshk—no recreational centers or movie theaters at all. In the whole town there is not even a public bath. The one public garden, a very small one, is located in the more modern section of town, near the railroad station.

It takes Cyrus and Baram only one day to get acquainted with the town. Baram has decided to stay with Shushi in his quarters, but there is no room for Cyrus. After some looking about Cyrus rents a room in the garage on the main street of the town. The only furniture in the room is a wooden bed. He makes it up as best he can using the cotton rug, blanket and sheet that he has brought with him. He puts up a shelf and on it he puts his books. He shoves the wooden case in a

185

corner of the room. It is a small dingy room but the rent is reasonable, and in addition the owner does not ask that it be paid in advance. And then too, the garage has a wide open yard which means every resident can pull out his bed and enjoy the pleasant night breezes. The garage has several other rooms, mostly similar to what Cyrus rents. In these rooms live truck drivers, mechanics, and semi-skilled laborers. Cyrus meets them the first evening but they do not impress him at all. It really doesn't matter, for Cyrus's chief concern is to obtain employment.

Sometimes early in the morning when the streets are still deserted, Cyrus walks out of the garage and washes himself by using the water pipe on the corner of the street so that he may be clean and ready for an interview later in the day. Each time he dresses neatly and puts on his only silk shirt. Baram has already succeeded in getting a job close to where Shushi works, but his work keeps him so busy that he hasn't had time to visit Cyrus and tell him more about it.

On this day, Shushi's brother, Ali, is taking Cyrus to the ration depot to seek a job. Ali is a young man about twenty years of age and from Cyrus's home town. He is a happy-go lucky, good-hearted youth and has talked to his boss about Cyrus. The Americans at the ration depot think highly of Ali: he has an excellent work record and has proven to be honest, energetic and friendly.

On their way to the depot, Cyrus asks Ali many questions about the place. Ali tells him what it does, how it started and where it is located. The ration depot is situated next to the station just outside of Andimeshk where the plains sweep toward the Persian Gulf. It is one of several centers where American supplies are stored and then transported to Russia. Its temporary boundaries are set off by high wires, and if need be its area can be extended to the Persian Gulf which would make it an area one hundred fifty miles in length. The amount of goods that pass through it depends upon the Russian demand and American mass production. Throughout the depot internal and external railroad lines run. Incoming and outgoing supplies are highly organized and classified. Supplies of different kinds are unloaded from freight cars which have come from ships anchored in the Persian Gulf. There are numerous kinds of cargoes —some of which do not even touch the ground at the depot: cranes transfer them from the freight cars into trucks which in turn transport them to the Russian border. Everything is done as speedily as possible so that the cars may return to the ships for more supplies.

The goods being unloaded are of many kinds. There are metals of all kinds, especially copper, bronze, iron, nickel and steel in the form of sheets, plates and even pipes. They are piled in one corner. Next to them are motor vehicles and airplane parts. They have their own special classification. For instance, Fords, Studebakers, Cheverlots and Jeeps are all sorted according to the make of the car. Next to these products of American machinery, in a more guarded area, are artillery, guns, ammunition of all kinds. Everything is carefully classified and stacked in neat piles. The need for them is so desperate that they have the highest priority in shipment—even before food.

A few yards from the weapons are stacked piles of tires all arranged by size: large truck sizes, medium sizes ones down to small cycle sizes. All are made in the United States and all are destined for Russia. The mountains of telephone cable, receiving sets and other equipment occupy another area. Even the food is sorted in certain prescribed ways. For example, sacks of flour, beans of different colors and piles of sacks of rice are all in one area. Close to it are cases of canned goods and packaged foods of many kinds.

Clothing is still in another section. Cloth is in one pile, ready-made clothing in another. Everything is sorted here before being sent on to the Caspian Sea, Black Sea or even Siberia. Woolen and cotton clothes are stacked high and sizes and types range all the way from clothing for grandmothers to that for newborn babies; but most of it is destined for official and military personnel.

Some of this Cyrus sees as Ali conducts him to the employment office. It is hard to believe that so many supplies could be collected in one spot. Cyrus feels the heat of the burning sand through his shoes and the sun bears down on him from above. He wonders how the manual laborers manage to work in such heat. Yet he thinks he will be able to put up with it as long as he can get a job. To Cyrus the thought of work is a blessing, not a punishment. He waits expectantly in a wooden office in the center of the ration depot until an army sergeant is ready to interview him. At the same time he is very worried that he still does not have his police identification card and this may keep him from getting the job, and Cyrus has explained this all to Ali. Now Cyrus is introduced to the sergeant and immediately the man starts to show him the process of checking. He doesn't ask Cyrus for any identification but tells him they will put him on a trial basis for three days. If he does well he will be hired.

The sergeant shows Cyrus how each truck is loaded. The checker must go over the number of cases in each truck, check its weight and tally the total weight. Paying attention to all that goes on, Cyrus soon catches on to the idea and goes at it with enthusiasm. By the afternoon the Americans are calling him "Cy".

It is a simple job and Cyrus is confident of his ability to do it well. Cyrus enjoys the checking, loading and calculating. He is quick, and during the loading he adds the weight of each case to the previous one. As soon as the truck is loaded he gives a good-ahead signal to the driver and a new truck rolls into position.

During the first three days Cyrus learns all about checking and loading the outgoing materials. If he feels uncertain about some procedure he asks Ali for help. On the evening of the third day when he is about to go home, the sargeant in charge of that section, Sargeant John, beckons to him. He informs Cyrus that he can have the job for eighty dollars a month. At the end of the first month he will receive an increase of twenty dollars. In addition, every other week he will be given a ration of five pounds of wheat flour, three pounds of sugar and half a pound of tea. Cyrus is more than pleased to accept and the sargeant conducts him to the central administrative building. It is built of wood like the others but is equipped with more modern facilities. There are fans running all the time and extra lighting is provided. Cyrus is introduced to the American colonel in charge of personnel and he makes an employment file on Cyrus.

Already during his orientation period, Cyrus has found that he must check goods and work at least once a day with a manager, a head checker, a crane driver and a few manual laborers. He quickly makes friends with them. Sometimes he helps the laborers in loading or setting the cases in the truck. Among this simple but sincere group he has become known as "Small Sir." Most of the laborers and crane drivers, and even a few of the managers are illiterate and when they receive their wages they usually make a finger mark as their signature. Cyrus decides to take it upon himself to teach them to sign their names. During lunch or after work—whenever he has spare time— Cyrus helps them.

In general, there are more than a hundred fifty such semi-

189

skilled workers and laborers in the ration depot. They all seem to know one another, for they all come from a tribe that has its quarters close to Andimeshk. Cyrus finds them all simple-minded and good-hearted. One of them tells Cyrus that when the Americans first started to work in the Persian Gulf region, the workers were paid two dollars a day and more. Now most of them receive at least a hundred dollars a month.

During the first four months Cyrus is promoted three times and in addition gets paid for a great deal of overtime. In this time he has become so fast and accurate that no checker can compete with him and even the head checker sometimes asks Cyrus to check his calculations for him. Cyrus likes to work and is grateful for the opportunity.

One day as Cyrus is loading cases of ball-bearings from a freight car to a truck the driver tries to signal to him several times. Finally he comes over and whispers in Cyrus's ear: "Load an extra case on and I'll give you a good tip."

Cyrus says nothing but moves to the other side of the truck so as to avoid having to answer the man. However, the driver is not put off so easily: he follows and repeats his offer, saying, "Nobody will find out. Everybody does it. Come on, kid, take the money."

Cyrus is hot with anger, and tells the man curtly, "I'm only a checker here, but I'd like to do my job honestly. Keep your old money—I don't want it."

He finishes loading the truck and dismisses the driver abruptly. Even after the truck has left, he continues to feel upset. Why do these men have to try to corrupt others? How have they been brought up? His anger spurs him on to work even more accurately. No truck driver is going to get away with more than his scheduled load. From then on he makes it a practice to mount each truck when it is loaded and count the cases a second time.

190

When it is an especially important load, Cyrus asks his co-worker, a Russian soldier to double check the truck. His one encounter with bribery has reinforced his desire to do a good job. On another occasion Cyrus meets a Russian driver from the province of Georgia. Much to Cyrus's surprise he speaks to him in Persian and tells him he wants a good load. If the cases in his shipment are broken or missing he will be severely punished. Cyrus learns that he is from Gandzeh the birth place of Nazami, a great Persian poet.[1] Cyrus is careful to load the cases gently onto the truck and wishes the driver good-luck on his return trip.

Some days later a new Russian soldier is assigned to the ration depot to check outgoing goods. He is poorly dressed and it is rumored that he has just come from the front lines. His name is George but there is little communication between him and Cyrus as neither speaks the other's language. Yet one day the two engage in a heated argument. With the help of a co-worker who speaks Russian, he boasts to Cyrus how the Russians helped bring about the exile of the Shah of Iran, who was finally taken to Africa on a British ship. Several hot-blooded tribesmen, working with Cyrus, become enraged and seize iron pipes and corner the Russian soldier. Sargeant John's sharp discipline and quick thinking bring order and quiet the men. George is transferred to another department.

Two other Russian soldiers replace George. One of them is called Joseph. He is short, industrious and clever: he knows a little Persian but speaks English fluently. Cyrus admires him because he seems so much more relaxed than the other Russians he has met. At the same time Joseph does his work well: he never makes a mistake in counting his cases. Sometimes when

---

[1] Up until 1823 the province of Georgia was a part of Persia.

there is a lull in their work, Joseph teaches Cyrus how to count in Russian from one to a hundred or he gives Cyrus a lesson in history and geography. In turn, Joseph is surprised at how much Cyrus knows already about his country. The two get along well together.

Cyrus does not have too much to do with Ivan, the other Russian worker. Nor does his severe unsmiling face particularly appeal to Cyrus. Cyrus keeps a record of supplies for the Americans and Ivan does the same for the Russian office. Sometimes he asks Cyrus to check his calculations, but other than that the two have little to do with one another.

Cyrus works hard and earnestly each day. There is seldom time for him to chat with his co-workers. One day however the American and Russian personnel cannot agree as to how a certain shipment of brass is to be handled. The men are ordered to stop work and Cyrus suddenly finds himself free for the afternoon.

One of the Americans who has helped Cyrus from time to time is a man called Mack. He is a heavy-set, muscular man of about 40 and his job is to direct the crane drivers in their work. On this afternoon Cyrus sees Mack stretched out in the sand lazily smoking his pipe. He joins him and Mack motions for him to sit down. For a long time Cyrus has wanted to know more about the States and now he asks his friend to tell him about America. The question is too much for Mack and instead he asks Cyrus what he already knows about the U.S.

Cyrus knows quite a bit about the geography of the U.S. and he gives Mack the names of the oceans surrounding the country, the major mountain ranges from coast to coast, the names of the Great Lakes, the tributaries of the Mississippi River and the names of as many states as he can remember. Then he talks about the American Revolution and such men as Washington,

Jefferson and Franklin. At this point Cyrus confesses that he doesn't understand why the British who fought against the Americans in the American Revolution are today being helped by the U.S. Nor does he understand why Mack should have left his family and friends to fight in such a war.

Up until this time Mack has said very little except to occasionally correct Cyrus's grammar. Now he takes his pipe from his mouth, knocks the ashes from it and speaks somewhat slowly and unsurely, "Well, there are lots of things I don't understand either. Hell, I don't care for this war; but it's those God-damm English and Russians who want to fight."

He puts his pipe back into his mouth, feeling he has expressed his thoughts sufficiently. Cyrus is just as puzzled as before, especially the way Mack uses the expression 'God-damm.' He's heard it used so often by Americans on just about every occasion: "those God-damm Englishmen," "the God-damm Germans," or "God-damm that pipe," "Where's my "God-damm" key?" "God-damm you!" or even "God-damm everybody!"

Cyrus looks up to see Sargeant John approaching with some candy he has found in one of the freight cars. He offers them some, and Cyrus takes a handful to the crane-drivers and laborers. They smile and wave their thanks to the sargeant.

Everyone likes Sargeant John. He is a pleasant looking young man who is courteous and considerate to all. He is Cyrus's immediate superior and he takes a kindly interest in the youth, sometimes advising him what he should and should not do with his free time. He has warned Cyrus to stay away from the brothel district, and Cyrus accepts his advice. The other Persian workers also listen to Sargeant John, and he exercises considerable influence among them. He has learned a few Persian words and expressions and uses them to direct the workers, but he

193

never orders them about. His tactfulness encourages the group to work more closely together and to do it cheerfully.

As a result Cyrus comes to work early. He often doesn't wait for the truck to pick him up with the other workers in the center of town. Rather he arises early, says his morning prayers and walks to the ration depot. He is generally the first to arrive, although sometimes Sargeant John is ahead of him. They talk a bit and then the sargeant outlines the plan of work for the day. Sometimes during the day Sargeant John asks Cyrus about his plans for the future. Cyrus talks about his family and his past schooling. The sargeant firmly advises him to return to school as soon as his job is finished because there is no future in it—it ends when the war is over. Cyrus listens carefully to what he says.

Frequently John brings Cyrus candy and Cyrus reciprocates with watermelons. Andimeshk is known for its watermelons and they are a most welcome treat in the summer. Cyrus eats watermelon every day and shares his fruit with the others.

The respect Cyrus has for Sargeant John is much different than what he feels for Joe, an American soldier who also works at the depot. Joe is an over-weight buffon who says whatever comes to his mind in front of high-ranking officers. He frequently comes to work drunk and it is rumored that he spends much of his time at a brothel.

As far as Cyrus is concerned, everyone is entitled to do what he wants in his private life, or even in public as long as it does not affect others. Sometimes Cyrus encounters Bob, another American G.I. He comes from Mississippi and is fond of telling wild tales especially after he's had a few drinks. Cyrus enjoys his good-natured friendly attitude but the heavy smell of alcohol about him is sickening.

Then there is the bus driver called Charlie. He drives the checkers to work every morning. A good natured, jolly and

194

husky fellow, Charlie gets along better with his fellow Americans than with the Persians whom he is inclined to mistreat. What annoys Cyrus is the way Charlie whistles at girls in the street and calls provocative suggestions to them.

After work Charlie drives the checkers and other workers to town. It is always a bus load of happy talkative men. Sometimes they gossip among themselves about Cyrus's quick promotion —they envy him and feel that he wants to be better than they are. He doesn't play cards or gamble, nor does he visit the brothels. They find it difficult to understand what enjoyment he has in life.

Consequently outside of work, Cyrus has few friends. Baram and Shushi live in another part of town and he seldom sees them. Ali, Shushi's brother, lives not too far from Cyrus and sometimes visits Cyrus in his room.

One week-end Ali and some of his friends from the ration depot decide it is time for Cyrus to become better acquainted with life in Andimeshk. They make their plans and then Ali goes to Cyrus. He tells him that he is planning to visit a friend on Sunday and he would like Cyrus to join him. Cyrus innocently accepts.

On that Sunday, Cyrus goes to Ali's house and the two start out. They walk some distance through narrow alleys and in parts of the city that Cyrus has never been. Several times when he asks Ali where his friend lives, Ali answers evasively, "Everyone enjoys visiting my friend. You will too." Cyrus is curious but not suspicious. Finally they cross a narrow line on the pavement and approach a small but neat looking house. From the cellar come the faint voices of some youths and a woman. Ali leads him to the door, knocks, then enters. A woman rises from the couch and Ali greets her saying, "I brought him."

Cyrus looks around the room and several of his co-workers

greet him with loud laughter. He is surprised to see them there and he suddenly becomes aware of where he is. In disgust he leaves the brothel and bangs the door. Ali runs after him and takes him by the arm explaining that it was just a joke to get him there. The boys don't really intend to do anything. Still upset Cyrus replies angerly, "I'll wait for you fellows out here."

Ali returns to the house and Cyrus stands outside. He passes back and forth trying to cool his anger. Several passers-by give him curious glances, especially the women who seem to measure him from head to foot. Being shy and reserved, he feels hot all over—not only because of the dry warm air but for the humiliation of having to stand in front of such a house. He hates himself, especially when he hears men's voices in the alley talking about their recent experiences with the girls. Undecided as to whether to wait longer for Ali, Cyrus goes back to the house to tell him he is leaving. With some hesitation he knocks. He tells the woman who answers it that he wishes to speak to Ali. In a minute Ali appears and tells Cyrus that he will come with him right this moment.

The following Friday Cyrus decides to meet Baram, Shushi and Ali for a walk. They decide to explore the modern section of the town—walking first through the park and then to the residental area where the Americans live.

It is late summer but the park still has a spring freshness to it, and the patches of green grass sway and dance in the evening breeze. It is almost sunset. Slowly the sun disappears in the endless Andimeshk horizon. Cyrus walks somewhat apart while the others enjoy talking about sex and the fact that at this time of year nature looks exactly like early spring in Shiraz. Cyrus is more intent on watching the scenery; although their conversation does not escape him, still he prefers to give the impression that sex is of no interest to him.

196

Suddenly Ali raises his voice and points to a young lady who is walking with an older woman, and he says to his companions, "She looks like a newcomer. I haven't seen her before."

Ali leads the others in following the woman into the street and then to the alley. Cyrus protests but Ali motions for him to be silent. Ali obviously admires her figure and by the time he gets a chance to talk to her, she has reached the door of a house. She enters but the door is invitingly left open. Just inside the door are two other women. Baram and Shushi start to follow Ali in, but Cyrus holds back Baram and asks him angerly, "What are you doing?"

One of the women smiles at Cyrus and remarks, "All are welcome here."

It enrages Cyrus still more, but the others take no notice of him. Baram calls to Ali that they will wait for him in the outer room. Cyrus blushes and sits down in the corner of the room nearest the door. He refuses to look at the others but stars pensively at his nails or at the floor. The ladies chat with the boys, and from time to time one of them tries to engage Cyrus in conversation. He maintains a stony silence and doesn't even look up. They tease him for being so shy in front of ladies but tell him that in time he'll get used to them.

At last Ali returns from one of the special rooms and they all leave the house. The woman who seems to be in charge thanks the boys for coming and tells Ali to be sure to bring his young friend again, obviously referring to Cyrus. The others are all amused by her interest in Cyrus. They tease him about it and embarrass him still further. Ali appears to have enjoyed his visit there, and Cyrus interrupts his remarks to exclaim hotly, "It really doesn't matter to me what you do with your own free time, but is there any reason why you have to drag your friends there too?"

Ali tries to soothe him and pats him on the shoulder saying, "Your attitude is too childish for your age. When are you going to be a man?"

The words sting Cyrus. He takes off his jacket to fight, but Baram restrains him and walks ahead with his arm around his friend in an effort to calm him. Shushi explains to his brother that Cyrus is deeply religious and different from the rest of them. Such relationships with women do not conform to his values and association with them would be sinful and self corrupting.

Cyrus overhears their remarks and is silently grateful to Shushi for interpreting his feelings to Ali. At this point he vows to keep away from Ali and his outside activities. At the same time Ali secretly respects Cyrus for his standard of social behavior, but he is sure that his morals will change the longer he stays in Andimeshk.

Cyrus returns to the small room in the garage where he lives. Although the neighborhood doesn't appeal to him it is all he can get, and he makes the best of it. The group of drivers who live in the other rooms usually stay in one day a week, and on that day the garage is a madhouse, but as long as he gets his rent the owner doesn't care. The drivers get together, eat, drink and then put on a real show. A few of the technicians who live close to Cyrus in the same building aren't as wild as the drivers but still their conversations are raw and filthy. Once in a while one of them is jobless for a few days and he has to borrow money. Cyrus is willing to lend it, but he wants no part of the group's activities. His experience with Ali has discouraged him from joining the social doings of his co-workers. On one occasion they invite him to go to Susa[1] with them, but he refuses saying

---

[1] Susa (Shushan of the Bible) was once the site of the old civilizations. It was the site of Elamites, Daniel and the Assyrians before the rise of the Persian kingdom by Cyrus the Great in the sixth century B.C. Dariush,

that he has to work overtime. He would like to go, but he is all too familiar with their way of behavior. He wants no part of it and desires just to be left alone. Not that he wants to isolate himself completely from them, for he makes a point of inviting them to his room for fruit or candy occasionally, but he refers to live his own way of life.

Sometimes the other roomers show an interest in Cyrus's work and his promotions at the ration depot. Brought up to be truthful, Cyrus answers all these questions honestly, even when asked how much money he makes.

From the very beginning, Cyrus has set up a plan of dividing his salary into three shares. He spends one part for his own personal expenses. He sends another share to his family, especially for his brother who wants to continue his schooling. Then he saves the third share in order to buy gifts for everybody in the family and to make a trip to Abadan and Tehran. And in a special place he tucks away the silver coins which he receives in change from his pay; this is being saved for Nazi. Sometimes Cyrus buys good pieces of material for each member of the family, and this he packs away in the wooden box. In the same box he saves some money carefully wrapped in his old coat. There is no bank in Andimeshk and this is all that Cyrus can do with his money.

One evening after returning from work, Cyrus enters the garage to find the door of his room unlocked. He is surprised because he remembers quite distinctly that he locked it after lunch-time. Entering the room, he sees his old coat on the floor. His face pales and he goes to the big wooden case and opens the

Cyrus's successor, erected his winter capital on the ruins of Elamite's capital. Ruined by Alexander the Great, the great Susa was rebuilt by Shapur II (310-379 A.D.) of the Sassanian Dynasty. It was sacked by the Arab invaders in the seventh century.

door with trembling hands. Everything is gone. "Nothing's left! How could such a thief be so cruel!" he exclaims.

Even the small coins are gone. Cyrus looks around hopelessly. "Why did they have to take the change too? It was only 200 rials and would have meant so much to Nazi."

He shakes his coat but nothing tumbles out. "Five thousand rials gone, just like that," he mutters.

Cyrus takes his prayer book from the shelf, feeling that it is the only thing which can overcome his grief at this point. He reflects, "So much hard work in the hot sun. So much hope with the things I'd bought for my family. So many plans for traveling and seeing Nazi's smile on seeing the silver coins. Now it's all gone."

He closes the door and sits on the cotton rug, his head bowed. In a moment he pulls all the money from out of his trouser pocket. It amounts to 4500 rials. He brightens up and silently exclaims, "Thank heavens! It's still three times as much money as I had when I moved to Andimeshk. Things aren't really so bad either: I've already sent about 5000 rials home and I've paid off the money that I borrowed for my fare."

He puts the money back in his pocket and straightens the room up. He is undecided as to whether to say anything about the robbery to his landlord. While he is thinking about it, he hears his next door neighbors talking to the landlord that they are missing a sheet. The thought immediately comes to Cyrus that the thief must have used the sheet to carry away his money. He leaves his room and calls the landlord to explain what has happened. A group gathers in Cyrus's room, everyone interpreting the crime in his one way. The owner remembers seeing a man leaving the garage with a sack over his shoulder, but he cannot identify him. One of the tenants of the garage is an older man of about 40 who has talked to Cyrus on several

200

occasions, and he now takes it upon himself to call a police officer.

The policeman arrives and immediately sets about questioning everyone present. He is immediately suspicious of Cyrus's two neighbors, two young brothers, and he asks them about their stollen sheet and how it could have been taken when their door was locked. He arrests them. It is a shock to Cyrus to think that these boys, his friends and neighbors, would have taken his money. Yet robbery is apparently a common crime in Andimeshk.

The next day Cyrus is summoned to the police station and informed that it will cost him 100 rials to feed and house each person suspected of taking his money until they can be made to tell what they did with the loot. Cyrus looks at the simple youthful faces of the two suspects and decides that nothing can be gained by such a procedure. He asks that they be released and pays for their day's imprisonment.

The news of Cyrus's lost money spreads through the ration depot and all express sympathy. Sargeant John is very sorry to hear about it, and Cyrus tells him that he is thinking of leaving the depot for good. The sargeant persuades him to stay on for another month and informs him that he is due for another promotion in a few days. Cyrus agrees to stay on that long.

In that month Cyrus works hard and puts in as much overtime as he can manage. He also writes to an old acquaintance of his father's at Abadan to tell him that he is planning to visit the oil wells. He receives a kind letter in return inviting him to stay with them.

It is pay day, and Cyrus receives his last earned wages. He waits until the others have all received their earnings and then he goes up to Sargeant John to say goodby. They shake hands and Cyrus tries to express his thanks for the sargeant's kind friendship. In turn Sargeant John gives him a certificate testifying as to his length of employment and his work record. It reads:

RAIL TRUCK DEPOT YARD
Andimeshk, Iran
5 December, 1943

TO WHOM IT MAY CONCERN:

This letter is in recommendation of Cyrus Amin who has worked at this installation for a period of six months. During his period of employment, I have found him to be trustworthy, reliable and efficient in his work. His duties were to check various kinds of cargo, both incoming and outgoing. His final classification was that of technical supervisor at the rate of 3500 rials per month.

He has asked to be released from this installation in order to go to Abadan.

(Signed)
First Lt. Department Commander

SEMA

ENCOUNTER WITH THE WEST

CHAPTER SEVENTEEN

A DARBAND PARTY

Autumn in Tehran. It swoops down from the mountains into the valley with a swish of wind, leaving behind a trail of trees with bright, feathery leaves. And although the branches bow to the wind, only a few of the more delicate leaves lose their hold and scatter.

Autumn is lovely in Tehran, sunshine throughout the day and only in the evening the sense of impending winter. Like a small child sent out to play, the wind skips this way and that, stirring up scraps of paper on the streets of the city and whipping up sand on the country roads beyond; harassing people by circling around them, blowing in their faces and whipping their clothes. Those waiting for buses clutch their bundles, warding off the tugs of the wind with their backs. Then, suddenly, the wind subsides, teasingly, for in a few minutes it is back.

It was about seven in the evening. From the cab window Sema caught occasional glimpses of people waiting for buses packed with after-work crowds and others out for an evening's entertainment beyoud the city. The new, American-style drive-ins were surrounded by cars whose cramped inhabitants gulped sandwiches and Coca Cola with all the bantering cheeriness of picnic crowds. The more familiar corner food stands with their charcoal heated grills were equally busy serving roasted ears of corn and charred bits of meat. Suddenly the thought of the entrails sizzling on the grills made Sema feel a little sick. Her awareness of this caught her by surprise. Sick at the thought of eating Persian food, she leaned back in the cab beside her friend Pari and brushed away the sick feeling and the shame at the same time.

Sema was looking forward to the evening ahead of them. The three weeks since her return from America had been a frantic cycle of relatives and reunions from which she had found herself longing to escape time and again. She had caught herself thinking (with amazement) of her terrible homesickness during the last weeks of her stay abroad. About to go home, to see her parents, friends, city, everything she had not actively missed for such a long time, she found herself suddenly and inexplicably homesick! True, she had been lonely when she first arrived, but gradually in a manner wholly unconscious, she had found her place in the university where she was studying. Her English had improved quickly and she made a few good and close American friends as well as discovered a number of Iranians with whom she could talk. On the whole she had stuck to her plan to learn about things American. For what was she there for, if not to see what it was that made all the talk—of power, of material wealth, of this superior freedom. And Sema was decidedly practical and determined about her future. At twenty-four years of age, she was equipped with advanced knowledge of public health methods and, while this was far from enough for her marriage-conscious parents, she believed it enough for her. For the moment.

As the car sped up Pahlevi Road on its way to the outer suburds Sema observed the unfolding scene—the rows of cypress trees behind which estates and gardens stood silhouetted in the dusk; the new, Western-styled buildings which made her unsure of her location in her own city. Teheran proper had spread out and areas which she had known as small mountain villages were now settled suburbs of the big city.

They were approaching Darband. The Hotel Darband in the middle of the village sent out a diffuse light through which its massive white façade banked by formal gardens could be seen. Coffee and tea were being served on the wide varanda. On either side of the hotel, at a respectable distance, small houses of mud, rock or wood clung to the slops of the mountains. At the foot of the hotel stood an old bus packed beyond any reasonable capacity with humans and their bundles. Waiting patiently to board it stood a group of women in dark, concealing chadhors. Next to the bus was the hotel's parking lot filled with what seemed to be a calculated display of Cadillacs, English sports cars, Volkswagons and a Russian sedan.

The cab had stopped in front of the hotel. The girls got out and followed a number of young women in evening gowns up the steps to the entrance. A uniformed doorman bowed them all into the lobby. Unattended ladies still shocked him; not outwardly, of course. Outwardly he bowed to all, to the foreigners as well as to the Iranians, to the American women who, with shoulders outthrust and cigarettes between gloved fingers, were as self-assured as the men they were with. And this was something the old doorman puzzled over. American men and women were so much alike.

The girls checked their coats and started up the wide stairway. Sema was the taller of the two and her slim black dress made her look even taller. Her white-gloved hands acted as exclamation marks to her quick, nervous speech. Her mother had wept and wrung her hands over her daughter's cropped hair and Sema herself had at first felt uncomfortable—the only female in her family with short hair. But it set off her strong features and she had almost begun to grow fond of her square, broad-bridged nose and overly wide mouth in a Western setting where they did not have to conform to a stamped ideal of Persian beauty. Her present air of sophistication impressed Pari who followed her closely, imitatively.

The girls had met in the States where Pari had spent a bewildering year studying education, methods a few of which seemed applicable to Iran. This did not bother her too much. She had met Sema who, as an old 'American,' already three years in the States, had taken her in hand. Pari, however, remained bewildered. She had now accepted a teaching position and was too busy with classroom problems to apply any of the methods she had learned abroad. This was the first time the girls had met since their home coming and they were celebrating; this was a party of Iranians who had been to America.

At the top of the staircase was a sign which read in Persian and English: "Association of Iranian Students, Returnees from the United States." An arrow pointed in the direction of a large ballroom. When the girls entered, the room was already full of people, some seated at tables around the walls, others standing in small groups, talking. Two giant chandeliers lit the room. The girls looked for an empty table, found one, and sat down. Sema noted the large number of Americans present and then, suddenly, recognized Mehdi. He saw her at the same time and waved. She nodded back and he, leaving his group, made his way towards their table. He had never seemed more carefully American as he greeted her in English. "Heard you were back. When did this happen?"

"Oh, I've been back three weeks. Mehdi, this is a friend of mine, Pari."

Mehdi shook hands. "Wow! Two pretty girls! I will have to introduce you to my friends." The Americanism rang unpleasantly in Sema's ears as she glanced at the table to which Mehdi was pointing. Obviously he meant for her to go there and she hesitated. At the other table were seated, in addition to several young men, two Iranian girls. Pari was already up, and somewhat reluctantly Sema rose. They joined the others, shuffling chairs about, and Sema found herself, not suprisingly, beside Mehdi. He offered her a cigarette and after glancing at it quickly she accepted. One extravagance she would continue, she thought: Persian cigarettes were not for her. Mehdi leaned over, touching her shoulder and Sema smiled and moved aside. Through eyes narrowed by smoke she observed him. His hair was clipped short and gis sports jacket was American. He could almost *be* American, she thought, at least in Iran. Then quickly, to cover her long gaze, she said, "What kind of group is this, Mehdi?"

"A social group. We have only been organized a few months. The idea is to have get-togethers a few times a year so that those of us who have studied in the States can talk over old times. Quite a few Americans come as our guests. In fact, at our first meeting, there were more Americans than Iranians! And," he grinned, "not like the States, there are always more men than women!"

Before Sema could reply she was swept down by Meri, an old friend from the years at the University of Tehran. After more introductions Sema looked around for a chair for Meri and then directed her gaze rather pointedly at Mehdi. He shrugged and got up. With a gesture of exaggerated gallantry he offered his place to Meri.

Meri held Sema at arms length and examined her jocularly but closely. "You have changed much, Sema." She spoke in her careful English. "You never wore makeup in college. And smoking! You always disapproved."

Sema laughed. "That was years ago. You have changed yourself."

209

"And you are half the size you used to be!" Meri's tone was lightly envious.

"I found out so many horrible things about food when I was studying that I almost decided never to eat a Persian meal again!"

"What!" Meri's shocked air was only partially put on. "You were so strictly Persian, Sema. Oh, how I do remember that!"

"I am just as much a Persian now," Meri." And then, to lighten her tone: "But you must not throw back all my old personality traits at me. I have carefully developed new ones and I want to keep them!"

"So! Maybe you have not changed after all. You are as determined as ever!"

"I want to be, Meri. But it is difficult. I mean, to come back after a long time and find that things have not changed much, if at all. And I suppose I had forgotten how they were, partly. It is hard to put aside four years of living a certain way."

"Why should you, Sema? The best of the East and the best of the West. That is what they say. Oh, look, Sema, the food is coming? How I missed *cheloo-kabab*, *khoresh-e-badenjoun* and *mast*!"

Sema knew her words had been stiff and not as she had wished them to be. But somehow the atmosphere irritated her, as did the sound of careful English, so much of it inaccurate. In America she had been so defensive of her country, to the point of a kind of intellectual dishonesty, for she had overlooked, even defended, the very faults she had been the first to criticize when she had been home. "I'm home now," she thought, "and I'm beginning to be annoyed with the same old things—imitation of the West and shame of one's own customs." And yet hadn't she looked forward to this evening? Hadn't she wanted to reminisce about experiences abroad? Why had she come, if

210

not to feel a bond with others who, like herself, had sought education in another country? But she was back home now and there were other things to think about, other than nostalgic tales of American life. At this moment, the years in America seemed so remote, so unreal. And now here was Meri telling her how sorry she was that her own year abroad had been spent almost exclusively in the company of fellow Iranians and how envious she was of Sema's greater initation into ways American, such a good and desirable thing. Sema listened.

In the midst of the talk a waiter appeared and began to set the tables for food. Mehdi, waving his arm, asked, "Now where would you get service like this in the States?" He paused dramatically before pronouncing: "That is one thing Americans do not know about—eating in style and enjoying the taste of food." His tone was proud and his orders to the hurrying waiter brusque, almost rude.

There followed the ordering of food: *cheloo-kebab* with *dukh* to drink. The *dukh* (yogurt and water) was refreshing and it seemed so unlikely to Sema that four years had gone by without having drunk it. She listened to some Americans at the next table talk about the food they were eating with such obvious enjoyment. Oh, they liked it, although they were critical of its fattiness. One even said he'd miss it back home. Sema had missed it, too, and it had taken her a while to get used to the blandness of American food. Apparently she had, for those first days home were as disturbing to her stomach as to her emotions. Now, the richly spiced vegetables and meats were beginning to be acceptable, more readily, she found, than certain customs she had thought to have only temporarily set aside.

Mehdi was asking Pari about her teaching and now turned to Sema. "You may find yourself teaching, too."

"I don't think so, Mehdi. I wouldn't like to give up the

211

idea of working in public health. It means too much to me. And I think it's important that we...."

A small orchestra began to play American dance music and Sema stopped in the middle of her sentence. A few people were on the dance floor, mostly, it seemed, Americans, with a sprinkling of the bolder Iranians. The poeple seated with her watched, Sema felt, with envy. She, too, envied those who danced so casually, so naturally. To be in the arms of a man one hardly knew, to make light, small talk to this man while he held you as closely as he dared, this was a difficult thing to get used to. She had, to some extent, done so, but here she found herself once again feeling strange. She felt, too the tightness and conformity of the group around her.

Mehdi asked her to dance. On the floor he spoke first: "You dance well, Sema. Where did you learn?"

Sema laughed. "Not in Iran, Mehdi. Where did you learn?"

"Oh, Arthur Murray taught me dancing in a hurry."

Mehdi talked on and Sema listened, sometimes trying to contribute to the banter. She was glad when the dance was over. Back at the table she noticed that Pari was dancing, and she had just sat down when she was asked to dance by a man she did not known. An American. She found herself acutely self-conscious and they ended up by dancing silently.

There were a few more dances for Sema, although she would have much preferred to sit and watch. She caught herself checking on the hour a number of times. And there had been so many things she had wanted to talk about—with Meri and Pari, even with Mehdi, but somehow it had not been the time or the place. She wondered about her own confusions and whether they were perhaps more personal than she cared to admit.

At about eleven-thirty the orchestra leader announced the

212

last dance. Mehdi had offered to drive the girls home and, reluctant but tired, Sema accepted for them.

Mehdi was full of chatter during the drive, teasing the girls, making Pari giggle unrestrainedly, but Sema was silent. The restlessness she had felt throughout the evening was still with her. An incompleteness. She was back home, home in Tehran, and she thought again of those last weeks in America when she had ached with homesickness.

The car stopped in front of Sema's house. She got out, said her goodbyes, and as lightly as she could, forstalled a meeting with Mehdi. As she walked past the gate she saw the light on in her mother's room and felt a sharp irritation at the familiar sight. Why, why was her mother up, waiting for her? Why did her whole family seem so anxious about her? As she was closing the door of her room, she heard the click of the light switch in her mother's bedroom. Her mother could now go to sleep— Sema was home. Her heart was pounding unreasonably and she stood for a moment in the darkness before turning on her light.

CHAPTER EIGHTEEN

AT HOME

Sema slept late the following morning. At ten o'clock she awoke, glanced at her clock and turned over, and pulled the covers back over her. Ten hours of sleep had failed to refresh her. A feeling of complete exhaustion seized her whenever she thought of getting up. It hadn't been that way in the States. Was it due to a change of altitude here, she wondered. Or perhaps, she soberly admitted, an inability to face the uncertainty of the days ahead, plagued her. Whatever it was, she didn't want to think about it now. Sleep was what she needed...sleep ...sleep.

Mr. and Mrs. Samidee had had their breakfast long ago. As was his custom, Mr. Samidee had an early breakfast before departing for work. He was a departmental chief in the Ministry of Finance and felt his position important enough to be punctual. His colleagues often joked with him that now as he had an important administrative position, there was no need for him to keep such strict hours. But Mr. Samidee kept to his punctuality.

At breakfast, Mrs. Samidee remarked to her husband, "I'm worried about Sema. Do you know what time she got in last night? Almost twelve-thirty. It's not right for her to be attending those late parties, without someone from the family with her. What will people say?"

"Well, they'll probably say that she's gotten all this foolishness from America," commented Mr. Samidee. "And they're probably right. What good did it do for her to go to the United States?"

Mrs. Samidee agreed: "It would have been much better for her to have stayed at home. She'd be married now, and we wouldn't have any worries. Or at least we should have arranged a marriage for her before she left, for she was so determined to go." Mrs. Samidee shook her head sadly as she reflected on the things that might have been.

"Well, maybe she needs a little time to get readjusted to things here," Mr. Samidee remarked sympathetically. "You know how thin she is. Wait a few more weeks till she gets fattened up a bit on Persian food."

"But that's just it," replied his wife. "She doesn't like our food anymore. She says our *pilo* and *khoreshes* are fattening, and she doesn't want to get fat."

This was new to Mr. Samidee. It was obvious to him that his daughter had not been eating properly in the United States and now here she was refusing the right food. It didn't make sense to him. He looked at his watch, and hastily picked up his briefcase and left the room. In the hallway, he exchanged his house slippers for his street shoes; for it is the usual custom for people to wear slippers whenever at home. He called goodbye to his wife.

Several times during the morning Mrs. Samidee looked in on her daughter to see if she had awakened. A few time Sema was sufficiently awake to be aware of her mother's presence in the doorway, but she gave no sign of stirring. What was the use of getting into another lengthly discussion and possible argument? No doubt her mother wanted to hear of last night's party; and most likely she would be shocked by what Sema said.

215

Not only a generation seperated mother and daughter, but the span of continents. Although Sema was now home in Tehran, her existence was more appropriate to New York. It was as if she lived in two places at the same time: only her physical presence presented itself in Tehran, the rest of her being remained in the States.

Sema's whole orientation was to American life. It had taken her four years to become acculturated to that life, and now she had to unlearn most of it, if she were to achieve contentment in Iran. But Sema, as yet, was not aware of what had happened to her. She only knew that her ideas were different now, and she felt that her present life's values were the real ones. What good would it do to discuss these things with her parents? How could she tell them that she needed more independence and the freedom to live her own life? To say this would only hurt them deeply.

And the truth was that her parents regarded her as the same twenty-year old girl who had left their home four years ago. They recognized the external changes that had occured in their daughter: her thinned figure, her bobbed hair, the exaggerated use of make-up and cigarette smoking. They were even willing to accustom themselves to this; but it never crossed their minds that their daughter had also brought with her changes in attitude. Sema was their daughter, bound to them by blood and by an intimate affectionate relationship built up from infancy, so characteristic of Persian families. It was expected that a child, particularly a girl, should honor and trust the judgment of her parents. Their values should be her values.

About eleven, Sema sat up in bed. Fatigued still, but weary of sleep, she propped herself up with pillows and reached for a cigarette. A few puffs revived her, and she looked about for something to read. On the bedstand was a currently popular

Persian magazine. She picked it up and idly glanced through it. Cheap love stories, and a lot of advertising. It sickened her, and she cast it aside.

Her mother now looked in again, and greeted her daughter cheerfully. "Good morning Sema. I hope you enjoyed the party last night."

"Oh, it was nothing much," Sema yawned; "just a reunion of people who had studied in the States." She obviously didn't care to discuss it further.

Mrs. Samidee wisely decided not to pursue the matter. Rather she turned to other matters. "Your aunt and uncle are coming for lunch today at one o'clock. Would you like some breakfast before then?"

"Oh no, mother, just some tea, thanks." Sema replied.

"Mrs. Samidee went out to get some for her daughter. Sema cautiously crawled out of bed, and looked for something to put on. Regretfully, she passed up her blue-jeans. It would not be the thing to wear when her aunt and uncle came. In fact, her father had been quite shocked the other evening when he found her wearing them about the house, but he'd said nothing right away. Later on that evening he'd asked her if she wanted to drive him to a friends' house and she'd accepted eagerly. Tossing a short topper over her shoulders, she'd stood waiting for him. He'd looked at her in amazement and exploded, "You mean to say you would go outside in these things? Surely, they don't even do that in the United States."

"But Father, all college girls in the States wear blue jeans. There's nothing wrong with them," Sema had protested.

Almost before she'd said it, she'd realized she shouldn't have. Without a word, Mr. Samidee had picked up the car keys and departed sullenly; alone.

Now Sima looked at her clothes, and picked out a casual

skirt and sweater. A pair of low heeled loafers and bobby socks completed the outfit. Her long dark hair was carelessly tied in a pony tail, and she applied just a dash of lipstick. A chance observer wouldn't have recognized her as the suave sophisticate of the previous night. Rather she looked a typical American bobby-sockser.

The morning passed rather quickly, perhaps because there wasn't too much of it. Sema wrote a few cards and letters to friends in the States. There really wasn't too much to say, for as she wrote to her best friend Jean, still at the University:

"I've only been home three weeks, but I'm bored stiff. After you've visited all your family and old friends, what is there left to do? Movies, you say? Ha! The films here are American films several years old. And when you go to them, everyone talks while the English dialogue is on, and waits for the Persian translation to follow. The whole continuity of the film is lost by these interruptions.

Last night, I enjoyed myself for the first time since coming home. I went to a reunion of Iranian students who had studied in the States. Homa and Peri were with me, and we met Mehdi there. He's a real charmer, but too American to be trusted. You know what I mean; he has a line of nice things that he says; but he say them to all the girls.

As for life at home: Mother and Dad just don't understand what America is like. They think a woman's ultimate goal is marriage, and they talk to me about getting married, although I don't think they have anyone in mind for me yet. You know, in Iran marriages are often arranged between families; without too much say-so on the part of the principals.

When I tell my family about my plans for working they look somewhat aghast. From their point of view, it was all right for me to get an education, but to spend my life working is another thing. Still they're willing to let me work a while. And I have high hopes of getting a job in public health, either through the Ministry of Health or through Point Four.

Jean, you'd really be interested in the house we live in. I was away so long, I almost forgot what it was like. We have electricity of course, and my family's gotten a refrigerator since I've been away. No washing machine as yet, and no central heating. Our drinking water is bought from a street peddler, who presumably gets it from

218

the mountains. I still don't trust it, and I have it boiled, just to be sure.

I don't know how I'm going to keep warm this winter. The evenings are already quite chilly lately. And all we have are small portable hand kerosene stoves, although in the living room we have a much larger one. Well, I suppose I'll just have to bundle up in sweaters and slacks. Which raises another problem: my father thinks it's very un-lady-like to wear slacks—so there I am.

But dont' let me give you the wrong impression of my country. I came back, because I wanted to help Iran make progress; and I know that once I start working ,I won't do so much complaining; I'll be doing more accomplishing.

Write soon, and keep me posted on University life.

Love,
Sema.

The doorbell rang and Sema got up to answer it; but the *bahjee* "Nannee" was ahead of her. Sema was still not accustomed to seeing servants about. She never quite knew whether to make her bed and wash and iron her own clothes, as she had done in the States, or whether to give them to Nannee. The first time she had tried it herself, her mother had been startled to see Sema washing clothes. In fact, she'd taken them away and given them to Nannee. When Sema got them back, some of her delicate American fabrics had been harmed by the harsh soap and water treatment of the bahjee. It just didn't seem fair.

Nannee ushered into the living room, Mr. and Mrs. Shahmanee, Sema's aunt and uncle. They kissed her fondly on both cheeks, even though they had seen her several times since her return. She felt somewhat embarrassed by this constant display of affection, but she put up no protest. Mrs. Samidee came into the room and greeted her relatives affectionately. The maid brought in the inevitable cup of tea, always a sign of welcome in a Persian home. Mr. Samidee came home some minutes later, and the family went into lunch. Missing was Nadir, Sema's eight year-old brother. He was away at school today, and usually ate there.

It was a hearty lunch of *bad-en-joun khoresh* (egg plant sauce), *pilo* (rice), *mast* (yogurt) and other things. Sema had always disliked this particular *khoresh*, even as a child; perhaps because it's served so often in Persian homes. Nevertheless she put a little on her plate, and dabbed at it politely.

The conversation centered on a trip that the Shahmanees were taking to Meshed. It was to be a pilgrimage to the Shrine of Imam Reza, the Eighth Imam of the Shi'a Sect. Both Mr. and Mrs. Shahmanee were devoutly religious, as was Sema's mother, but her father much less so. Mrs. Shahmanee proposed, "Why don't all of you come with us. Our children are staying home to study for their examinations, se we have planty of room in our car. It would be so nice for Sema. I remember when she was in high school she said the best graduation gift she wanted was to visit the Shrine of Imam Reza, and somehow she never did." Mrs. Shahmanee turned beemingly to Sema for confirmation.

Sema was startled. It was so unexpected. She searched her mind to recall her high school dreams. "Yes, I guess I was quite religious in high school," she admitted to herself. After entering college, even in Tehran, she had gradually forsaken religious observances and it had been a long time since she had observed daily prayers, visited a mosque, or followed fasts. Everyone was looking at her now, expecting a reply. She knew that she couldn't offend her relatives or her parents, so she replied hesitantly. "It's so nice of you to ask me, Auntie and Uncle. I've always wanted to visit Meshed, and I really wish I could go with you next week. But the truth of the matter is. I have some important appointments to keep, as I'm going to be interviewed about several jobs. I promise that the next time you go, I'll join you for sure."

Everyone was truly unhappy that Sema was denying herself this opportunity to visit Meshed, bu they accepted her reasons unquestionably. Mrs. Samidee mentally protested that Sema was becoming like her father, giving work as an excuse for not going. On the previous two Fridays, Mrs. Samidee had asked Sema to accompany her to the mosque, but each time her daughter had found an excuse for not going. Mrs. Samidee had been hurt but had said nothing.

After some deliberation, Mrs. Samidee was persuaded to accompany the Shahmaness to Meshed. It would be at least a week's trip in all. Sema's mother was worried about how the family would get along without her, but Sema soothed her by saying, "Now, now Mother, it won't be the same with you gone, but we'll manage for the time you're gone. Nannee is here to help, and you'd be surprised how much cooking I learned in America. Maybe I'll even make some pies and cakes whole you're away."

For the first time since her return home, Sema felt a heightened warmth and closeness to her mother. In some small way she would be able to help her mother enjoy a well deserved vacation. At this moment, Sema experienced nostalgically the total impression of all her years in the States: the monthly check that they'd sent her each month and the small homey gifts from time to time. Never once did they complain in their letters of the sacrifices that they were undoubtedly making for her. All they expected from her in return was a weekly letter. But being home now, she knew they expected her to fall into her old patterns of life. Was the price of an education to be conformity and denial of her own self expression.

CHAPTER NINETEEN

INDECISION AND DECISION

The next few days were busy ones for the Samidee family. Sema helped her mother prepare for the journey to Meshed. To the daughter the trip seemed a very casual ordinary occurrence. American oriented as she was, the several hundred miles represented merely a day's journey by car. Sema couldn't understand why her mother viewed the preparations as such a tremendous

To the mother, the trip was of great significance. Primarily, it was a pilgrimage, a reaffirming of one's religious beliefs. As such, it was an important event in Mrs. Samidee's life and one that required enormous planning. There were certain religious articles that she would need: a *chedhor* to wear inside the shrine, prayer beads, and of course, a Koran to protect her on the journey, as well as for reading. Then too, she purchased gifts for the many relatives they would be visiting along the way. And indeed, there were necessary items for automobile traveling in Iran: fruit, nuts and seeds, along with blankets and pillows to make the ride more comfortable. Even then the passangers could expect a great deal of discomfort, Persian roads being what they are: winding, narrow, dusty roads traversing mountains and valleys.

Nor was Mrs. Samidee accustomed to traveling. The family's vacations were almost always spent at their summer residence near Tehran, or occasionally they drove to Damavand, a summer resort a few hours' drive away. Furthermore, the rest of the Samidee family was not going. Mrs. Samidee couldn't help but wonder how her husband and the children would fare without her. She was seldom away from them, and she felt a keen responsibility for them. Sema had assured her several times that she would manage the household in her absence, and of course there was Nannee to do the actual shopping, much of the cooking and cleaning. Still neither Sema nor Nannee, Mrs. Samidee felt, could handle an emergency should one develop. This feeling she conveyed to her husband several times. With casual indifference he tried to reassure her, "Nothing will happen while you're away. If it does, they can telephone me."

With reassurance from all sides, Mrs. Samidee still faced the departure date with both anticipation and hesitation. The day came. Family and friends were at the gate to bid them good-bye. Perhaps it was fortunate that Sema had not planned to come, for little space was left for sitting after all the luggage had been stowed away. Tearfully, Mrs. Samidee fondly kissed her husband, Sema and little Nadir, even Nannee. With school books in one hand, Nadir held on to his father's hand with the other. He shifted from one foot to another anxiously. His mother had told him she would only be gone a week, but here she was crying as if she were departing from life itself. He began to worry and looked up to his father for reassurance. Mr. Samidee sensed his son's anxiety, and whispered comfortingly, "Don't worry. Your mother'll be back soon. You see, she's crying, because she misses you already."

As the car started up, Mrs. Samidee called out last minute reminders to all: "Azem, don't forget to phone the carpenter tomorrow; Sema, pick up the clothes at the dressmakers; Nadir, remember to come home right after school, and obey your sister; Nannee, don't buy any more kerosene until Thursday."

223

Her last words were lost to the wind as the car pulled away. A few minutes before there had been a multitude of people, all talking at once. Now only Mr. Samidee, Sema, Nannee and Nadir were left. All were silent momentarily. Mr. Samidee glanced at his watch, mumbled good-byes and was off; Nadir dashed off in the other direction, forgetting to take his lunch box. Nannee noticed it and picked it up; and went off after the youngster hoping to catch up to him. In it was his noon-day soup, which he would heat up on a stove in school.

Sema went indoors. The house seemed unusually big and depressing. She felt swallowed up in it. All alone, she wondered what to do with herself. She didn't really have many household chores to take care of. Nannee, who had been with the family for many years, was efficiency plus. Sema sat down on the sofa and lit a cigarette. Why was she stalling, she asked herself? For several weeks now, she had been lolling about the house, making all sorts of grandiose plans for working. But always she had found excuses to postpone it. Now that her mother was gone, the time had come. For hadn't she told them all that she couldn't go on the trip because she had job interviews to keep?

She pulled her feet up under her, and lazily blew smoke rings in the air. What was her trouble, she questioned herself? It wasn't the first time that she had gone job hunting. She had had several jobs in the States, but of course, she had gotten them through the University Placement Bureau. She smiled inwardly as she remembered the first day that she had gone hesitantly to Miss Larson's office in Student Personnel. When she had first come to the States she had never thought of working at all. Coming from Iran, she had the idea that work of any kind, especially for a girl, was associated with manual labor. To work, meant to put yourself into the lower class. Yet many of the American girls that she came to know and to admire were paying some of their school expenses by working. Many of them, she learned, were not from the lower class, but from moderate well-to-do families. They had really wanted to work. And what particularly surprised Sema was that they enjoyed their jobs. So much so, that she spent many pleasant hours listening to them relate their experiences.

As time went on, she began to feel a little left out of things. She wondered if she, as a foreigner, might be eligible to work. Her friends encouraged her to visit student personnel. Miss Larson, the director, helped her fill out various application forms and seemed hopeful that she could find something for Sema. In a few days Sema was notified that a job was available in the departmental library: ten hours a week.

The job proved to be a great adventure for Sema. She made many new friends and found that she too had interesting happenings to relate to friends. Not only that, but she became better acquainted with library facilities. Later on, she worked in Student Health, and while there acquired a practical knowledge of first-aid treatment. And of course, not to be forgotten was her monthly paycheck which helped supplement her income from home.

So accustomed was she to the idea of work, that she wrote home a happy report of her experiences in working. Her family was greatly shocked to receive the news and sent her a large sum of money, thinking that acute financial straits had prompted her to take up work. In subsequent letters, Sema tried to explain that it was a custom for American college girls to work. She was never sure that they fully understood.

Now back home, the problem was still present. Her family had taken it for granted that she would be content to stay at home, and help manage the household and entertain, until some suitable marriage was arranged for her. When Sema had first

225

mentioned that she intended to work, her father had reassured her, saying, "Now, Sema, I appreciate your wanting to contribute to the family income; and I know many Persian girls do work these days. But I have a responsible position at the Ministry, as you know, and we have a little property. There's no need for you to work. In a short time you'll be married and have lots of household responsibility. You might as well enjoy yourself now."

Sema had replied somewhat hotly, "But Father, you don't understand. I studied in the United States to train myself to do something useful and to help my country. Now you tell me to sit home and twiddle my thumbs. Maybe I'd enjoy working for a few years, before getting married."

Both parents had been somewhat taken aback by the directness, and yet earnestness of her speech. Her mother pleaded, "But Sema, maybe it was all right for you to work in the States, but in Iran, men don't like to see women working. You'll ruin your chances for a good match."

Sema had become exasperated, "Can't you two see that times are changing? Iran needs well trained people, both men and women. By staying home, I'll helping delay progress. Is that what you want?"

Mr. and Mrs. Samidee acknowledged their daughter's logic, but emotionally they were still tied to traditional views. With a great deal of misgiving, they at last gave their consent to Sema to work, but on a temporary, provisional basis. She would of course, take a job in Tehran, and one in an office. Any job that required her to inspect health facilities in the villages or field work of any kind was out of the question. Sema reluctantly agreed.

Mr. Samidee had offered to find her a position in the Ministry of Finance, but she had refused, saying, "Thank you, Father, but I want to make use of my training in public health."

From these and other statements, Mr. and Mrs. Samidee assumed that their daughter had already made some contacts for getting a job. But the truth was that Sema had no idea of where to start. In Iran there was no vocational guidance bureau to help her get oriented. This was one of the reasons why she dilly-dallied so long in starting.

Now, reclining on the sofa, Sema finished up the last drags on her cigarette. Here she was, and this was the problem: "Where to start?" It faced her in large capital letters. Over and over again, she mumbled half aloud: "Where should I start?"... "Where should I start?"....

"What good is education?" she asked aloud. "Education! that's it," she exclaimed. "I'll go to the Ministry of Education, and see if they can use me in their school health department. Why didn't I think about it before?"

Jumping up, she walked through the house humming a popular tune. There was only one thing to do, and to do it now. That was to phone for an appointment with the Minister of Education. She dialed the number quickly and asked for his office. After being transferred several times, she was able to talk to his secretary. Sema explained, "I'm a graduate student who has just returned from the States, and I wonder if it would be possible to see His Excellency, the Minister."

The strong male voice assured her, "Why, yes, I believe he can see you. By chance, he is free tomorrow morning at eleven. Can you come then?"

For a moment Sema held back. It was soon. She hadn't really thought of what she wanted to say. But she remembered an old American expression, "Opportunity knocks but once." This was her chance, and she knew she must take it. "That would be fine, My name is Miss Sema Samidee. I will be there at eleven."

She had taken the first step now. Tomorrow loomed ahead as a big day, but inwardly she felt an inner glow. It wasn't everyone who had an opportunity to see the Minister, and she felt confident he would be interested in her training and would be able to place her in some school health program.

The closing of the front gate interrupted her day dreams. Peering out the window she saw Nannee returning, empty handed. She had apparently caught up to Nadir and given him his lunch. Poor Nannee! She looked so tired and worn.

Around her waist was knotted the ends of her torn chedhor, which partly covered a faded pair of loose pajama-like trousers. The apex of the chedhor was pulled around her head and could be pulled over her face should she pass a group of strangers, particularly men. On entering the yard, she had let it fall back, revealing straggled hennaed hair, so common among the older generation of Iranian women. Her face was wrinkled in deep furrows and her shrunken chin gave her a grandmotherly air, which accounted partly for her nickname of "Nannee." She was a widow from the small village of Marvana in the south of Iran. When her husband had died ten years ago, she had journeyed to Tehran and had joined the scores of villagers who come each week to the big cities to seek employment. Luckier than most, she had stayed with relatives in Tehran and through them she had met the Samidee family. Mrs. Samidee, having had a succession of servants come and go, had taken Nannee on hesitantly. She was obviously getting along in years and in a few years would be unable to work and thus dependent on the Samidee family for support. Most families who employ servants generally make some arrangement to provide for their servants in old age. Mrs. Samidee could not be choosy, for she had been without a servant for several months. So Nannee became a member of the Samidee household. Among other problems, Mrs. Samidee found it extremely difficult to train Nannee to do things the way she wanted it done. Too often Nannee did things as she had been accustomed to in the village. No matter, how much Mrs. Samidee supervised the kitchen, Nannee always managed to impart her own flavoring to the cooking. There were other problems too: Nannee had a sharp tongue and made no effort to soften it in the presence of her employers. If she disagreed or disapproved of the action of the Samidee family she made it known to them. No one was spared, not even Mr. Samidee. Nadir was most affected, for Nannee had entered the household before he was born. It was she who helped welcome him in the world, and most of the time she had dressed and fed him in infancy. She kissed him in affection, and slapped him in anger. Now that he was at school, he was less under her influence, but she still exercised considerable control. Nannee was stricter with Nadir than his own parents were, and it was she who saw to it that Nadir studied each evening.

Before others, Mrs. Samidee was always quick to cite Nannee's faults; but if anyone had suddenly volunteered to take the aged *bahjee* off her hands, she would probably have retorted, "Oh, no, you wouldn't want Nannee. She's getting old and is slowing down. We'll soon need to get a younger girl to help her. Besides, we've spent a lot of time and effort training Nannee. It would be silly to let her go now."

The truth was that Nannee had changed her ways very little since joining the Samidee family, and it was they who had been trained not she.

So anxious was Sema to relay her good news to someone, that she followed Nannee into the kitchen. "You won't believe it, Nannee, but tomorrow morning I'm going to see the Minister of Education. Without doubt, he'll know of a school health program where I'm needed. Isn't it wonderful!"

Unimpressed by it all, Nannee's only comment was: "Wait and see. The end of *Shahnahmah*[1] isn't in sight yet."

It didn't bother Sema. Since coming home, she had developed new respect for Nannee. Here was an elderly woman who had spent all her life in a small village. Because of need, she had journeyed to the big city and found employment for herself. And it was no easy job. While the rest of the household lived leisurely, Nannee toiled from early morning till bed time. Before she had gone to the States, Sema had never paid much attention to Nannee: she was a kind of fixture in the house, like an electric light, to be there to serve others and subject to their command. In the States, Sema had found that servants were relatively uncommon, and even then they were often day laborers who did a day's work and went about their own business. They had no real interest in or loyalty to the family they served. Lately, Sema had come to feel a certain kinship for the old woman, and she sometimes resented the sharp tones in which her mother treated Nannee. For the first time since she had known Nannee, Sema was interested and curious to learn more of the *bahjee's* life. As an opener, Sema asked, "Nannee, do you have any relatives in Tehran?"

"Oh, I have many nieces and nephews here," she grinned toothlessly. Having found an audience, she then proceeded to enumerate them, one by one, with description of their families, homes and jobs. Nannee talked on and on. Sema moved farther into the kitchen, and took up a paring knife and began cutting up some of the vegetables. Nannee strongly protested, and tried to take the knife out of her hands, saying: "You shouldn't dirty your hands with this rough work. After all, you have lived in America and they don't do that over there."

---

[1] An epic poem of 60,000 verses.

Sema held onto the knife, and tried to explain to Nannee that American women had no servants and worked themselves in the kitchen. Nannee couldn't believe this at all and was sure Sema was jesting. Yet Nannee was secretly pleased and flattered that Sema should want to help out. She was even more amazed when Sema volunteered to prepare the evening meal for the family. "Oh, no Khonem; it is very kind of you to offer to prepare it, but it is not your job in life to cook meals and do such things. Your parents would be very angry with me for even letting you into the kitchen. They didn't send you to America to learn to cook."

There was nothing Sema could say to make Nannee relent. From past experience, Sema knew that when Nannee said "No," she never changed her mind. But circumstances intervened that afternoon. Nannee decided to pay a visit to some sick relatives in the far section of town, and she told Sema that she would be away for several hours, but would return in time to prepare supper. Sema bade Nannee good-bye and gleefully wondered what Nannee's reaction would be when she returned home later. As soon as she had departed, Sema checked the refrigerator and cupboards to see what food was on hand: she found ground meat, potatoes and vegetables, as well as other staples. Sema wanted it to be as American a meal as possible; so she decided on making a meat loaf, roast potatoes and vegetables. There were also ingredients for making a lemon pie. The oven was much less up-to-date than what she had been accustomed to in the States. It was a small portable one that could be set on top of the kerosene stove. Nor did she find all the kitchen gadgets she had used before. Yet determined to carry through her project, she substituted a milk bottle for a rolling pin, and a small cooking pan for a pie tin. There was just enough room in the oven for the meat loaf, potatoes and pie.

Several hours later, when Nannee returned home, the meal was well under way. Nannee entered the kitchen, sniffing the air and asking, "What is this I smell. It's new to me."

"Oh, it's just your supper," teased Sema. And she let her look into the oven. Nannee was completed dumbfounded. She had never thought that Sema really wanted to cook in the kitchen when she had first suggested it. Yet she had gone ahead and done it. The food smelled good, but it looked strange. What would Mr. and Mrs. Samidee say to all this? Nannee was not afraid of them, for she knew she could handle them; but she knew they would disapprove. She shook her head in wonderment and went away exclaiming, "*Khonem* is very talented. She not only knows how to read and speak English, but she can cook American food too." Nannee was obviously pleased, but as was her custom, she hid it underneath her persistent scolding. Secretly she wondered if Sema had spent her time working in the University kitchen, rather than in the library as she claimed. That would explain how she learned to cook.

That evening Mr. Samidee and Nadir sat down to the meal prepared by Sema. When Sema told them she had made the supper, they approached the food with some hesitation. But the first taste won them over, and they complimented Sema again and again. Nannee enjoyed the food too, but her only comment to Sema was, "It's hard to eat such strange looking food."

Yet Nannee vowed to herself that she would learn how to cook these new dishes. It wouldn't do for Sema to become the mistress of the kitchen.

After supper, Mr. Samidee retreated to the study to write some business letters. Nannee came to the doorway of the living room to remind Nadir that it was time for him to study his lessons. With a sight of disgust, he ran his fingers through his wavy brown hair. With his other hand, he yanked the briefcase off the table and spilled out his various schoolbooks on the floor. Throwing himself down beside them, he gingerly sorted them out in neat piles, got up and filled his pen and sharpened several penclis. His usual impish face wore a mask of boredom, and he performed his tasks mechanically with half-closed eyes. From behind a magazine. Sema watched. She was amused by all the subterfuges that Nadir employed in order to delay studying. With a start, she realized she hardly knew her brother. Even though he had grown considerably while she had been away, still he was small for his age. Yet his small size did not prevent him from being an active member of the neighborhood soccer team, as well as a popular student at school. When he applied himself to his studies he did well, but more often than not, he was lazy and avoided studying as much as possible, even with Nannee's prodding. Several times Mrs. Samidee had asked Sema to help Nadir with his English, for this was his hardest subject. Sema had put it off and Nadir had never really come to her for help. Now Sema wondered how she might offer help. Nannee helped solve the problem. Nadir had gone to the kitchen for a glass of water, and came back with Nannee at his heels. "I told you to study your lessons," she declared. "Here your sister is waiting to help you with your English, and you're not even prepared. For shame!"

Nadir looked up inquiringly at his sister. Sema took the cue from Nannee, and remarked, "Bring your English book here. I'd like to see it."

He did as he was told. For the rest of the evening, Sema drilled him on his English pronounciation and spelling. As an extra, she taught him to say a few short phrases and sentences. With a great deal of accomplishment, Nadir went in to say good-night to his father and to show off his skills. Then with many hurried thanks to his sister, he went off to bed.

Mr. Samidee came into the living room to compliment Sema, well as you do."

"You're the first one who's been able to help Nadir with his English. He told me tonight he wants to learn to speak it as

Even Nannee added her thanks, for she was happy that Nadir had had a good lesson that night. Sema was elated by all the day's happenings: her resolution to see the Minister, the appointment, cooking dinner and teaching Nadir. She felt a sense of accomplishment such as she had never felt before.

CHAPTER TWENTY

JOB HUNTING

The early November morning was sunny and crisp, with just a hint of approaching winter. Sema had awakened before the alarm and shut it off in advance lest the noise disrupt her tranquility and flow of thoughts. She was wide awake and eager for the day to begin. The things she wanted to say to the Minister were well in her mind now. In addition, she had written a short formal note giving her reason for wanting to see the Minister. Her father had suggested this, as he had had many years of experience in dealing with government protocol. Sema also had letters of reference from several important government officials in Tehran. She felt confident that the Minister would be impressed by her record and would help place her.

She took a taxi to the Ministry Office and arrived almost twenty minutes before the hour. Poised and confident, Sema felt little uneasiness about seeing such an important man. In her years in the States, she had had many opportunities to meet with the president and deans of the college, as well as other distinguished people who visited the campus from time to time.

The Ministry Building was old but stately. An extensive garden surrounded it and added to the dignity of its surroundings. Sema asked the attendant inside where the office of the Minister was. He gave her the directions, and she found the office without undo difficulty. There were many people in the

235

outer office, and she gave her name to one of the people at a front desk. He went into a second room, and another man then checked her name with a large appointment book. Then he led her into the Minister's office and asked her to wait there. He explained that it would be a half hour yet before the Minister could leave the meeting.

The half hour gave Sema ample time to study the room: it was a moderately large room with several large windows facing an inner courtyard, which Sema surmised was probably a garden in the summertime. A massive desk at one end of the room was piled high with papers of all kinds. The opposite wall was lined with bookcases. It contained mostly fat heavy volumes of documents.

There was a flurry of voices outside the door. Then the door opened and a stout bespectacled man stepped in, followed by several aides, each carrying a sheaf of papers. They deposited them on his desk and stepped out. The Minister turned to her and extended his hand, "Khonem..." he paused and looked at a sheet of paper in his hand... "Khonem Samidee, how do you do?"

Sema acknowledged the greeting and began, "It was very kind of you to give me this time to talk to you. I realize that you're very busy and I don't want to take much of your time."

"Not at all. *Befarmaid* (please)," replied the Minister, although from time to time he glanced at his watch, as if expecting another appointment.

Sema continued, "Several weeks ago I returned from the States. Now that I'm back in Iran, I would like to put my training to use. My first thought was that I might be able to participate in your school health program."

"What did you study in America?" he asked.

"Public health, primarily. I also had some work in nutrition."

"And how long did you study there?"

"About four years," Sema answered. "I have my master's degree from an American university."

The Minister suggested politely, "Perhaps it would help if you wrote out a summary of your background and sent it to us. Then we'd be better prepared to help you."

Sema was quick to reply, "I've already done that, and I have it with me, along with several letters of recommendation."

She took them out of her purse as she was speaking, and handed them to him. He glanced through them and said, "Everything seems in good order. I'll be glad to give you a referral to our personnel director, Mr. Kargozin." He wrote out a note: "This is to introduce Miss Sema Samidee who has had training in public health. She has a summary of her educational background, as well as letters of reference. Please advise her and help her apply for any existing positions, in accord with personnel policies."

He handed it to her, and then stood up and offered his hand. The interview was obviously at an end, and Sema thanked him for his kindness. Outside his office, she asked the way to the Personnel Office. It was a short distance down the hall. At the doorway, a guard was posted. On inquiring, Sema learned that Mr. Kargozin sees poeple only before eleven. The man suggested she come early the following morning and at that time she might get a chance to see him. The personnel director was a very busy man. To make an appointment would take several weeks. Sema nodded and agreed to his suggestion.

The following morning Sema arrived at the personnel office, promptly at eight. It was already filled with people. When she inquired about seeing Mr. Kargozin, a secretary informed her that he was at a meeting with the Minister and would not be free until ten. From ten to eleven he would have time to see his regular appointments, and others, if time permitted. Sema sat down to wait. Looking about her, she saw some other people standing near-by, obviously waiting to see the personnel director too. Listening to their conversation, she learned that one of them wanted to be transferred to another district, and several were seeking promotions. Still others were job hunters, just as she was. She was well aware of the fact that the Ministry of Education is the only ministry that can take an additional employees. In the other ministries there is a surplus of workers, and employment is frozen at the present level.

Time passed slowly for Sema. Only 8:30. Then another long period: 9:00. Waiting...waiting. At 9:30, she left, having decided to return the following day.

The next day she again arrived early. As she entered the lobby, she heard some one address a man near-bye: "Good morning, Mr. Karzogin."

Looking in the direction of the voice, she saw a man of slight build, briefcase in hand, acknowledge the greeting with a curt nod. Sema hurried after him, and caught up to him as he started up the stairs to the second floor. "Excuse me, Mr. Kargozin," Sema intruded hesitantly. "I've been trying to see you for several days."

"Yes, yes, what is it?" asked the personnel director in an annoyed manner.

As briefly as possible, Sema outlined her need for employment in the Ministry of Education. When they reached his office door, he metioned for her to follow him to his office. There he asked her to sit down. He pulled a box of cigarettes from her drawer and offered her one. The cigarettes were a Persian brand, and Sema politely refused. With a direct, straightforward manner. Mr. Kargozin began: "Khonem, you have received a very good education in the United States, but the only way that the Ministry of Education can employ you is as a high school English teacher. There's a need for them in the provinces. Even that can't be arranged now, because the school year has already started. Later on, your request will have to go through the Office of Provincial Education. If you want to apply for a similar job in Tehran, you should apply through the Office of Education for Tehran."

"But I don't want to teach English," protested Sema. "I spent several years studying public health in the United States."

"My dear young lady," he addressed her in a condescending manner, "just what do you think your training in public health qualifies you to do? If you didn't want to teach, why did you come to the Mininstry of Education? Wouldn't it have been better for you to have gone to the Ministry of Health?"

Sema too was annoyed, and forgetting her tact and restraint, she replied, "I came here because I thought I could participate in your school health program. And the Minister of Education led me to believe that you would help me to apply for such a job. Apparently, your office doesn't accept the suggestion of the Minister."

"Amazing, Miss, amazing," exclaimed the director. "I thought you were familar with the procedure of the Ministry. When the Minister writes "in accord with personnel policies" he means just that. According to Civil Service Law, Article 25 the Minister of Education can hire only teachers, and that of course means teachers who have been educated through Iran's National Teacher's College."

Provoked and exasperated, Sema made no further comment. She stood up and said crisply, "You were kind to give me this time. Good-bye."

Outside the office, she paused momentarily, undecided what to do next. Infuriated and worn out from her recent encounter, she decided to postpone her visit to the Director of Education for the Tehran District.

In the following week, Sema made efforts to see Mr. Jamal, the Director of Education in Tehran. She had as much difficulty seeing him as she had had the other officials. Yet he proved to be kinder and more interested in helping her. But even his pleasant manner could not hide the fact that he too had nothing concrete to offer Sema. He was willing to hire her as an English teacher for the following fall, provided she had her university credentials evaluated by the Council on Education. On their recommendation, she could then be given a job. With polite thanks, Sema shook hands with him and left.

Walking down the street, she stared at passers-by in an angry, hostile manner. Suddenly one of them caught her eye: it was Hoori, an old school chum from the States. They greeted one another warmly, and stopped to chat a moment. Hoori asked, "What are you doing these days?"

"Oh, job hunting," lamented Sema. "Being a graduate of an American university seems to be more of a handicap than a help."

"Yes, I know how it is," sympathized Hoori. "It took me three months to get my diploma evaluated, and then they couldn't offer me much of a job. Fortunately, I found a job with the USIA Library in Tehran. It fits in well with my major in Library Science."

There were many things that Sema wanted to ask Hoori, but she sensed that Hoori was in a rush, so she suggested, "Why don't you come over to our home for tea this afternoon? I'm having some other friends in, and I'd really like to talk to you more."

Hoori accepted the invitation, and the two friends went their separate ways.

240

Sema went home about lunch time. Her mother had written them from Meshed. She seemed to be enjoying her visit there. Only Sema and her father were present at lunch this day. He noticed her moodiness and remarked, "You're eating even less than usual, these days. What seems to be the matter?"

"Job-hunting trouble," complained Sema. "I'm ready to give up the idea of working all together, I'm so discouraged." She explained her recent encounters at the Ministry of Education.

"Well, that's what you have to expect here," answered her father. "Iran isn't like America. Everything takes times here. While you're waiting for your academic records to be evaluated, why don't you try some of the American agencies. And if none of it works out, I may be able to find you a job in our department," he suggested encouragingly.

Sema was grateful to her father for his words of encouragement. She resolved to talk to Hoori about American employment possibilities in Tehran.

About five o'clock Sema's guests started arriving. Many of them were Persian friends she had known in the States. Hoori brought another girl whom she introduced to Sema as Soria. Sema learned that Soria was working in public health in a new organization that had just been organized in Iran by WHO in cooperation with the United States and Iran. Sema was eager to learn how she had obtained her job. Soria told her that she had previously worked with ICA and had transferred to the new set-up when it was first announced. She suggested that Sema try ICA first.

Sema related to her friends her frustrating experiences at the Ministry of Education. Everyone nodded. It was nothing new to any of them. All of them had similar experiences to relate. Many of them were now employed by American agencies, and they shared the view of one girl who declared, "It's not the

241

job that I really wanted, but it came through the fastest."

Sema wanted to know more about American agencies in Iran. She asked Tooba: "What kind of problems are there in working for American agencies?"

"Well, I don't know about all the agencies," Tooba responded. "But I work in the administrative section of the University. Part of it has been organized by an American university, and many people consider it the best American operated agency in Iran. On the other hand, I can tell you it has made plenty of mistakes too. For instance, the American staff that they've sent over to Iran to teach Administration is hopelessly unfamiliar with the specific administrative problems that we have in Iran. They think they can directly apply American principles to Iran. It just isn't so."

Hoori joined the conversation and added, "I've heard rumors that they're in somewhat of a predicament. They're short of money and they need funds from the American government to continue. As it is, they've had to bring over second-rate professors. They'd never consider hiring as teachers Iranian professionals who've studied abroad—except as interpreters. Then to make it appear that they're graduating a lot of students, they've even hired private tutors for the slow ones."

"Well, anything for money," commented Soria. "From what I've seen of Americans in Iran, they seem, for the most part, to be money grabbers. Many of them were probably misfits in their own culture, and they've come to Iran to take advantage of the situation. At last they feel that they've gotten a chance to succeed, and they're determined to make the most of it while here. Their goal is to Americanize all Iranians. Their way is always the right way."

"That's true," agreed another girl. "In that way they're like the British. In fact, both Britain and American have encouraged

242

islik e and distrust by bringing in economic and military aid But there's a difference too. The English didn't bother investing much in the country at all, they just took out oil and whatever they needed. The Americans want to pay for it, in terms of economic aid; but they bungle the situation so, that the result's the same: antagonism and dislike."

Sema finally succeeded in putting in a few words, "Don't forget that the well of Iranian society is dry these days, and no one from above can make it a well simply by pouring buckets of water in it. And that's what American aid is doing. What about Iran itself? How do you think our own Ministry of Education functions? After weeks of running from one office to another, they still refuse to recognize my diploma in public health. They'd prefer to hire me as an English teacher, and thus I'm rated as less than a professional teacher with a salary of 3000 rials a month ($40). Can you blame Americans for this too?"

"Yes, yes," they all acknowledged, "Iran has problems too."

It was time to serve tea. Sema brought it in, along with many cakes, pastries and other sweets. There was a piano in the house, and one of the girls played many popular American tunes and they all joined in. Except for that, everything else was Persian: the other household furnishings, the food, and even the enjoyable custom of tea-time. As the guests took their leave, one by one, Soria suggested to Sema that she come and visit her at work the next day.

The following day, Soria took her around and introduced her to several WHO and ICA officials. They gave her application blanks to fill out, but warned her that it might be several months before there would be an opening in her field. One of the Americans suggested she temporarily teach English at the ICA Language Center.

Skeptical as she had become, Sema didn't want to rely on the promises of any one agency. She went from one American agency to another: from ICA to NEF, then to CDO, PAD, IAA. It took several more weeks to see all these people. And then she had to wait, occasionally filling in time by teaching evening courses in English at ICA.

Then one day she received a telephone call. There was an opening in ICA's Public Health Organization, as an assistant to the public health director of Tehran. It paid 10,000 rials a month ($135.) and Sema was delighted to accept. Her job hunting days, at least for the present, were over.

CHAPTER TWENTY-ONE

SOCIAL AWARENESS

Mid-December is often cold in Tehran. There is little snow, but the wind never seems to tire. Loose shutters beat a sharp staccato against the outside of the house, and the noise of it is a constant reminder of the gusts outside. Everyone is glad to be indoors. Of course, the heating systems in Persian houses are never as adequate as those in the States: there is no central heating, and kerosene and oil stoves are not satisfactory substitutes, especially for those accustomed to American ways. Sema would have been the first to acknowledge this. On this particular morning, she awoke before the alarm. She turned it off and blissfully pulled the covers up over her head for a few minutes more of sleep. There was no fear of oversleeping this morning. Today would be her first day on the job, and she was eager to begin.

Sema dressed with care, "First impressions are so important," she reflected. She knew exactly what she would wear, for she had given it careful thought. She slipped the skirt over her head, buttoned the tiny jacket of her trim gray tweed suit. A touch of white at the neckline femininized it and accentuated her dark eyes and hair, and slender figure. Black suede shoes and bag, white gloves completed her ensemble. Her long black hair had been carefully set in a chignon, and it made her look older and more sophisticated than her years.

245

Breakfast consisted of a cup of Nescafe and some coffee rolls. Sema still found it difficult to drink tea for breakfast, or to eat the thin slabs of bread that most Persian families have for the first meal of the day. With a hurried good-bye and a kiss for her mother, Sema left for the office. It was just seven minutes to eight when she arrived there, far more punctual than most. Her immediate boss was Dr. Jenkins, a youngish man whose receding hair line made him look older than his years. He was an American doctor of public health. He took her around and introduced her to the Americans and Persians whom she would be working with. Many of the Americans were interested to hear that she had studied in the States, and asked her about her various activities there. The Persians were also friendly to her.

The job was all important to Sema. For the first few weeks, she concentrated hard on it, and tried to learn all she could of the functioning of the organization. But as time wore on, she discovered that her own participation was relatively unimportant in the over-all working. Not only that but the organization itself was ill-equipped to handle the problems of public health in Iran: in terms of adequate medical staff, laboratories, drugs and programs for educating the public. On the whole, however, she felt herself in a friendly environment and there was little formality in the relations of the senior and junior staff. Even though she could not put all her training into practice, still she was satisfied that she was accomplishing something.

Quite often the staff went out to lunch together, frequently at the Iran-America Society; and from time to time there were staff parties at the homes of the American staff members, as well as Iranian homes. Sema herself entertained some of her newly acquired American and Iranian friends at tea in her own home.

Two months later, during the Noo-Ruz holidays, the office

246

decided to hold a picnic in the countryside, just outside of Tehran. It was the job of the girls in the office to plan the cooking. Because there were so few girls on the office staff, especially Iranian girls, the responsibility of planning for the food fell to Sema. She wanted the party to be a huge success, and to be sure that everyone would enjoy it, she unobtrusively surveyed the food likes and dislikes of the entire staff, and planned a menu that would have something tasteful and appealing for all, both Persians and Americans. With the American girls on the staff, she planned a menu of hot dogs, hamburgers, baked beans, tossed salad, potato chips, soft drinks and beer to please American appetites; and *boghelee pilo*, yogurt, and *dukh* for the Persians.

The men in the office decided on a favorable site for the picnic and arranged transportation for all. It was a family affair, and wives and children joined in. There was enough food prepared for twenty people.

The picnic was held in a lovely grove of trees near AbeAli, famous in winter as a skiing resort. Near by was a small stream. The American children had brought their baseball bats and balls and they had a great deal of fun teaching some of the Iranian children how to play the game. The adults were busy carrying food packages from the car to the picnic site. In the midst of all this preparation, a servant arrived from a farmhouse in the vicinity. He brought several carpets with him, as well as a samovar for preparing tea, and he graciously offered them to the guests for their use. Such is Persian hospitality!

The men helped spread the carpets out, and then a small charcoal fire was built to heat some of the food. Meanwhile, one of the Persian men unpacked his *santur*, an old Iranian musical instrument, resembling in appearance and tone, a zither. He sat down on the rug and plucked out several Persian melodies,

247

apparently familiar ones; for several Iranians joined in singing. At times the melody seemed lost to Western ears, and even dissonant. Another of the Iranians present, was by nature a talkative fellow and given to story-telling. He soon had an audience of both Americans and Persians around him, as he narrated some of the adventures of Mullah-nasra-din, a sly, clever wag who always manages to be victorious, whether in social or political encounters.

As delicious as the food was, it seemed to take second place to the merry-making and joking that went on. One of the Americans had brought a guitar and he led the singing of many old American favorites. The Iranians who had studied in the States joined in the singing of such oldies as "You are My Sunshine," and "Stardust."

With much encouragement, some of the Persian girls agreed to perform some Persian dances, which they did very gracefully. Sema did not join in, either because she had forgotten how to do the dances, or because she felt embarrassed. Perhaps it was a bit of both.

With the setting of the sun, the merry-makers packed up their belongings and headed back to town. Everyone agreed that the picnic had been a giant success.

For Sema too it had been a very pleasant Friday outing. When she arrived home her family was waiting to have supper with her. Although they didn't directly say so, they had obviously missed her. Her mother described how quiet their day had been, and how much effort she and Nannee had put into preparing Sema's favorite chicken *pilo* for supper.

Since she had started to work for the American agency, Sema had divorced herself more and more from her own family's activities. Her lunch was usually eaten away from home, in the company of her co-workers at some place close to the office.

Whereas her father worked Iranian government hours of eight to two, Sema worked eight to five, five days a week. In the evenings, she was often invited to the homes of friends.

Her return to Iran had also stimulated her interest in women's rights. There were many women's organizations that she wanted to know more about, such as the Women's Club of Tehran, the Red Cross, the Women's Social Welfare Organization, and other charitable groups. She readily accepted their invitations to speak before them. Most of these women's organizations got their start in the last decade, shortly after Reza Shah banned the wearing of veils by women. However, these groups act rather passively in the cause of feminine rights, as Sema soon discovered. Yet she wanted to be a member of the Women's Club of Tehran, the most active of the groups. One of the members, an old school chum, nominated her for membership. She was accepted.

In her acceptance speech, Sema spoke out strongly, and declared, "It is a great honor for me to become a member of your organization. Just a few years ago, it would not have been possible for any woman to have joined such an organization. Now we are free to do so. But that does not mean that everything is won, it is only the first step. The next step, and it is a big one, is for women to gain the right to vote. Iranian law makes it possible for an illiterate man to vote, but denies the same privilege to an educated woman. Is this kind of law just? Perhaps some of you, raised in a very religious family, may say that it is contrary to Islam for women to have such a privilege. This is only a weapon used by fanatic Moslems. Tell them to show me the passage in the Koran, if they can. You women here are the educated women of Iran, and it is you who must lead the way."

Sema sat down amid a flurry of applause. Mrs. Narzam, the

chairman remarked: "All of us were inspired by Miss Samidee's speech. Several of our members have questions they would like to ask our speaker."

One of the older members of the group, Mrs. Bandi, rose to her feet, and haltingly framed her question: "Miss Samidee, women in America are different than Iranian women. They act like men, and at times want to take over the role of men; but in Iran we still want to be women." (Gentle laughter greeted her statement, but there was also an affirmative nodding of heads.) "Therefore if we fight actively for the rights of women, we will lose our femininity, and we will be rejected socially. Have you forgotten the popular song that came out a few months ago called 'Let the Women be the Legislators'? It has caused a great deal of discredit to our group. Don't you see that we must work slowly and let public opinion be the instigator in getting us our rights."

Sema stood up, incited and aroused by these words. "No, I do not believe that passivity is the way to make progress. Let them sing their songs; in time they will completely forget about it and accept the situation as a natural one. Remember, a few years ago there was another song: "Beware of the Woman Who Drives.' And yet women did learn how to drive, and now everyone takes it for granted. Activity, not passivity, should be our guide."

There were other questions asked, but of lesser importance. Sema's response to the first one aroused such a great deal of feeling, pro and con, that little attention was paid to the regular affairs of the club. At the close of the meeting, Sema had acquired recognition, both favorable and unfavorable. "Well, at least, they're thinking about these things; whether they accept what I say or not. That's the important thing," reflected Sema.

This meeting had stirred up Sema too. She felt strongly motivated to contribute more to the problems of her sex. In conversations with her fellow club-women, she hit upon the idea of starting a magazine for women alone. In her wistful thinking, she called it 'Health and Happiness.' But the idea was shortlived. When she applied for a license at the Ministry of Education, she was told that the publisher must be at least 30 years of age. She was not yet 30, and so it was out of the question. However, one of the officials at the publication office suggested that she speak to Mrs. Kamandar, the editor of *Banavan Iran* (Iranian Women).

Some time before, Sema had written an article concerned with the development of women's rights in different countries. It was really an elaboration of ideas she had presented in speeches before various club meetings. With this manuscript in hand, she sought out Mrs. Kamander and introduced herself. The editor of *Banavan Iran* was a heavy-set robust woman in her early 50's. She wore a tailored black suit, and her hair was severely parted in the center and pulled back in a knot at the nape of her neck. Her features were strongly drawn: a prominant nose, full lips that might have relaxed more, and an intense gaze that made some people ill at ease. Mrs. Kamandar had heard of Sema's speech before the Women's Club and was immediately interested in knowing more about the young girl. She accepted the manuscript willingly and promised to read it at her earliest convenience.

About a week after this initial encounter, Mrs. Kamandar telephoned Sema at her office and invited her to tea at her home. Sema accepted, and was inwardly thrilled at this honor, for she had learned that Mrs. Kamandar was a leading member of several important organizations, especially the Iranian Blue Cross, where she served on the executive committee.

The home of Mrs. Kamandar was in the better section of Tehran. It had a large garden, and was surrounded by many trees. Inside, the house was elegently furnished with art objects from abroad, especially Europe. Sema noted that the tea service was English, the china German and the tea was an Indian variety but brewed in the Persian manner. Mrs. Kamandar served her many Swiss chocolates. Mrs. Kamandar had read the article thoroughly and complimented Sema on the material and her style of writing. She promised to publish it in a fortcoming issue of the magazine.

Sema's hostess was eager to learn more about her guest's background and training, and Sema was more than willing to have an audience. She explained how she had been influenced to study something that would be serviceable to her country when she returned. She was interested in health, but did not want to be involved in direct medical practice as a doctor or nurse. Public health seemed the answer. Mrs. Kamandar inquired, "And what have you been doing since you returned to Iran?"

"I've had a job of looking for a job," quibbed Sema. "It took me a long time to find my present job in the American Public Health Organization."

"And how do you find it?" asked the older woman.

"Well, it could be more stimulating than it is," responded Sema.

"And how is that?"

"What I mean is, it doesn't give me an opportunity to deal with public health problems directly. I'm merely an office worker, rather far removed from the actual problem. I guess, the work isn't as glamourous as I imagined."

"Yes, I see what you mean," commented her listener. She paused and smoked her cigarette thoughtfully. "How would you like to be more actively involved in public health?" She didn't even wait for an answer, but continued, "The Blue Cross needs a person with your background to serve on its committee for emergency aid. Would you like me to suggest your name to the executive committee?"

252

Now Mrs. Kamandar waited for an answer. "Why, yes, I would be honored to become a member," answered Sema trying to keep the excitement out of her voice. The Blue Cross was *the* organization in Iran, to which all the important social leaders belonged.

Mrs. Kamandar was true to her word. At the next executive board meeting, she presented Sema's name, fully expecting the committee to welcome the presentation as a gift from Heaven. But she was mistaken, for the other committee members expressed grave concern that Sema was an American graduate. One of them echoed the feelings of the group when he said, "American graduates do not have the same respect for authority and tradition that the European trained graduates do. What assurance do we have that she won't try to dominate the group and tell us all what to do?"

Het sponsor smiled a little to herself, but she realized that Sema, with her recently acquired training in public health and her enthusiasm for promoting change, might seriously threaten the out-moded and forgotten beliefs of the older members of the committee, most of whom had been trained in Europe. She too had been trained there, but she had grown along with the times, perhaps because her children were all attending American universities and she was pleased with their progress. However, she was now careful to acknowledge the opinions of her colleagues, "Friends, a young woman such as Miss Samidee can never really influence the over-all planning of the Blue Cross Committee. Rather, she is a specialist in one small area that is called upon the do very specific jobs at the request of the executive committee."

Mrs. Kamandar was able to put them at ease, and Sema was elected as a member of the committee for emergency aid. Needless to say, Sema was thrilled, and for a while it overcame some of the disappointment she was finding in her job.

At the Office of Public Health there were several sore spots that irked Sema. Mostly it concerned her own social status in the organization. On the one hand, she discovered that many American wives of American personnel were working in public health. With no training in that field and often with little college education, they were earning three times as much as she. Those Americans who had a master's degree in public health were earning ten times as much. On the other hand, there were Iranian girls hired as clerks and typists who earned almost as much as she. Even they resented the fact that her salary was more than theirs. All in all, it was a highly unsatisfactory situation for Sema, but she was reluctant to speak to any of her bosses about it, for fear she would lose the job entirely. And so she drifted into boredom, coming to work late and leaving early. Whatever interest she had in public health was now delegated to the Blue Cross, where she served as a vigorous volunteer member of the emergency aid committee.

CHAPTER TWENTY-TWO

THE CALL OF DUTY

In October, a severe flood occured in Kashan, south of Tehran and close to Isfahan. It had already ruined several villages, and threatened to engulf more. To meet the crisis, all medical and social organizations in Iran were sending supplies of food and clothing to the stranded families. The Blue Cross and the Ministry of Health, aided by American supplies from the Public Health Organization, sent medical supplies and equipment. Several officials from Sema's office were dispatched to survey the damage and make suggestions to the Iranian government for alleviating some of the destruction.

The emergency aid committee of the Blue Cross stepped up its meetings until there was almost one scheduled for every day. Sema was very much involved in its activities, and her advice was sought by all. About a week after the flood had been in progress, Mrs. Kamadan approached Sema and asked her if she would be willing to go to Kashan and help direct some of the relief work that was needed there. For the first time since she had returned to Iran, she felt really needed; and she accepted without hesitation. But she realized she would have some difficulty persuading her parents, for she had promised them long ago when she first started to work that she would never leave Tehran as part of her job. Yet the seriousness of the flood situation had impressed all of Tehran, including Mr. and Mrs.

Samidee. They knew of Sema's participation in the Blue Cross, and they were openly proud of their daughter's acceptance into such a national group. When she told them that she had been asked to go to Kashan by the Blue Cross, they expressed concern for her own health and welfare. But they knew she was needed there and they let her go.

Sema did not have much time to pack. In a few hours, a sturdy station-wagon was scheduled to pick her up at the Blue Cross Headquarters. She knew she would be away several weeks, perhaps more. There would be no fancy parties or need for frivolous clothes. Her American tailored slacks and blue jeans were the main-stay of this wardrobe; and she was singularly glad she had no discarded them as her father had asked her to do. Warm shirts, sweaters and socks, as well as sturdy shoes and boots were all carefully packed away in her suitcase.

With hasty farewells and promises to write, Sema hurried off to the Blue Cross Office. She had come and gone in such a short time that her family had not yet gotten accustomed to the fact that she would be away from home for several weeks; or it's likely that Mrs. Samidee would have cried still more.

The Blue Cross transport left at ten that evening and drove all night. Her companions were two physicians, two nurses and a public health doctor, as well as the driver. There was little time for talk: the medical supplies that they were carrying had to be checked carefully and packed in water-proof containers. Sleep was precious, and everyone dozed throughout the night. At day-break they neared the flood-swept areas. As they looked out the car windows, they saw acre after acre of farm land under-water; only the roofs of houses were visible in some places. In others the gushing torrents of flood-made rivers had uprooted buildings and carried them downstream. Here and there were the carcasses of animals swept ashore. The road was filled with

256

foot-weary travelers, men, women and children all fleeing the flood; but going nowhere. Small babies were carried low on their mothers' backs in slings made of cloth or blankets. It was a pitiful scene, and the human caravan often signaled the car to stop and give aid to them. The Blue Cross team was tempted many times to stop and administer to the sick and wounded, but they had been told to proceed directly to Kashan where the damage to property and life were reported to be the greatest. Many times the roads had been flooded too, and the small truck strained and pushed its way forward. A few bridges had been washed out and it was necessary to make detours around them. At last they arrived at Kashan, which ordinarily is a moderate sized, prosperous city. Now there were few buildings intact in the whole city. Some of the municipal and government buildings had survived the swirling waters, and the school was one of them. An emergency first aid station had been set up there, and the other municipal buildings served as hospitals for the badly injured. Sema's team had been ordered to proceed to the first aid station and relieve the other Blue Cross Group who had been on almost constant duty for ten days. Blue Cross units from other cities were also participating in the relief program. The doctor in charge of Sema's team suggested that during the day they all work in pairs; at night, they would have to sleep on a split shift arrangement, each one sleeping only half the night, from 10 to 6.

Dr. Aszan, the public health doctor, set out to tour the damaged areas. He suggested that Sema accompany him. Sema put on over her shoes, high rubber boots, and bundled up in her warm nylon jacket that she had once used for skiing in the States.

It was still early morning, and not everyone had risen. In the higher levels of the city, the inhabitants had made all kinds of

257

make-shift shelters in an effort to keep warm and dry. But this was impossible: rain blew in through the cracks of the hastily constructed huts, or heavy winds ripped the sides and roofs loose. There was little fuel to begin with, and what there was, was completely wet. Occasionally, some families resorted to burning animal dung, although even that was scarce; for most animals had perished in the early days of the flood.

The fortunate refugees of the flood had been able to find some sort of shelter, but there were many less fortunate who roamed the streets, ill-clad and ill-fed for such an occasion. Their scanty clothing was badly torn, and hardly appropriate for the chilly winds that blew about them. Some had shoes, but what shoes they were! For the most part, they consisted of pieces of cloth or wood tied round their feet. It made walking of any kind difficult, not that these people had either energy to move, or a destination to go to. Groups of people huddled close to one another, in any kind of semi-enclosure where the winds were less likely to penetrate. There were men, women and children: no one had been spared. Everyone wore his full share of clothing; that is, whatever he possessed, and usually that wasn't very much. Many women had wrapped several chedhors about them, in a futile effort to keep warm. Small children clung to their mothers' skirts, and the tiniest ones hardly able to stand, often hid under the loose flapping robes.

These were the scenes that Sema witnessed as she walked about the city with Dr. Aszan. Her face was contorted with anguish as she gazed upon the misery of the people around her. They all looked so hopeless and forlorn. What could she do for them she asked herself?

Dr. Aszan seemed to sense her thoughts, for he remarked, "It's a pitiful scene, isn't it. It's not just a few people, but thousands. All over the countryside it's like this. Makes you want to do something, but you ask yourself, 'What can a few people like us do to relieve the misery and unhappiness of so many?' Then I think of all the sickness and ill-health that has just begin, as a result of the flood. Dysentery, typhoid and all sorts of intestinal troubles that result from poor sanitation and malnutrition. And the children are the first to suffer. This isn't the first flood scene I've witnessed, but it still affects me the same way as when I first came to help out. Well, there's work to be done. Let's get back to the school and see how much progress is being made there."

The school building was filled to overflowing with semi-invalid people, many aged ones along with those who had been injured in one way or another, as a result of the flood. They were not ill enough to be hospitalized, and yet hardly able to fend for themselves on the outside. Some sat about on wooden benches, others squatted on dirty rugs or stood in doorways. A meager breakfast of tea and bread had been served to them. Food supplies were low and rations were being kept to a bare minimum, even for the public health staff. As yet, no food supplies had been distributed to the homeless thousands on the outside, although shipments were expected in the next few days. Sema and Dr. Aszan went into the make-shift kitchen, and helped prepare tea and bread. They also supervised the boiling of drinking water to which some chemicals were added, for it was vitally important to prevent the spread of disease.

After a hasty breakfast, Sema went out to the municipal buildings which served as temporary hospitals. One usually thinks of a hospital as clean, orderly and functional. By these terms then, one would hardly have called these structures "hospitals." Improvised litters with the sick and dying lined the halls. Sheets of any kind were not to be seen. Most of them were lucky if they were covered with a blanket, quilt or even coat of some kind. As she walked down the hall, a chorus of moans and out-stretched arms, as well as feeble attempts to call out 'Help me' followed her. In the upper floors of the building were housed the more serious cases. Pneumonia, typhoid, severe dysentery and diphtheria were common. There were also some cases of people who had been injured severely as a result of falling beams when buildings collapsed. It was obvious that medical services were terribly understaffed. Sema spied one of the nurses who had accompanied her on the way down. She greeted her, and asked if she could help with some of the medical care. The nurse still hadn't had time to get breakfast, and she asked Sema to relieve her while she was away. Awkwardly, Sema began to move from bed to bed, bathing the ill and tending to their needs as best she could. She had always been slightly squeamish at the sight of blood and open wounds, so she tried not to look at their injuries. Yet their helplessness and pain tore open her heart, if not her eyes. She soothed their feverish brows and tried to make them comfortable. Sometimes a pleading mother would beg, "Try to find my family and tell them that I'm here. What's become of my children? I need them here with me." Or at other times, a child cried out in helplessness, "I want my mother. Bring her to me."

The nurse returned from breakfast with the news that Dr. Aszan was looking for her. Sema hastened back to the school-house, where she found the doctor making an inventory of supplies and also drawing up plans to improve the sanitation of the hospital. He greeted Sema and made several suggestions to her, sandwiched-in between remarks to the various workmen about him, "Miss Samidee there's an urgent need to get this inventory of supplies finished and sent back to Tehran. Also you'll have to closely supervise the kitchen to see that food rations are used wisely and sparingly. It would also be a good

260

idea to talk to some of the village leaders and tell them that we could use the help of some of the local people, especially carpenters, electrical workers, etc."

Sema listened carefully to what he was saying, asked several questions, and then left to carry out his requests. The inventory took the rest of the morning. She checked the kitchen supplies, had a hasty lunch and left the hospital grounds to search out some of the village leaders. She particularly wanted to speak to the major and some of the important merchants and farmers in the area. Most of these people were comparatively well off. Their houses had been of sturdier construction and had stood the flood pretty well. They had taken in as many relatives and friends as their houses could possibly hold. At one merchant's house, Sema was greeted very cordially and offered tea and fruits and sweets. She accepted the tea, but politely refused the other things knowing that their food rations were probably low too. Everyone was anxious to know the full extent of the damage and what was being done to repair the blighted areas. She told them what news she had, and then asked them to cooperate with the relief staff. If they were at all talented in construction work, or knew of someone who was, then they could help hasten the return to normalcy. Sema also appealed to the women to serve in the hospitals as aides.

From house to house she tramped, enlisting the help of more and more people. The first evening she returned to the school building at nine in the evening, tried and worn. She had promised to relieve one of the aides there at two A.M; so she crawled into the station wagon to get a few hours sleep until then. At two she was up and on duty in the main hall of the school, ready to administer to the ill, should they need help during the night. At six in the morning she was in the kitchen supervising the cooks. For the rest of the day, she led a volunteer group of

261

civic leaders through some of the city, and pointed out to them the most apparent and appaling health problems of the people on the streets. Again and again, she wished she had food and clothing to hand out to these people, instead of mere words that 'help was on the way.'

Supper was again late for Sema, followed by a few hours of sleep. This frenzied schedule lasted about two weeks. Some food and clothing had arrived and Sema helped distribute it. This was a major task in itself: there was not enough to go around, and how was one to decide who was needy and who was not, when obviously all were in deperate need. With the village leaders, she helped set up a crude system of rationing. It helped apportion the goods to those most in need; but even then there were a lot of complaints of mismanagement.

In the midst of all this relief work, a torrential rain broke loose and continued for two days. The incidence of illness and disease increased still more. Many of the efforts that Sema had made to improve the care of the sick and injured were brushed aside. There were no facilities, staff or drugs to handle the deluge of victims. Sema's own strenght and stamina were at a low ebb. One morning she failed to report for duty, and an aide was sent to look for her. Covered with blankets and coats, she lay huddled up in the staff room, shivering and in a delerium. They carried her to a hospital bed that was hastily made up for her, and gave her some antibiotics. In a few days her condition had sufficiently improved for her to sit up in bed, but she was still far too weak to get up. A new supply of medical personnel was expected that evening. A fatigued and exhausted group was returning to Tehran that same evening. The consensus of opinion was that Sema should return to Tehran with them.

At the appointed hour, they bundled her up well and put

her into the car. The other occupants of the car were mostly doctors and nurses who had come to Kashan about a week before Sema. They were too tired to talk, and most of them dozed in the car. It wasn't a pleasure ride for any of them, especially Sema. The recent rains had left water-filled holed in the road, and mud was much in evidence. Several times the car stalled, and the had to get out and push it through the mud. Travel was slow. Some of the bridges were still washed out, and detours had to be found. It took 12 hours to reach Tehran, and Sema was considerably weakened by the ordeal. In the early hours of the morning, the car drove to the front of her house. One of the doctors helped her out and into the anxious, waiting arms of her family. She was home at last.

CHAPTER TWENTY-THREE

WHAT MIGHT HAVE BEEN

Sema's arrival home was completely unexpected. There had been no time to notify the Samidee family that she was coming home. They really had not expected her for at least another week. And then to discover that she was desperately ill was still another shock. Mrs. Samidee put Sema immediately to bed, and telephoned their family doctor. He arrived, and found Sema in a serious condition which he diagnosed as pneumonia. Complete rest was prescribed, and he also gave her some antibiotics to reduce her fever. Mrs. Samidee and Nannee took turns for the next few days, keeping a constant vigil at her bedside. Mr. Samidee and Nadir looked in on Sima several times her first evening at home, but Sema was either asleep under sedation, or else in a stupor unable to recognize her surroundings.

The first night, Sema moaned and groaned in her sleep. Nannee who was on duty in the room was greatly disturbed, and awakened Mrs. Samidee thinking Sema was in pain. The two of them listened closely to her breathing and discovered that she was talking in her sleep. It seemed to concern her recent experiences at Kashan, for she mumbled again and again, "Oh, those poor people, standing in line, hour after hour for a cup of tea and a small piece of bread...that poor whimpered baby that died in my arms before I could get it to the hostipal...

that old crippled man who hadn't eaten in a week and was so emasciated that we had to carry him to the car...

Mrs. Samidee and Nannee shook their heads. It must have been a terrible experience for Sema to have gone through. Mrs. Samidee commented to Nannee. "I shouldn't have ever let her go in the first place. It was all my fault to have given her permission. Such a place isn't good for a woman. There are plenty of men around. Why don't they send them? But Sema's so eager to relieve suffering that she'll volunteer for anything. She wants to change the country overnight. And then look what happens to her. She should be at home, planning for marriage, not thinking about a career."

Such was Mrs. Samidee's view. She would have expounded still more, if Sema.s voice from the other room had not alerted them. They heard her say in a loud clear voice, "No, no, you can't have any more clothing for your family. I know your children need more, but we have to ration out our present supplies, until more come... But doctor, you mean to say that those two youngsters who died were the children of the woman who was in the other day complaining so much? They're dead from exposure?"...

And then Sena commenced to sob hysterically. Mrs. Samidee and Nannee hurried to her side, but the young woman couldn't be roused. She was, as if in a hypnotic trance, recalling all the events of the past ten days that she had not been able to express consciously.

Mrs. Samidee sat down at Sema's bedside and quietly stroked her daughter's forehead, hoping to soothe her. In time Sema fell into a deep, but restless, slumber. She tossed and turned for the rest of the night.

The doctor visited the family the following day and gave Sema more medication. Mrs. Samidee related the nightmares

265

that Sema had been having, and the doctor nodded. He told her that this kind of reaction was one that many sensitive people were likely to have after encountering such distressing scenes. There was nothing to be afraid of, as long as Sema could be encouraged to talk about her experiences with her family and friends. Then it would cease to trouble her at night.

In a few days, Sema's fever had subsided enough for her to sit up in bed and be more aware of what was going on around her. Mrs. Samidee, Nannee and some of the neighbors came in to chat with her the first day she was up. In the evening, Mr. Samidee and Nadir amused her with funny stories from work and school. In the following week, personal friends and people from her job came to visit her. Among the visitors was a young couple who had been Sema's classmates in college in Tehran. She had known the Kevehs before they were married, and now seeing them together she remembered their wedding and how happy they had been. And they seemed happy now too, she thought as she looked at them. The husband was now teaching in a high school, and his wife occasionally taught school when she was not busy with her young son.

"Life is so easy for them," thought Sema. "They haven't had all these problems of wanting to change the world. They're content to live their own lives and not meddle in the affairs of others. How I envy them!"

The Kevehs had brought her some red roses, and after they had left, Sema looked at them admiringly. It brought back memories to her. Memories of a college romance. She had met Faidoun when both were students at the university. In fact, they had sometimes been a four-some with the Kevehs. On special occasions Faidonu had always remembered that she liked red roses and had brought them to her, always presenting them with a favored line of poetry from Khayyam:

> Look to the Rose that blows about us—"Lo,
> Laughing," she says, "she says, "into the World I bow
> At once the silken Tassel of my purse
> Tear, and its Treasure on the Garden throw."

She recited them now to herself, half aloud, wistfully recalling the face of the loved one: dark laughing eyes, occasionally saddened by some inner sorrow; a prominant nose, and a flashing smile of warmth. His hair still retained some of the curliness of youth, although he tried much to hide it, by combing it back.

They had been so happy together. Every day after their classes they had met to stroll down Shah Reza Avenue, talking about their ideas on life and what they hoped to contribute to it. "Teaching is for me," Faidoun had often said. "Give me the child, and I will fashion the man... You talk about changing society, but how do you propose to change it?" he often asked her.

"But it takes so long for children to grow up and influence others. Isn't it better to do something yourself to actively change the existing social situations?" she answerd him in turn.

"I suppose it's all a point of view," he would acknowledge graciously.

There was never a hint of an argument between them. They enjoyed so much together. Whenever the weather was sunny, they sat under lovely chenor trees on the campus and prepared their lessons together. When they were saturated with reading, one might start out:

> Why, all the Saints and Sages who discuss'd
> Of the Two Worlds so learnedly, are thrust

And the other would continue:

> Like foolish Prophets forth; their Words to Scorn
> Are scatter'd, and their Mouths are stopt with Dust.

267

On holidays they were accustomed to joining one another's family and all went on picnics together. Sema's family was very fond of the young man; and Faidoun's family also thought highly of Sema. Graduation time came for Faidoun, two years before Sema. He had previously made arrangements to teach in the provinces, but Sema knew that he would return to visit his family from time to time. They parted sorrowfully, but not tearfully. There had been no talk of marriage between them, perhaps because Sema had not encouraged it. Somehow she had not felt prepared to discuss it at this point in her life: a career in public health was all important to her.

Of course she had met other men in the States, Americans, Europeans, and Persians. Yet none replaced the feeling that she had carried for Faidoun, even though she had ceased to hear from him. At times she thought he might be married by now.

Looking again at the rose, Sema was reminded of the sweetness and simplicity of her life in the days when she had known Faidoun. "Those days are gone forever," she reminded herself. "Love and marriage are for the young and innocent. Who wants a career-minded 'old' woman of 25 like me?" she reflected bitterly.

Her thoughts ran on. "How funny it is in Iran to be considered old at 25, and beyond the marriageable age. Yet in the States, many women marry at that age or later. Not that I could go back there and live. No, America is not for me. I have to make my place in Iran, no matter how difficult it may be."